THE TWO OF US

THE TWO OF US

My Life with John Thaw

SHEILA HANCOCK

BLOOMSBURY

First published in Great Britain in 2004

Copyright © 2004 by Sheila Hancock

The moral right of the author has been asserted

Bloomsbury Publishing Plc, 38 Soho Square, London WID 3HB

A CIP catalogue record for this book is available from the British Library

ISBN 0 7475 7020 5

10 9 8 7 6 5 4 3

Typeset by Palimpsest Book Production Limited, Polmont, Stirlingshire
Printed in Great Britain by Clays Ltd, St Ives plc

All papers used by Bloomsbury Publishing are natural, recyclable products made from wood grown in well-managed forests. The manufacturing processes conform to the environmental regulations of the country of origin

When Clare Venables was dying, her friend Peter Thompson wrote her this letter.

My much-loved friend,
It matters to have trodden the earth proudly, not arrogantly, but on feet that aren't afraid to stand their ground, and move quickly when the need arises. It matters that your eyes have been on the object always, aware of its drift but not caught up in it. It matters that we were young together, and that you never lost the instincts and intuitions of a pioneer. It matters that you have been brave when retreat would have been easier. It matters that, in many places and at many times, you have made a difference. Your laugh has mattered. Your love has mattered. Above all, it matters that you have been loved.
    Nothing else matters.

The sentiments he expresses apply equally to my husband John Thaw. I borrow them in dedicating this book to them both.

I also wish to pay tribute to John's brother Ray, who died in June 2004.

It takes two.
I thought one was enough,
It's not true;
It takes two of us.
You came through
When the journey was rough.
It took you.
It took two of us.

It takes care.
It takes patience and fear and despair
To change.
Though you swear to change,
Who can tell if you do?
It takes two.

– 'It Takes Two' from *Into the Woods* by
Stephen Sondheim

ACKNOWLEDGEMENTS

My deepest gratitude to Alexandra Pringle, without whom this book would never have been started, and Victoria Millar, without whose gentle guidance and advice it would certainly never have been finished.

Also thanks to many people I have interviewed to fill in the gaps in my knowledge of John's life.

Some of the proceeds of this book will go to The John Thaw Foundation which aids young people who need a helping hand.

The John Thaw Foundation
PO Box 38848
London
WI2 9XN

Contents

Prologue

3 September 2000
Walking in our field. A soft mist of rain. The sun shining behind the drizzle. A rainbow forms across the sky behind me. It reflects in the raindrops on grass and trees. Millions of multicoloured baubles, iridescent, extraordinary.

John, quick, come and look.

Racing back over the wooden bridge, into the conservatory, I toss aside his script, grab his hand and pull him, limping and protesting, to my magic vision.

It's gone.

Oh, great. Miserable wet trees, pissing rain and soaking wet trouser legs – thanks a bunch.

But it was beautiful.

Well, you daft cow, why didn't you stay and enjoy it?

I couldn't enjoy it properly without you.

Oh, come 'ere, Diddle-oh.

Arms pulling me tight, hands on bum, wet faces nuzzling, laughing. An aging man and woman, happy in a wet field.

You should have known it wouldn't last, kid.

He meant the rainbow.

The Girl

26 January 2001
Been asked to do the narration in a recording of a musical
version of Peter Pan at the Festival Hall. Was playing a
demo of the score, which is charming, when I noticed John
lurking.

I, THE GIRL, Sheila Cameron Hancock, was born on the Isle
of Wight on 22 February 1933, nine years before him. He, the
boy, John Edward Thaw, was born in Manchester on 3 January
1942. The intrusion of World War II was not the only similarity
in our childhoods. Varying degrees of fear, abandonment and
delight were common moulding influences. As was a performance of *Where the Rainbow Ends*, a musical play for children
about St George's quest to slay the dragon.

As the girl was the first to arrive, we'll start with her.

When I was three years old I sat entranced in the Holborn
Empire watching a beautiful sprite called Will o' the Wisp floating about on rainbow-coloured wings. When my mummy
whispered that it was my sister Billie leading Uncle Joseph to
the end of the rainbow I absolutely believed in magic, because
I could see it there, in front of me, on this enchanted place called
a stage. So dumbfounded was I by my sister's transformation

that I had a massive nosebleed. I refused to leave, preferring to ruin the cotton hankies of half the audience in the dress circle. People didn't use tissues in those days.

My father worked for the brewery, Brakspeare Beers, that put him and my mother into various pubs and hotels around the country as managers. They were working at the Blackgang Hotel on the Isle of Wight when I was born. Its windswept Chine, with the skeleton of a whale in the garden, looks pretty bleak in photos.

We moved directly after my birth so I remember nothing of it, but my parents told tales of smugglers and incest in that cut-off part of the island. My seven-year-old sister lived in dread of the adders that infested the garden and of the cliff adjacent to the hotel crumbling into the sea, as it often did. Now the Chine is a rip-roaring amusement centre, but in 1933 it can't have been a very jolly place from which to greet the world.

After a brief spell in Berkshire we landed up in a spit and sawdust pub called The Carpenter's Arms in King's Cross. We lived in the flat above the bars. It reeked of stale beer and the whole place shook and glasses rattled as trains passed the back-yard. Sleep was not easy. I was often still awake when Dad shouted, 'Time, gentlemen, please,' hoping that the shouts on

4

the pavement outside would not be accompanied by too much breaking glass and thuds and screams. The jollity was equally raucous. I was not allowed into the public or saloon bars, or Dad might lose his licence, so I sat on the stairs leading up to our quarters, listening to the adults letting loose. Mummy played the piano for Daddy to sing 'The Road to Mandalay' and then both of them silenced the babble with:

> If you were the only girl in the world
> And I were the only boy
> Nothing else would matter in this world today
> We would go on loving in the same old way
> A garden of Eden just made for two
> With nothing to mar our joy.
> I would say such wonderful things to you
> There would be such wonderful things to do
> If you were the only girl in the world
> And I were the only boy.

I too entertained the customers. Fired by my sister's triumph in *Rainbow*, I regularly performed the whole of *Snow White and the Seven Dwarfs*, playing all the roles to the captive audience of women hoping for a quiet port and lemon in the Ladies' Bar.

27 January
Remembering John's addiction to Sondheim's Sweeney Todd *when I was in it at Drury Lane and wondering if he might enjoy a break from telly coppers and lawyers, I played a Captain Hook number while he was in earshot. It's good. Funny-scary.*
  'You could do that.'
  'Nah.' But he twinkled a bit.

My first school was St Ethelreda's Convent in Ely Place in Holborn. I am not a Catholic, yet I learned my Catechism and all the rules and regulations like a good little child of the faith.

I could not abide the smell of incense though. The nuns did their best to save my soul but I retched and went green whenever the priest shook his thurible anywhere near me, and eventually I was allowed to sit with the nuns behind a glass screen at the back of the chapel, watched from the pews by my mortified sister.

There was plenty for the nuns to pray for. Alarming things were happening in Hitler's Germany. In 1932 Broadcasting House had opened its impressive new quarters in Langham Place. Inside was a mural declaring, 'Nation Shall Speak Peace Unto Nation'. The message eluded Adolf Hitler. In 1933, the year of my birth, he became Chancellor of Germany and after a suspicious fire at the Reichstag, used the excuse of a Communist threat to prevent freedom of speech, burn books and forbid public assembly. His spin doctor, Goebbels, took over the airwaves. His message was not one of peace. Ethnic cleansing had begun. Dachau had opened, Jewish shops were being boycotted, and rumours of a programme of sterilisation of disabled people in Germany were circulating. In 1936 only a few token Jews were allowed to take part in the German Olympic Games and Hitler refused to shake hands with the winning black athlete, Jesse Owens. Closer to home there were Fascist rallies in London led by Oswald Mosley, vigorously opposed by some of our friends and neighbours.

My family history is a bit vague, but there were several related Cohens that we visited in Lewisham and a photo of a portrait of a crinolined woman who I was told was a relative called Madame Louisa Octavia Zurhorst. She reputedly fled Prussia from an earlier pogrom. My mother lost a Polish fiancé in 1917 and both my parents had their youth blighted by the horrors of that war to end wars. The signs of more trouble from Germany must have alarmed them.

29 January
A gentleman called Mohammed Wali, the Taliban religious police minister, has forced Hindus in Afghanistan to wear labels. Oh dear.

Life in King's Cross for a child innocent of Jarrow marches and nasty Nazis was bliss. Every Sunday morning I donned my best dress with matching apron, made by my mum, and collected a pint of winkles and shrimps for our tea from the barrow on the corner. I laboriously took off all the hard brown lids with my pin and then twisted the grey morsels from their shells, competing with my dad to get a winkle out intact. I lingered to sing jolly hymns with the Salvation Army band outside the pub, sometimes bashing a tambourine, and sat on the stoop with my fizzy lemonade and a bag of crisps with a twist of salt in blue paper inside. From the door, I watched the Salvation girls in their bonnets collecting from the respectful customers and helped them count the money in their little velvet bags. On Sunday afternoon there was the Walls ice-cream man, ringing the bell on his tricycle with a square box in front full of goodies. The lip-licking choice between a triangular water ice, a small drum wrapped in paper to peel and put in a cone, or a wrapped flat brick with a couple of wafers to make a sandwich was a very serious matter. Food seems to feature prominently in my memories and probably accounts for the somewhat chubby child in the very few photos I have of myself then and for my father's nickname for me: Bum Face. When I got older and thinner, Bum Face alternated with the then more accurate nickname Skinny Lizzy or, mysteriously, Lizzy Dripping.

The Royal Family were central to our lives. At any royal occasion we were there cheering among the crowds, me heaved on to my dad's shoulders for a better view, and after the procession, rushing down the Mall hoping for a balcony appearance. I did not realise that the enthusiasm of the crowd at the Coronation of George VI in 1937 was fuelled by their confusion at the abdication of the Duke of Windsor, but I was thrilled that there were now two little girls in the new Royal Family. I loved the diamonds and pretty frocks and golden coaches. Life was colourful and exciting for a child. It was accepted that some of our customers were dodgy but the police from the station over the road kept an eye on things. There was a code of behaviour among villains that protected my parents from harm. When a drunk smashed a glass with the intention of jabbing it in my mother's face, the local gang leaped on him and made sure he never entered the pub again.

My parents worked long hours. When the pub was closed my mum cleaned, washed glasses and prepared bar snacks, and Dad did his complicated work among the wooden barrels in the dank cellar. It involved thermometers and little brass buckets for slops. And quite a bit of tasting. Up in the bar too Dad began to respond more often in the affirmative to 'Have one yourself, Rick.' Often he would make it a short. Eventually, he or the brewery or, more likely, my mum, decided he should try another career. In 1938 they left the pub life and moved to the suburbs.

31 January

Today John was persuaded to go over a couple of numbers with the musical team for Peter Pan. *He was, of course, sensational. The bastard. Is there nothing he can't do when he sets his mind to it? The result is he is going to offer the world, leastways Radio 3, his all-singing, all-dancing Captain Hook. Joanna is on board testing her versatility by playing sundry pirates, mermaids and Tiger Lily so it's a Thaw show.*

After the rough and tumble of King's Cross, Bexleyheath in Kent seemed dreadfully dull. My parents thought it was a step up to have a home separate from their work, which they were buying on the never-never. It was an entirely new concept for people like them to own their own home – eventually. Everyone's ambition was to have a detached house and we were on our way with a semi. A long street of identical pebble-dashed: two beds, boxroom, bathroom and, great luxury, separate loo, upstairs, and two rooms and kitchenette downstairs. In the garden was a shed where I helped my dad make and repair broken furniture, holding planks of wood in the clamp while he sawed them, and stirring the glue bubbling in the black iron pot. Maybe the fumes from it contributed to my elation. Every day I laid out his brushes and yellow dusters and opened the tins for the daily shoe-cleaning ritual. I was barred from the shed before Christmas when Dad did secret things there. The anticipation was thrilling as he sneaked furtively out of the shed and made a great show of locking the door. As well as the apple and orange in my sock, I would find at the foot of my bed a jewel box or a wooden puppet, and, one extra specially exciting year, a sewing box on legs lined with quilted pink satin, left over from their newly made eiderdown, and equipped with needles, cottons and a thimble and scissors just like Mum's.

All the houses in Latham Road had identical gardens back and front and there were – very much admired, this – little sticks along the pavement that would grow into cherry trees. We had definitely gone up in the world. We left behind a life of beer and skittles or, in the case of The Carpenter's Arms, shove-halfpenny and darts, and became lower-middle-class. Dad got a job at the Vickers factory in Crayford and Mum worked in a family-owned store called Mitchells of Erith. It was a sedate emporium where my enterprising mother worked her way up from gloves through lingerie to setting up a little café and theatre booking office in the shop.

In their free time my parents set about transforming the house to show we were not going to be swallowed up into conformity. I aided my father in building a mini Tivoli Gardens in front of the house, using an antique stone bird-bath as a centre-piece. He and I nicked it by dead of night from a derelict house, a

provenance my father was never quite comfortable with. The garden had irregular flower beds and a sunken crazy-paved area.

I mixed the sand and cement with his huge spade, hollowing out the centre of the heap, pouring in water and flopping the mixture about ready for Dad to use. We worked in companionable silence, pegging out shapes and heaving the stones about, then sitting on the front wall with an orange squash admiring our work in progress. My profound love and respect for my father was consolidated doing that garden. Years later I discovered some soulless fool had demolished it to provide a concrete stand for his Ford Escort.

1 February
Took delivery of my Jaguar XKR in advance of my birthday. I've christened her Mavis to stop her getting above herself. Went for trial run. Does she go. 'Yes, all right, calm down dear, take it easy,' But he was beaming. He loves giving presents.

An Italianate garden may seem a strange choice for a grey suburb of London, but not for Enrico Cameron Hancock. The son of a man who worked for Thomas Cook, he was born and spent his childhood in Milan. It was rumoured that Enrico Caruso was his godfather, feasible if Grandfather booked the star's travel, but I never met my relative to ask him. Where the Cameron, which I have inherited, came from, heaven only knows. My mother, Ivy Woodward, had worked in a flower shop in Greenwich and a pub in Lewisham before falling madly in love with my handsome dad and remaining so for the rest of her life. She was a beautiful girl and made all her own frocks, coats and hats, which were modish copies from magazines. She was clever with her needle. She made all our clothes too and covers for the furniture and bright curtains to enliven the interior of our box-like house. She washed all the bed linen and clothes by hand, rubbing them clean on a ridged wash-board. I sometimes turned the handle of the mangle to wring them dry and then handed up pegs as she hung the clothes out in the garden on Mondays. It was not done to hang out washing on any other day. The flat irons went on the stove. It was my job to test them with spit. She managed all this on top of working six days a week at the shop. On the few occasions she sat down for a nap with her eyes closed, her hands continued to work away with the knitting needles. Dad laid the fire with faggots of twisted paper and chopped wood for me to light when I got back from school. I cleaned the house from top to bottom on Saturdays, bright-eyed and bushy-tailed with pleasure when they came home from work and praised me.

Even the presence of my two grannies using our front parlour as a shared bedroom didn't trouble me, although it must have been hell for my mum and dad. The two old girls hated each other. Grandma Hancock was 'piss elegant' in her moth-eaten fur tippet and Nanny Louisa 'Tickle and Squeeze 'er' Woodward resented her put-on airs. She, after all, had slaved all her life and saved a few quid while Grandma Hancock had swanned around Europe with Cook's being the hostess with the mostest and not a penny to show for it.

They had furious rows over their nightly game of whist that ended with a lot of 'Who do you bloody well think you are?'

and 'Don't speak to me like that, woman.' It wasn't helped by
Grandma Hancock's descent into dementia so that she couldn't
remember which suit was trumps. I loved her childish behaviour,
going to the pictures to see the same film over and over and
doing stately dances in the street using a lamp-post as a partner.

3 February
John learning his numbers for Peter Pan *already. I only
have to play a phrase once and he knows it, he's got such
a good ear. He's enjoying himself. Particularly relishes the
phrase 'Blood will spill, when I kill Peter Pan.' Have to
remind him it's a show for kiddie-winkies. 'Well, that'll
shut 'em up,' he says.*

Our piano had come with us from the pub and family gatherings always ended with a sing-song. Dad often gave us his Ridice
Pagliacci, reducing us and himself to tears. Then a rousing chorus
of his version of the Riff Chorus from 'The Desert Song':

> Ho so we sing as we are riding ho
> Now's the time you best be hiding low
> It means the Ricks are abroad
> Go before you've bitten the sword.

Mum's speciality was:

> You must remember this
> A kiss is still a kiss
> A sigh is still a sigh
> The world will always welcome lovers
> As time goes by.

Her glances towards him were guaranteed to make Dad blush
and, of course, cry. He cried at everything, happy or sad. We
blamed his Italian childhood. He laughed till he cried and cried
till he laughed. He seldom finished a joke, so convulsed would
he be with the telling of it. The sight of him spluttering and

weeping with laughter, doubled up and groaning weakly, 'Oh Christ' had my sister and me rolling on the carpet. We also enjoyed it when he got incoherent with sentiment and yet more tears would cascade into his sodden, overworked cotton handkerchief. Particularly after a few drinks.

Gradually, I warmed to the security of routine in this new way of life in Bexleyheath. I enjoyed playing in the street with the other kids – no one owned cars then, and I remember no threat of any sort from strange adults or the growing crisis in Europe, and anyway, I knew my parents would protect me from any harm. At five years old, without fear, I walked the two miles to school on my own.

At Christmas, a big event pushed my fascination with performing a bit further. Upton Road Junior School decided to mount my party piece, *Snow White and the Seven Dwarfs*. It never occurred to me that my teachers would not cast me in the lead. Hadn't I thrilled the old girls in the Ladies' Bar with my winsome Snow White? I knew every line of the role. It was a sad six-year-old who broke the news to her family that she had been cast as Dopey. Daddy threatened, as he always did, to write a letter, while Mum went into 'best of a bad job' mode and set to work with Billie to make me a costume that would outshine all the others. My red dressing-gown had a little train sewn on, pointy felt slippers were fashioned out of an old mat, and the crowning glory was a cotton-wool beard, fixed with elastic round my head under a green nightcap. I still felt pretty bitter towards the girl with hair as black as ebony and skin as white as snow, who squeaked her way through rehearsals of my coveted role. Just because she's pretty. It's not fair. Ah, little girl, it was ever thus. But you will learn that one day her ebony hair will go grey at the roots and her white skin will crinkle and people will say 'How sad', whereas, with a bit of luck they'll say, 'She's perky for her age' about the woman who played Dopey.

When the great day of the performance dawned, I put on my much-admired costume and set off heigh-hoing up the wooden steps of the platform behind the other six tiny dwarfs. Somehow my train got caught in my legs and my slippers were well named for I slid flat on my face. There was a gasp from the audience which I quite enjoyed because it drowned the *sotto voce* Snow White's line. I straightened myself up, twanging my beard, which had settled round my eyebrows, back in its place. What was this? A huge, relieved laugh. This is a good lark, no one's looking at Snow White, particularly when I contrive another fall and repeat the business with the beard. My lack of subtlety can be traced to this day. Drunk with success, I fell about all over the stage, to the delight of the audience and the fury of my teacher. Not to mention Snow White's mother. A triumph rescued from the ashes of my humiliation. A lesson learnt. Making people laugh was a good ploy to deflect attention from Snow Whites.

4 February
Letter from someone asking me to support a campaign against the closure of Upland Junior School. Because it is an old building and to save money it is being amalgamated with another school. They wouldn't do that to Eton.

For some reason, I hope unconnected with this event, I was moved to another school, Upland Junior, and here, under the guidance of an inspirational headmistress, Miss Markham, I developed my performing skills. Participation was the teaching method employed here, probably to grab the interest of the fifty-plus kids in each class. We acted everything, even geography – I was Japan and my best friend, Brenda Barry, was Singapore. In history, being tall, I got pretty good at playing kings and was a dashing Hannibal, thoroughly enjoying trampling over several small Alps. In science, Brenda, as the earth, did a pretty nifty revolve round my sun and our eclipse was a triumph. The only mild anxiety in my life was whether, in the playground, I would be last to be chosen in 'The Farmer's in His Den'. 'Ee, aye, ante oh, we all pat the dog' could be pretty scary. Even worse, 'We all gnaw the bone'. They were golden days with only small childhood fears.

The adults, meantime, must have been terrified. The Nazis had entered the Rhineland and Austria. In 1938 a deal had been struck

by Chamberlain to give them the Sudetenland in return for 'Peace in our Time'. Chamberlain was a man who, like my parents, had experienced the lunacy of the 1914–18 war, and it is understandable that he tried every trick in the book to appease Hitler. His despairing cry, 'I am a man of peace to the depths of my soul. Armed conflict between nations is a nightmare to me', reveals his anguish. I have a photo of him in stiff collar and cravat, watchchain draped across his waistcoat, with two sceptical sober suited Englishmen behind him. He is shaking hands politely with a bulletheaded, ludicrously uniformed Mussolini, backed by a posturing Daladier and Goering similarly attired for a musical comedy. A gentleman at sea with a group of thugs. Yet the likes of my Dad in those days trusted their leaders to save them. They knew best, the upper crust. They were educated and knew what's what.

5 February

Meeting in the flat at Number 10 to discuss luvvies' (God how I hate that word) involvement in the election campaign. I found myself having a go at Tony Blair: 'You surround yourself with men in Armani suits, and the man people elected is submerged in spin. They wanted your honesty, your raw idealism, etc., etc. Why are you running this campaign for the Daily Mail?' *I went on about prisons – 'Have you ever visited one?' – and the vilification of asylum seekers. Was appalled by Hague's speech in Harrogate saying Labour will leave Britain 'a foreign land'. Shades of Enoch Powell. Why hasn't he denounced such language? I couldn't stop. I could hear myself ranting, it was awful. The woman from* Coronation Street *said, 'I don't know why you're 'ere.' Then others came to my defence and the whole meeting was soured. Blair was rattled but then so am I. Don't think he is used to people disagreeing with him. I like him and especially Cherie but when in power people seem to shed their ideals and are only interested in staying there. He pointed out no Labour Government had had a second term so I suppose he has to watch what he says. But it's sad. Get me. Silly actress telling off the Prime Minister. Mummy would be horrified. My Quaker friends would be pleased though: 'Speak truth to power.' Went home and told John, 'There goes your knighthood, pet.'*

The days of the polite politics of Baldwin, Ramsay MacDonald and Chamberlain were about to collapse in the face of the savagery to come and with them my peripatetic but carefree childhood.

In February 1939 people in Latham Road began to take delivery of Anderson air-raid shelters, but not my father. Was he still clinging to a belief that sanity would prevail? He knew the SS had ordered the destruction of Jewish properties in November 1938, and some Germans, probably in fear of their lives, had watched while their neighbours were beaten up. *Kristallnacht* must have convinced most people that this was some evil force that had got out of hand and become very dangerous. Not my dad. A scrupulously honest, loyal and compassionate man, maybe he just didn't believe it could be true. When Hitler entered Prague in March he did nothing. Only when they invaded Poland and Russia in September did he dig a hole in the garden. Too late to get the corrugated iron panels to complete an Anderson shelter, he managed to acquire some railway sleepers to cover the hole. On 3 September 1939 we gathered round our wireless to hear Chamberlain's weary admission that in response to his ultimatum that Hitler should retreat from Poland, 'No such undertaking has been received. Therefore this country is at war with Germany.'

Immediately after the broadcast the heart-sinking, swooping howl of the siren warned of an air-raid. Panic. My father frantically pushed myself, Billie and Mummy down the garden and ordered us to sit in the wet hole while he single-handedly dragged the final railway sleepers across. He then, in a frenzy, shovelled earth on top. The stones rained in on us in the darkness and for the first time in my life I saw my mother nakedly weeping. 'Not again. Oh Christ, not again.'

Mass evacuation started. There was the possibility of us going to America, but when Dad heard that the little Princesses were staying put in London he decided so would my sister and I. My father was put on secret work for Vickers and joined the ARP, whilst my mother continued to work at the shop. Business as usual. Even the local police station had a notice saying 'Stay good. We're still open.' Blackout went up in all the windows and the world went dark. 'Put that light out,' shouted my dad in the street. Slogans like 'Keep it dark. Careless talk costs lives', 'Dig for victory', 'Be like Dad. Keep Mum' (excuse me?) and 'Is your journey really necessary?' became common currency. The Germans, and later the Japs, became objects of our ridicule. 'We'll get the Hun on the run' and jokes about Hitler's one ball were rife, even among us kids. Humour was our only weapon against an all-powerful enemy. That and Churchill.

10 February
The Tories have taken to standing Hague on a soapbox and letting him loose amongst the people. Only trouble is, in the newspaper photos, the people listening look bemused and bored.

In contrast to our ribaldry, Winnie's rhetoric was superb. We all crowded round our wirelesses when he was on. 'I have nothing to offer but blood, toil, tears and sweat.' I found him much more exciting than Laurence Olivier or James Mason. He was the best actor of the lot, sounding as if he really believed what he said.

His gift for oratory got us through that well-nigh hopeless situation. I saw how my parents perked up and set their jaws after he spoke. 'Let us therefore brace ourselves to our duty, and so bear ourselves that, if the British Commonwealth and its Empire lasts for a thousand years, men will still say, "This was their finest hour."' The British Empire has not lasted a thousand years, and as the people who experienced the war die off, few recall how fine was the hour, but young as I was, I do.

When the Battle of Britain started we were situated in Bomb Alley between Woolwich Arsenal, Vickers and the City and docks. We were the defence area. Down our road were black cylinders that produced a smoke screen, on the waste land behind our garden were a mobile searchlight and an ack-ack gun that split your eardrums. Above in the sky were hundreds of barrage balloons into which the more dimwitted Germans were meant to collide, I suppose. Concrete blocks appeared across the roads confidently intended to stop the German tanks.

My sister, mother and I slept every night on bunks in our now completed 6 feet 6 inches by 4 feet 6 inches Anderson shelter, the bangs and shudders not disturbing my sleep at all. My main fear was that a German airman might be shot down in our garden, but I slept with my hand on the spanner for the escape hatch to deal with that. I still sleep with one hand above my head. Occasionally someone would say after a huge bang, 'That was close,' and peer out to see if the house was still standing. We were lucky. It always was – just. The roof went several times and most of the windows; eventually, my father gave up repairing them and just covered things up with tarpaulin and planks of wood.

Come daylight, we went to school in a crocodile, with tin helmets and gas masks at the ready. On arrival, we went down more shelters. Long corridors, underground, with benches either side. Here we did our lessons, but if the air-raid got very close and noisy it was my chance to shine. Lessons were stopped and as a distraction I was allowed to entertain. I must have been the only person in Bexleyheath who wanted the bombs to fall nearby. I puzzled my young audience with impersonations of Ciceley Courtnidge, Evelyn Laye and Suzette Tarrie – none of whom I, and they, had ever seen, but my sister had been in a panto with the impressionist Florence Desmond and I impersonated her impersonations of them. I had heard little Julie Andrews and Petula Clark on the wireless and I had a go at them, although my Andrews coloratura was a bit of a liberty.

14 February
Valentine's Day. John gave me an odd-looking teddy bear to add to my collection. He says it looks like him – grumpy with little short legs. It does give a familiar anguished bleat when you press its tummy.

We stuck out this mole-like existence, as usual making the best of a bad job. I competed with my friends for the finest shrapnel collection. Pieces of a bomb were prized, as were machine-gun bullet cases. We were still in imminent threat of invasion. In June 1940 the French surrendered to Hitler in the same railway carriage in Compiègne where General Foch had made the Germans agree to humiliating terms in the armistice of 1918, so Hitler was just across the Channel, photographed dancing with glee. We were not overly confident that the Home Guard marching down the street with rusty old rifles and pikes and cutlasses from the local museum would be able to beat back the Hun. There were dog fights overhead night and day, bomb sites everywhere and friends being killed. The Spitfires dodged and weaved above our heads, puffing shots at the relentless 1,000 bombers a day that came over Britain. 'Never in the field of human conflict was so much owed by so many to so few.'

In December 1940 the City of London was ablaze and on 11 May 1941 there was a raid in which one 1,400 people died. In one night all the buildings that represented our way of life were struck: The British Museum, Westminster Hall and Abbey, Big Ben, the House of Commons, St Paul's, all the railway stations and Buckingham Palace. For the first time, people were weeping in the streets. Enough was enough. It was agreed that my sister and I should be evacuated to the country. I had no idea where.

As I stood in a shattered King's Cross Station, clutching my suitcase and gas mask, I thought I was being sent away for ever. The station was full of people in uniform. Nearby was a group of Navy officers, showing off to a couple of Wrens in their jaunty tricorn hats.

'Where's the bloody train?'

Dad whispering, 'You see, girls, gents like that can get away with swearing. It sounds all right in a posh voice, but you mustn't do it.' He continued to run desperately through a crash course of defensive behaviour:

Little girls should be seen and not heard.

Blessed are the meek.

Don't blow your own trumpet.

Keep yourself to yourself.

Keep out of trouble.

By the end of it I was convinced the country was the Dragon Wood, and I was no St George. I was an eight-year-old girl, with a solid rock in my chest and a huge lump in my throat. The train steamed in and my fifteen-year-old sister dragged me away from my father. We undid the leather strap of the window in the corridor. He shouted through it, panicky, 'Bum Face, what's your identity number again? In case you get lost.'

'CJFQ29 stroke 4.'

As the train chuffed out of the station I saw my father bent over, his hands on his knees, head hanging down, unable to look at us as we disappeared waving, weeping.

26 February
Sweet ceremony in Oxford giving Colin Dexter the freedom of the city. After we had a romantic meal and a night at the Manoir aux Quat' Saisons. We were like a couple of kids. Agog at all the luxury, you'd think we'd be used to it by now but we still feel they might turn us out if we misbehave. Which we did in the privacy of our luxury suite.

My sister and I were billeted in Wallingford, then in Berkshire later to be transplanted into Oxfordshire, on an old couple called Mr and Mrs Giles. They had no children but doted on a snuffly

Pekinese called Dainty, who rode in the basket of Mrs Giles's sit-up-and-beg bicycle. Dogs they understood. Children were a mystery. The big girl was OK, pretty and self-possessed, but the little 'un was a puzzle. I was painfully thin on wartime rations, monosyllabic with despair, face contorted with a tic. Every few minutes my mouth gaped wide open and described a circular movement. Then my teeth clamped shut into a tight grin and my shoulders shrugged up to my ears. It made me look demented. Trying to comfort me, Mrs Giles made little egg custards from real eggs. I had only had dried eggs since the war started. Too frightened to refuse one, I forced the slippery pale yellow spoonfuls down my contracting throat. Half an hour later my stomach dissolved. I was given a torch and made my way down the garden path to a hut at the end. Inside was a hellhole. A black pit over which was a scrubbed wooden seat. My feet could not touch the ground and I clung to the sides, vomiting now as well. My bottom was much smaller than the hole, I could disappear and never be seen again. Or alternatively be bitten by the tarantulas hanging above my head. I cleared up my sick as best I could by torchlight with the neatly cut squares of newspaper that hung from a piece of string on the door. The endless path back to the house, surrounded by pitch blackness, was definitely the heart of the Dragon Wood.

I was settled in for the night on an old brown leatherette settee. Everyone else went upstairs. The latch of the wooden door at the foot of the stairs clunked shut. I stared out of the window at the stars, begging them to watch over my mum and dad. As I lay there, the pillow either side of my face became wet with tears although I dared not make a sound. Then I felt a warmth in the bed. I had soiled it. Like a baby. I lay unable to move or speak to ask for help, my cosy world disintegrating. The Blitz had been fun but this strange country world was dreadful.

My sister Billie soon went back to London to pursue her dancing career, dodging the bombs in London and all over England on tour. Later she joined ENSA (the Entertainments National Service Association) and weaved between torpedoes to Africa, where she ventured into godforsaken places to brighten up the troops. She was fifteen when she started, so she grew up

fast. I worshipped her. She was so glamorous in her uniform and she and her variety friends were outrageous and funny. This separation from her and the rest of the family was grievous. I knew there was a very good chance they would be killed in the inferno I was leaving behind.

1 March

Taking a break in France before Peter Pan. *Stopped off at Vasaly on the way down to Provence. I wanted to climb the steep hill to the church to light a candle for Jack who is having his brain scan check-up today. We passed an ancient building on which was a plaque which said some saint had stopped there on his journey and founded this hospice on the site. John struggled on a bit, panting, then sat on a stone, lit a fag and said, 'I think I'll stay here and found a hospice if you don't mind, kid.' I snarled, 'Well, I hope it'll be a non-smoking one,' and went on to the top. He's nine years younger than me, for God's sake.*

2

The Boy

IN THE YEAR OF John's birth all the church bells rang. Up until then they had been silenced, only to be rung when Britain was invaded, but a victory at El Alamein in 1942 marked a turning point in the war, and Churchill ordered the bells to celebrate it. But, always brutally honest, he warned, 'This is not the end. It is not even the beginning of the end. But it is, perhaps, the end of the beginning.'

1942 did, however, mark the beginning of the life of the boy. On 3 January of that year, John Edward Thaw was born in Longsight, Manchester.

Churchill was right to be cautious about premature rejoicing over El Alamein. In the same month as John's birth, two ugly events had illustrated that further horrors were being planned. Both prompted television programmes later in the life of that baby, who was destined to become one of the medium's biggest stars.

Reinhard Heydrich, right-hand man to Himmler, held a secret meeting in which a group of Nazis cold-bloodedly planned the extermination of the Jews – the Final Solution. Sixty years later, Heydrich and his team's clinical decision to set up gas chambers and killing camps was chillingly portrayed by Kenneth Branagh and his fellow actors in *Conspiracy*. John, no longer able to perform himself, watched it with profound admiration.

The British also embarked on a programme of mass killing in the month of John's birth. Bomber Harris decreed that his Bomber Command force would 'scourge the Third Reich from end to end' with blanket bombing that had no specific military target but was aimed at lowering the morale of the German people. With our modern approach of so-called clean bombs and avoiding collateral damage this may seem shocking, but perhaps it is more honest. John's portrayal of Bomber Harris on television in 1989 pulled no punches but, with his usual empathy for the characters he portrayed, he made it easier to understand how the man and the country felt, bearing in mind that simultaneously news came through of the slaughter of Jews in the Warsaw Ghetto. Hatred was in the air. Into this grotesque world came the baby who had 'the whitest hair and bluest eyes you've ever seen'.

His mother, born Dorothy Ablott, was one of ten children. His father, John Thaw, commonly known as Jack, was one of seven, two of whom had died in childhood. They married when Dorothy was nineteen and Jack twenty. Their engagement party did not bode well for the relationship of the two families. Aware that the Ablotts were even needier than they, Jack's mother dispatched her daughter Beattie with her fiancé Charlie on the long walk from their home in West Gorton to the Ablotts' home in Longsight, with a laundry basket full of crockery for the party. The party itself was an awkward affair as the families sized each other up but all went reasonably well until the day after. Beattie and Charlie returned with the empty basket to collect the loaned dishes. 'You're not touching them pots till she gets 'ere to see what's what,' said Mr Ablott, despite the obvious superiority of the Thaws' precious best china to their own.

3 March
Bought some pretty new plates in Marseilles plus a desk, bookshelves and chair in flat packs from Habitat. John cursing and growling in the salon trying to understand the diagrams. I put World Service on loud and do a lot of

cooking. Eventually I am summoned to search for various nuts and screws he's lost and share his disgust at the 'fucking idiots who designed these things'. He is inordinately proud of the slightly skew-whiff bookshelves and wobbly desk and chair that he completed. I tightened a few nuts while he was in the garden.

Dorothy's father was a frightening man. A cripple from birth, he had a deformed hip and a shortened leg on which he wore a hefty raised boot. In later life John too had a withered leg, which he put down to copying his grandfather's walk, although a more likely explanation was a neglected ankle injury from a car accident causing him to drag his foot and therefore under-use his calf muscles. If Dorothy and her siblings were scared of their father's physical violence, they doted on their mother. A tiny woman, with several fingers missing on one hand from an accident at work with an industrial sewing machine, she managed to keep the family going despite her husband's brutality and habitual unemployment.

As a result of the engagement party débâcle, none of the Thaw family attended the wedding at St Cyprian's Church round the

corner from the Ablotts' house. Jack and Dorothy started married life in a rented house in Stowell Street, West Gorton. The terraced rows of two-up, two-down houses had back-to-back cobbled yards with one outside lavatory shared by four neighbours. Once a week, a thorough wash was done in a tin bath in front of the kitchen coal stove, the water shared to cut down on the boiling of pans to fill the bath. Jack's mother and father lived next door, his sister Beattie and her now husband Charlie up the road, his sister Doris and her husband Mark on the opposite side. The Thaws ruled the roost in Stowell Street, especially Jack's mother.

Mary Veronica Mullen, Grandma Thaw, was an ebullient woman of Irish descent, fat and raucous and overflowing with energy. On top of running her family she worked as a caterer in Hunter's Restaurant during the day and at Belle Vue Pleasure Gardens in the evening. She was a wonderful cook and fed anyone who was down on their luck with leftovers she brought home from work. Every Christmas George Lockhart, the famous ringmaster in the annual Christmas Circus, chose to stay with her. One year an entire Welsh Rugby Team, playing a Christmas match at Belle Vue, camped out in the various Thaw houses.

Mary Veronica thrived on work. On her marriage certificate, instead of the usual blank for the bride's rank or profession in that period, she is listed proudly as Grocer's Assistant. Her husband is entered as an Iron Slotter, though sadly not a lot of iron needed slotting and he was frequently unemployed. He could play any tune on the piano, a useful skill for a family that enjoyed a good old sing-song. On one occasion during the war, Grandma Thaw was enjoying just such a knees-up in the local pub when a buzz bomb cut through the roof and landed at the back, mercifully failing to explode. Everyone fled but Grandma, who, surrounded by debris, refused to go till she had finished her Guinness.

I once caught John with tears in his eyes as he watched a TV performance of mine as the battling mother in D. H. Lawrence's *Daughter-in-Law*, because I reminded him of his gran. She was a Catholic. Her husband disapproved, so she gave her children rather ambiguous moral guidance by sending them secretly to the local monastery to buy holy water: 'Don't tell your dad.' She fought many battles against injustice for her neighbours, but was not best pleased when her small daughter was banned from the local football ground for a month when she ran on to the pitch and beat up a player who had kicked her brother.

Into this rumbustious environment Jack brought his young bride. A feisty peroxide blonde, smart and knowing, she kept a clean house and got on well with everyone. Perhaps too well with some. A year after the wedding their first son, John, was born.

10 March
The family arrive. This is a wonderful place for the grand-children. They can run wild. They play with the Romany kids camping in the hameau – everyone plays boules with the locals. We relish one another in the sun. How lucky we are.

The war made it difficult to have a stable married life. Jack was exempt from military service as he had broken his spine as a child, playing leapfrog over apple crates, so he worked making munitions in Fairey Aviation Factory, often working nights. He was also a volunteer rescue worker with the Fire Brigade. After one raid his sister Beattie, who worked on a mobile canteen, came across Jack crying and vomiting into the road, having just dug out of the debris a pair of child's wellingtons with the feet still inside.

Twenty-year-olds everywhere were exposed to horror but Dorothy still managed to have a laugh. She kept her son and everyone else amused when she went down the public air-raid shelter in the nearby croft, but mainly they got under the table or the stairs if there was a bad raid. She fell about when she heard that Beattie had refused to leave her new bedroom suite when the bombs got close, resolutely holding on to the mirror until the planes passed over. In 1944 another son, Ray, was born. At the same time Jack was sent to work in the mines and was away even more. It could have been worse. Many of their friends who had been at the front were missing or killed in action.

The end of the war was greeted with great rejoicing. Ray and John attended street parties dressed in their MacDonald tartan kilts in honour of their great-grandmother, called illustriously Flora MacDonald. The implications of the atom bombs on Hiroshima and Nagasaki were not allowed to spoil their celebration at having, against all odds, got rid of something vile. Heedless of the war-weariness of the grown-ups, Ray and John, now two and four years old, began to have the time of their lives.

11 March
Our dear friends David and Liz took us for a picnic right up in the Luberon mountains at Silvergue. Magic.

With the war over, Belle Vue, just by Stowell Street, regained its former glory. Founded by John Jennison in 1836, it had grown to be a wonderful pleasure garden for the working class. Sixty-six acres of it. John and Ray went to the speedway track with their dad and mum. They watched the rugger and football, getting in free because Uncle Charlie was a coach. Sometimes their dad, fag hanging from the corner of his mouth, would play football. They rode on the helter-skelter, the scenic railway and the magnificent Bobs roller-coaster. There was an open-air ballroom alongside a lake for the grown-ups, where many a romance blossomed. Young women in their Sunday best danced gracefully to Bonelli's Band, hoping someone beautiful would have the last waltz with them and walk them home. John's mother got a job as a barmaid at the Longsight Gate where Grandma Thaw was still working as a cook. The zoo housed camels, lions, polar bears, tigers and monkeys. Phil Fernandez, the Indian elephant keeper, lived over the road, and the two boys helped him march extra elephants through the street, from the station to the zoo, for the annual circus. Young John became very fond of Ellie-May, mucking out her stall and having rides, clinging on to her huge back. Very often the gibbons

and monkeys escaped over the wall into the surrounding streets. The kids helped round them up in nets. Belle Vue was their huge back garden.

John heard his first classical music when the great Halle Orchestra played at Belle Vue, as well as developing a life-long passion for the brass bands he heard there. One year the magnificent annual pageant, culminating in a spectacular fireworks display, was made doubly exciting when his father got a walk-on part. Jack always maintained that his role in the Belle Vue pageant demonstrated the talent that he bestowed on his offspring. His delivery of his one line, 'Seize that man', dressed in a toga, holding a spear, was apparently the talk of Manchester. His grandchildren later conceded, when he frequently re-created his triumph for them, that his profile was acceptably Roman, but his accent less so. He challenged them to prove it was less Latin than their posh English.

12 March
Lovely to be in France. Weather really hot. John slaving to learn his lines for Peter Pan. *He doesn't have to, it's a*

broadcast, but he says pointedly, the live audience will be short-changed if he has his head in the script. They're not paying anyway – so sod it, as far as I'm concerned. Asked me how to pronounce 'floreat Etona', Hook's dying words. When I joked, 'Why? Didn't you learn Latin in Burnage?' he snarled, 'We didn't even learn English. Mind you, we'd have rowed the arse off those Eton tosspots on Belle Vue lake.'

Grandad confessed that his chief motivation for appearing in the pageants was the three and six a week he got for doing it, a Brechtian attitude that his son inherited. As soon as the young Thaw realised he had a talent for entertaining he used it to make money.

He started to hone his potentially lucrative gift in his Auntie Beat's house in Stowell Street. Uncle Charlie acquired an old microphone and rigged up a studio for John under the stairs. As a four-year-old, he seated the family in the front parlour to give them a wireless performance. Like me, his speciality was impersonation. Crouched in his cupboard, he mimicked radio personalities like Al Read, Stanley Holloway, Max Miller and Jack Warner.

A paucity of toys made him adept at make-believe. His first bosom friend was his 'mulk nut' – a coconut brought back by Uncle Charlie on leave. Auntie Beat became alarmed by his unnatural attachment to this nut, which grew hairless and filthy as a result of all his hugs and kisses, so she accidentally-on-purpose smashed it – a trauma the young John took in his stride, transferring his affection to an imaginary motorbike. Everyone was forced to do a detour round this treasured vehicle. He polished the phantom bike meticulously, sometimes forcing his cousins, Sandra and Jackie, to join in. They thought it was pretty soppy, but his ferocious seriousness cowed them into a half-hearted compliance.

The career John would have chosen at the time would not have provided the money for a motorbike. He longed to be a coalman. He wanted to drive the horses that pulled the cart; he practised with cushions heaving the sacks on his back and emptying them down the coal hole. One day he overacted the tipping part and hit his chin on the rung under the table. His dad carried the bleeding child to the local hospital to patch him up, but he bore the scar on his chin for the rest of his life.

Accidents and illness were much feared. Doctors were seldom used, except when absolutely necessary, in those straightened circles, until in 1948 the newly elected post-war Labour Government brought in the NHS with its free cradle-to-grave care. People were depressed by the slowness of recovery from the war. Rationing continued, there were some dreadfully hard winters, and the divorce rate rocketed as men and women had to adjust to normal family life after the separations of the war.

Dorothy and Jack were not finding it easy either. Jack took a job as a long-distance lorry driver which meant Dorothy was increasingly on her own with the two boys. One day a three-year-old John shouted to his Auntie Beat, 'My baby's crying.'

'Tell your mom.'

'No, he's crying for you.'

'I'll come in a bit.'

'No. Now.'

Tucking her Sandra under her arm, she went over, to find his mother had disappeared. There was a pile of clean clothes from the wash-house on the table but Dorothy was missing, leaving the kids on their own. Rumours of her wayward behaviour became the talk of Stowell Street. She was frequently absent for a day or two. Sometimes she took young John out and about with her; he had to lie about people and places that she visited. On one occasion an irate woman caused a rumpus in the street, rowdily searching for Dorothy because she had dallied with her husband.

Eventually the gossip in Stowell Street became intolerable and the family moved to Dorothy's parents' house in Norman Grove. Grandma Thaw was incensed that they could leave their nice little home to crowd in with the Ablotts. She wanted an explanation and to see her grandsons. She stormed round to Norman Grove. Mr Ablott barred the way as usual. There was a shouting match, culminating in Grandma Thaw hurling a child's scooter through the bay window. The police called by Stowell Street to investigate, but were won over by Mary Veronica's homemade cake and dropped the case.

13 March
I was swimming in the crowded public pool and he was watching from the café up on the terrace, noshing an almond croissant. Suddenly he shouted down in his colonel voice, 'I say, I say, excusez-moi, Madame – has anyone ever told you you have a ver' lovely derrière?' When I shouted back, 'Bugger orf' he spluttered with outrage to the startled French around him, 'Good God, did you hear that? I say – that's a bit uncalled-for, isn't it?'

Dorothy was used to her father's fights, but the boys were not. John solemnly swore to Ray that one day he would have a beautiful house with a big garden that had a wall round it that no one could get over. The fierce battles between Jack and Mr Ablott raged around them until, one day, the boys came home from school to find all their belongings dumped in the front garden. The family was off again, this time to a council flat in Wythenshawe. In the days of no cars, it was a long way from both families and, rows notwithstanding, the bonds were still strong. Girls went home to Mum to have their babies. Dorothy had gone back for the birth of both her boys. Jack's sister Beattie had had her Sandra in her mother's kitchen in Stowell Street with John playing whip and top in the yard. When the newborn baby was held up by the midwife he yelled through the window, 'Yuck, a skinned rabbit.' They missed all that intimacy, so within a few weeks they moved again.

The Kingsway Housing Estate in Burnage, an exemplary council venture, was nearer to their families. It was laid out in crescents and cul-de-sacs either side of Kingsway, which led up to both family homes. Like Bexleyheath for the Hancocks, it was a step up for the Thaws. There were green spaces, little gardens and trees. A man in Daneholme Road had, ominously as it turned out, been deserted by his wife and was happy to swap flats with the Thaw family. Compared to Stowell Street and Norman Grove it was paradise. It was the fresh start the battered family needed. The boys began to settle in.

But Dorothy did not. She gave a lovely party for Ray's fifth birthday and shortly afterwards disappeared again, this time for good. Having toiled to make her happy, Jack cut her out of his and the boys' lives for ever. Unbeknown to his father, seven-year-old John made one last effort to get his mother back. He dressed his brother and himself in their best grey flannel suits, and went round to where, with his inside knowledge of her movements, he guessed she would be. Their mother would not even let them in. She gave them sixpence each, told them to go away, and shut the door in their faces.

3

The Adolescent

AS AN EVACUEE IN Wallingford, I had little choice but to follow my father's advice of 'Keep yourself to yourself.' The local kids hated us 'bloody vaccies'. We overcrowded their schools and spoke a funny language they could understand no better than we could theirs. I was frightened to death of cows, sheep and horses and they were everywhere. I walked miles around fields to avoid them. We vaccies were considered dirty and undisciplined, which the local church school tried to cure by raking our hair for fleas and liberal use of the cane. My walk to school involved crossing a big field called the Crinny. There were strange, possibly prehistoric, mounds all around it. Here I would cower until the coast was clear and then run hell for leather across to the relative safety of the school playground. Sometimes a whooping gang would catch me out and then I would be jostled and jabbed and sneered at. At eight years old in a supposed place of safety I learned about fear.

One family in particular took agin me. I was a bit of a twitching wimp – fair game in a world where survival of the fittest ruled. There were a lot of Joneses – a veritable army of boys and girls, all with purple faces from their treatment for impetigo. I longed to be their friend and tried everything to ingratiate myself with them. I stood on my head, showing my knickers to the boys, and made daring jokes in class regardless of the rule to sit silently with your arms folded. Nothing worked until I too appeared with spots of gentian violet on my face and simultaneously had my fleas announced to the whole school and received the cane for biting the teacher who tried to dip my head in vinegar. Now I was one of them. From then on no one dared touch me or they'd have the Jones boys to answer to. If you can't beat 'em, join 'em. My Dopey experience proved useful. I became their clown. We went stealing turnips together, playing kiss chase and sliding off haystacks and romping in the cowslips. The Gileses were never fussy about when I came home, so my life was wild and free. I began to enjoy the country. I lay face down on the grass drinking in the smell of the earth, listening to the insects and grasshoppers, feeling the sun on the back of my neck and knees. If I was sad I had a secret hillock where, if I ran down it as fast as I could, my cotton frock flapping on bare brown legs, my spirits would soar into gasping delight.

14 March
On the drive back from Provence stayed at lovely hotel at Moulin des Ruans. Banks of bluebells. Took us both back to childhood. Cycling out of town and bringing back bunches of bluebells with their white stalks tied to the saddle rack. Then putting them in jam jars and the perfume and the luminous blue lighting up the house.

Since El Alamein the raids had become less frequent, so, aware that I was getting out of control in Wallingford, my parents whisked me away from evacuation. Mr and Mrs Giles had lavished awkward love on me and made no demands; back in Bexleyheath it was not easy to settle into my parents' more disciplined approach. In the Dragon Wood in Berkshire I had learned to stand up for myself verbally and physically. Thanks to the Jones boys I could land a nifty right hook. 'Blessed are the meek' had proved less effective than 'Do that and I'll 'ave yer guts for garters.' My school report after I returned said, 'Sheila is a born leader but must be careful to lead in the right way.' This may have been a reference to my behaviour one day in Wet Break. A teacher caught me, stripped down to my serge knickers and liberty bodice, executing a frenzied improvised dance to the rhythm of the rest of the class clapping their hands and banging their desks. A shocking sight at a time when the Valetta and the Dashing White Sergeant were the usual dances at the socials in the church hall. My parents struggled to control me and impose some routine on my life.

We began to sleep in our own beds, only going down to the shelter when the sirens went. But Hitler had another little trick up his sleeve. Well, two tricks actually. In June 1944 the Allied troops landed in Normandy and began to take France from the Nazis. The same month, just when we thought it was all over, Britain had to contend with a mysterious new weapon. I could identify any plane by the sound of its engine – 'OK, it's one of ours' – but this one puzzled us. A loud, deep, mechanical throbbing sound which would suddenly stop, followed soon after by an explosion. These were Hitler's V-1s that were christened buzz bombs or doodlebugs. The chugging, pilotless plane approached and, so long as it kept going, you were all right. If it stopped, everyone fell flat on the floor. We had just adapted our way of life to this when the V-2 or rocket came on the scene. Their approach was silent but they caused a massive explosion and extensive damage. At least with the normal air-raids you had warning and could take shelter, but these were lethally unpredictable. So off I went again. This time to Crewkerne in Somerset, accompanied by my mother to keep an eye on me.

I was billeted on a distant relative who was a medium and fascinated by my aura. I, in turn, was fascinated by a boy called Keith. I was ten and he was sixteen. My first real crush. I worked with him on a local farm for pocket money, heaving three hay stooks at a time into a wigwam shape and gleaning after the reaper had done its job. It was gruelling work, with the stubble cutting my ankles, and horrors such as the slaughter of rabbits that ran from the ever-decreasing circle of the machine, to be beaten to death by local youths. The things they did to cows were not pretty either. I bore all of it to work alongside my country lad. One day, sitting under a tree playing Truth, Dare or False, he said it was true that he loved me, frightening me to death. I ran off in a panic and then, to cover my embarrassment next time I met him, invented a twin called Wendy who was shy. I kept up this subterfuge the whole time I was in Crewkerne and came to enjoy being flighty one minute and inarticulate the next. He was completely taken in, due more to his gullibility than my acting talents.

Because of the war and my parents' work I did not have holidays as a child, but while I was in Somerset I visited my best friend, Brenda Barry, in Dorset. She had been evacuated to an idyllic cottage on the cliffs above the sea at Langton Matravers. One night we were allowed to run across a field and clamber down the cliff to a rocky platform known as Dancing Ledge. In the middle of the rocks was a large hole which filled with seawater. When the tide receded and the sun shone, it warmed the water, leaving a perfect swimming pool. It was dark and deserted so Brenda and I stripped off our clothes and plunged in. We floated on our backs, hand in hand, naked in the velvet water, listening to the waves crashing beside us on the rocky ledge. No dragons here. Ablaze with stars, the sky that had rained bombs and bullets on us, now embraced us. We were at one with each other and the universe. Like running down my hillock in Wallingford, I experienced ecstasy, transcendence. People could be vile, but nature was kind.

The Americans were kind as well. I had never seen any except in films, but in Somerset the GIs were glamorously in the flesh. 'Overpaid, oversexed and over here,' said the grown-ups, who mocked their sloppy uniforms and marching. We loved them. 'Got any gum, chum?' would always bring handfuls of chewing and bubbly gum, Lifesaver sweets and chocolate. There being no shrapnel, I started a collection of American badges. These strange people were gentle, funny and generous. They too had been uprooted from their homes and they sympathised with us evacuees.

20 March
The new President Bush on TV news. Another one?!
Reformed alcoholic, born-again Christian, eyes too close
together and very odd arms, he makes me feel nervous.
Seems to know nothing about foreign affairs but then only
8 per cent of Americans have passports so perhaps they
don't care. John says we must think of Singin' in the Rain.
And Mel Brooks and The Producers. *You've got to love a*
country that can come up with those.

My behaviour was still fairly wayward, but despite my disrupted education (I went to seven different schools before I was eleven) my teachers said I was potentially bright. My mum and dad wanted a better start for me than theirs; both had left school at thirteen and been pushed into work to earn a living. They thought it worth braving whatever Hitler threw at us for me to try for a scholarship to grammar school, so back we went to Bexleyheath.

The exam for ten-year-olds sorted kids into streams. Grammar school if you could afford to pay or got a scholarship, technical college if you were not quite so bright, and secondary modern for the rest, an invidious selection system that blighted lives. Miss Markham reckoned that I could get a scholarship, but the night before my exam there was a huge raid. When the All Clear went, Mummy took me out of the shelter, shook the debris off her handmade pink satin eiderdown and let me lie in bed with her – a great treat – staring at the night sky through the holes in the roof. She psyched me up to determine that however tired I was, I would not let this one opportunity to better myself slip by. A few months later Miss Markham picked Brenda and me out of class and said that we could run home and tell our parents that we had won a scholarship to Dartford County Grammar School.

Everyone in Mitchells of Erith cheered me as I did the round of the counters with my news and then I waited outside Vickers' gates for my dad. I knew he would cry and he didn't disappoint me, stopping complete strangers on the way home to tell them about his brilliant daughter.

In 1944 the Education Act opened the doors of grammar schools to all free of charge, but in 1943 you had to pay and even though both my parents were working all hours of every day, we just could not afford that, so a scholarship was essential. As it was, my mother had to make my uniform rather than buy it. On my first day I was more nervous about revealing my homemade shirt and tunic than coping with Latin and Algebra.

18 April
First rehearsal of Peter Pan. *Both pretty nervous which I remained all day. But John is so focused when he works that he has no time for nerves. He wants to get it right. Musicals are a whole new world to him but all the dancers and singers were wowed by his willingness to try anything. He keeps himself to himself, head in script, when not rehearsing but when he is he really goes for it and sets the pace. Poor buggers were shocked to discover he's learnt it all – now they have to too. Not me, I am the narrator – well, that's my excuse. The rehearsal room is opposite Heal's. I'll have to restrain him from refurnishing the whole house.*

Not long after I started at the grammar school the war ended. The grown-ups went mad and we kids stuffed ourselves with junket and jelly, with evaporated milk as cream, at the street parties. Our neighbours arrived home from the battle front and prisoner-of-war camps. My support for the war was shaken by the return from Japan of the son of the Frickers who lived next door. He had been fond of me as a child and I was asked to try to get him to talk. This speechless wraith staring blankly at me made me realise there was not much to celebrate. Other friends had problems with the arrival of unfamiliar men in the family. My dad made me absorb what happened in the concentration camps. I still have a photo that he showed me of beefy women warders tossing skeletal bodies into a vast pit of festering corpses – 'This must never happen again. It's up to you.'

His faith was shaken. As with many people, the war transformed his attitude. His generation had trusted their leaders to know best, even after the leadership of the 'donkeys' in World War I. The examples of Hitler and Mussolini shook Europe. Their ugly deaths underlined the squalor of their regimes and the unbelievable idiocy of those who followed them like sheep. Unlike many, Dad believed it *could* happen here if you didn't ask questions. Exhausted by a war in which fifty million died, no one seemed to question or oppose President Truman when he threatened that the US would 'unleash a reign of ruin from the air the like of which has never been seen on this earth'. So he did it. Twice. The atom bombs of Hiroshima and Nagasaki killed and maimed civilians. And the world was irrevocably changed.

The enormity of the atom bomb was difficult for a twelve-year-old to grasp. It terrified me, especially when, a couple of years after the war, my school sent me to a family near La Rochelle to improve my French. They took me to see Royan. I kept a diary of the trip for my dad.

13 August 1947

In 1940–41 just before the French surrendered, our planes suddenly came upon Royan. For two hours there was hell on earth after which the whole town was razed to the ground. When I say the whole town I mean it. I have never seen anything so awful in all my life. It's the bomb damage we are used to increased by a hundred times. Like an atom bomb, I suppose. You could stand and look at miles and miles of ruin. Thousands of people were killed, hardly any survived in fact. All this would not be so terrible if it had been to some purpose but it wasn't. The British have admitted it was a terrible mistake. There are notices up saying, in French, THIS TOWN WAS DESTROYED BY MISTAKE. It was done two days before the surrender. I don't know how they could ever forgive us. I was awfully glad to leave the town. It had a terrible atmosphere of death. I stood for some time looking at the white stones strewn on the ground with odd walls silhouetted against that blue sky. I had the sort of

feeling we used to get after a raid when we looked at the damage. I would like to take all the politicians and war mongerers to that place and say, look, this is the sort of thing you are responsible for. You ruin beauty, you kill – we ordinary folk are the ones to suffer. Why don't you grow up and realise what's at stake?

A mite pompous, even for a fourteen-year-old, but it shows the beginnings of my commitment to pacifism.

In July 1945 the 'ordinary folk' made their voices heard. Much as they loved the charismatic Churchill and were grateful to him, he was rejected for the ordinary Attlee, whose quietly confident assertion, 'We are facing a new era. Labour can deliver the goods' won a landslide victory. The Labour Government was led by visionaries, some, like Aneurin Bevan, from the working class, in itself a revolutionary concept in government. A colourful knockabout started between the old guard and the new. Churchill called Bevan 'a squalid nuisance', and Bevan called the Tories 'lower than vermin'. The Labour Party achieved change in all areas of life. In a few short years, my parents' burden of worry over illness, old age and education was considerably lightened. The new Labour Government founded the Welfare State.

23 April
John has a really good singing voice. He's learning all these
new things and taking to them like a duck to water. They
all love working with him but he gets a bit irritated by the
usual musical company jolliness. They keep saying what
'fun' it all is. He hates all that campery. 'Acting isn't fun,
it's a fucking job.'

Life for me was full of hope. I loved learning. Our teachers
were dedicated to improving our chances at a time when good
jobs for women were thin on the ground. Even grammar school
girls were guided towards nursing rather than aspiring to be
doctors or, God forbid, surgeons, and all the professions were
deemed too difficult to combine with the obligatory first priority
of marriage. Which is probably why my teachers were either
spinsters, who may have lost fiancés in World War I, or lesbians.
Whatever the reason, I remember only one who was married;
their lives were dedicated to us girls.

I heard my first classical music, apart from Dad's arias, with
Miss Tudor Craig. She told us what to listen for, then sat drinking
it in with knees apart, showing a glimpse of passion-killer drawer
elastic just above her knee. In Music Appreciation class she
played us Tchaikovsky's Fantasy Overture to *Romeo and Juliet*.
The build-up of the orgasmic melody gave me the same sensa-
tion as running down my secret hill in Crewkerne and floating
in the water of Dancing Ledge. I rushed to the local music store
with my money box and asked for the record, with some difficulty over the pronunciation. They did not have it but kindly
suggested alternative pieces by Tchaikovsky or works by other
composers. I rejected them, not believing anything could be as
lovely as the one I wanted. What a lifetime of joy lay ahead of
me discovering how wrong I was. Under Miss Tudor Craig's
guidance I started a vinyl collection for my wind-up gramo-
phone and searched the wireless waves for more magic music.
Years later I did a play called *Prin*, about a head teacher, in
which I based my characterisation on Miss Tudor Craig, hoping
to repay a little of the debt I owe all those inspirational women.

They introduced me to history, literature and culture. Everything I hold dear in my old age was first shown to me by them. They encouraged me to believe I could achieve anything – however humble my origins. Them and my Dad's constant urging to be the best.

'I was second in maths, Dad.'

'Oh, who was top?'

I was all set to try for a State Scholarship to university when I was fatally diverted. Dartford Grammar was an all-girl school. The boys were in a separate building, where later Mick Jagger would start the Rolling Stones. Our concentration on our studies was absolute. Or supposed to be. My raging hormones made me the best bat in the cricket team because, with a bit of luck, in the practice net I could hit the ball into the boys' playing field adjacent to ours. I was also a keen member of the Young Farmers' Union as the rabbitry ran alongside their fence and, whilst cleaning out the creatures' unsavoury hutches, I could peek at the boys through the wire. I volunteered for bell duty on the days their sixth form used our chemistry lab. However much I flashed my quite nice long legs running down the corridor and violently shaking the bell as I passed the laboratory glass door, I elicited not a glance from these paragons. I was very tall, a terrible embarrassment in those days, and resplendent with acne. No wonder they were more interested in the Snow Whites who acted cool and hard to get. I hadn't got a chance. Until I was cast as St Joan in the school play directed by Mrs Wilby, our only married teacher whom we all treated as a friend, very unusual in those overly respectful days. She concealed my spots with theatrical Five and Nine make-up and I threw myself into the role. The next day, when I did my usual frenzied bell ritual, the blond, devastatingly handsome head boy, Alan Coast, beckoned me over and asked me to accompany him to the end-of-term dance, telling me that he thought I was 'all right' in the play. The die was cast. An ignoble reason for going on the stage, but a succession of Greek gods and glamorous parties seemed infinitely preferable to more school, as I imagined university to be, never having been near one.

My Quaker headmistress, Miss Fryer, tried to persuade me to go for something safer, using my good brain, but when I was adamant, she pointed me towards RADA and suggested I should get some help to prepare for the audition. My accent and appearance can't have inspired her with confidence about my chances in my chosen career. Miraculously, she persuaded Kent Education Authority to award me a scholarship – the first for drama in that county – covering my fees and some subsistence, subject to my being accepted at RADA.

Someone in the shop told Mummy about a wonderful old actor laddie who directed amateur shows and would be prepared to give me intensive elocution lessons. Mr Hadley Prestage and I slaved over my vowels and consonants, driving my family mad with my vocal exercises. My sister designed a New Look outfit for me and my mum made it up on the treadle Singer sewing machine. The austerity of the war had been replaced by ballerina skirts, waists nipped in with waspy corsets, and layers of frilly petticoats. Dolled up in this outfit, I walked through the door of the Royal Academy of Dramatic Art in Gower Street rigid with fear, but determined not to let down Dad, waiting anxiously outside.

I had prepared a piece from *A Midsummer Night's Dream*, playing both Titania and, in a different voice, Bottom. I stood up for Bottom and sprawled on the floor for Titania, jumping up and down like a yo-yo. Maybe they liked my cheek, or they felt sorry for this spotty, gangling girl with an awful voice and a desperate glint in her eye, but they accepted me.

26 April

We did it! I almost forgot to have stage fright, so scared was I for John. And what happened? He sailed through it loving every minute, and I was all over the place. He actually went so far as to admit afterwards that it was 'fun'. He was so cocky he even giggled at Jo's divine Red Indian war dance as Tiger Lily and twinkled at me as he declaimed 'Floreat Etona'. The grandchildren loved it but looked a bit askance when they first saw him after the show. I think they were relieved he had survived the crocodile. It was a glorious, happy, triumphant evening. Someone suggested he should play Professor Higgins. He could too. Something for the future?

It was the last time John ever performed.

4

The Teenager

'TURN YOUR BACKS.' Jack sat the boys down. 'We're on our own now. We've got to look after each other; and you must turn your back on any trouble. Just walk away, don't get involved, or they'll take you away from me and put you in a Home.'

Turn your back. Potent advice.

As a little boy, despite his family's grinding poverty, John had been happy. When his adored mother walked out of his life, leaving him to be brought up by his often absent father and responsible, at the age of seven, for the care of his five-year-old brother, everything changed. Her desertion inflicted a wound that took the rest of his life to heal. From that day forward he followed his father's advice. The Back Treatment became his chosen weapon of self-defence.

Jack went to court to get custody of the boys, which the magistrate allowed, subject to Auntie Beattie supporting him – an almost unheard-of decision in those days when fathers were considered incapable of looking after kids. Dorothy stayed away from the court, and her mother and her sister, Cissie, remained silent throughout the hearing.

The Thaw family and the neighbours rallied round Jack and his sons. Auntie Beat took the tram to Burnage twice a week with ham and pea soup and other goodies. The conductor would ask, 'What's on the menu this week?' If Charlie hadn't had much work that week, she would walk. The people in the flat above checked that the boys were in bed by nine and they, or some other neighbour, would make sure that they got off to school in the morning. Jack was still away a lot on the long-distance lorries and it is to the everlasting credit of those kindly people that the seven- and five-year-old boys were not taken into care. It became easier when their dad got a job driving ambulances and was home more.

27 May
Filming EastEnders. *I was like a sad fan gawping at all the characters. Martin Kemp took me to see the Albert Square set. I couldn't have been more thrilled if it had been* Ben-Hur. *Rushed home to tell John. What with* EastEnders *and* The Archers *our tastes are not exactly highbrow. But I still maintain there is more good acting and camera work in* EastEnders *than many other shows. And God, do they work under pressure. Kick, bollock and scramble all day, however emotional the scene. No wanky discussion and analysis – just do it. I told John it would suit him down to the ground. 'But not the money, darling.'*

One day the boys saw their mother outside the flat sitting in a car with a man. She didn't talk to them. Ray never saw her again. Beattie saw her once. Dorothy came up to her in the street.
'Hello, Beat.'
'What d'you want then?'
'Could you give the boys this?'
'No – they don't want money, they want a mother.'
And that was that.
Broken homes were rare in those days. Whether from shame or fear, the boys kept quiet about their absent mother. The teachers at Green End Junior School only found out about it when John arrived clutching a dirty hankie to a bad cut on his

hand. When questioned, he explained that he had done it opening a can of beans for their breakfast.

With their mother's barmaid's income gone, there was even less money. The pawn shop was a regular trip, and diving behind the sofa when the rent man came was a favourite game. For the rest of their lives John and his father would never answer a doorbell if they could help it.

'Who's that?'

'I don't know – go and see.'

'No, no, kid – you go.'

John took his little brother everywhere. In the absence of a mother, Ray doted on John. They wandered the streets a lot but had a good time. They went to see Manchester City at Main Road. (Ray and Jack were besotted with the team – it had, after all, started in 1880 in West Gorton as St Mark's FC, the very church that Auntie Beat had married in. John, too, supported City until February 1958 when an air crash in Munich killed seven of United's Busby Babes, three staff members and seven journalists. Out of sympathy John switched his allegiance to Manchester United. His father and brother never quite forgave him.) Auntie Beat took the two boys on the tram to grimy Manchester for knickerbocker glories and milkshakes in the café in Lewis's. John incongruously joined the Young Farmers' Club and dreamed of country life. He also joined the Boys' Brigade, the Church Army and the Cubs, but only long enough to qualify for the outings to Blackpool. Various uncles and aunts visited, and Grandma Thaw, or Beattie, did a lovely Sunday dinner back in West Gorton; and afterwards Uncle Charlie took the boys and all the cousins to Belle Vue.

There were regular holidays in Charlie's tiny caravan in Rhyll. While there, young John started a business gathering golf-balls from the local links and selling them, a racket that ended when John, over-zealously, took a ball that was still in play, and, like one of his later scenes in *The Sweeney*, ordered his brother and cousin Sandra to run to the caravan, lie flat on the floor and deny they knew each other if anyone found them. Another scam was the result of a kindly local chemist offering money for rosehips.

John got all the kids on the site working for him, producing sack-fuls of booty for the startled chemist. When the man hastily ended his contract, John wailed, 'Oh no, just when we were getting a good trade going.' He became yo-yo champion of the area when he discovered there were competitions with money prizes.

John's chief source of pocket money was his talent. He now turned his experiments with Uncle Charlie's microphone under the stairs in Stowell Street to practical use. The impersonations were worked on and added to, to form a stage act. He sought out every talent competition in the area, which he invariably won, dividing his prizes between his brother and cousins to buy sherbet fountains and ice cream. His own share was spent on books of jokes, which he put into his act, trying them out on his long-suffering family: 'I'm going to treat you all.' Every Saturday morning he did his stand-up in the local cinema in Burnage,

where he became the star turn. His Charlie Chaplin was espe-cially fine and he quaintly took off Bransby Williams, a very grand old actor whom he had seen doing monologues at Ardwich Hippodrome. He discovered that though his mother may not have found him beguiling, other people did. He could command their attention and make them clap and laugh. All right, he had to go home with Ray to an empty flat, but he would occupy his mind in planning new acts, inventing material from his accurate observation of other performers. His confidence grew. He'd show 'em. Or her.

In 1952 the musical play *Where the Rainbow Ends*, which had so impressed the girl at the Holborn Empire, was to affect John profoundly too. The ten-year-old made his acting debut at Green End Junior School, as Uncle Joseph in pursuit of the same old rainbow. This was proper acting in a play, creating a character as he imagined it, not just mimicking other people. He would much rather have played the flashy Dragon, but he had no trouble, then as later, playing much older than his age. 'I was born old.'

> **29 May**
> The Glass *is aired. John not thrilled by it. Nor me. The casting of him in romantic competition for Sarah Lancashire, with Joe McFadden, our Peter Pan, who looks two years old, as his rival, is an executive's fantasy. He must choose better than this. He's nervous of the future, I can tell. Absurd of course, he is inundated with offers but the death of Morse was the end of an era and he must start again. This is not the way. He is a wonderful actor even in this ill-conceived venture and it will happen.*

He showed stage presence as Uncle Joseph, and the headmaster's meticulously handwritten log-book records that the performance was 'well received by the parents'. John was praised and applauded. He resolved there and then to be a proper actor, although he had little idea of what that was or how it happened. He knew he enjoyed being someone else. Maybe because at that time he did not much enjoy being himself.

A short while after his triumph in *Where the Rainbow Ends*, by the skin of his teeth and after some pressure by his father, John got into Ducie Technical College in Moss Side. It was no longer the salubrious neighbourhood that Charlotte Brontë wrote about when she stayed with Mrs Gaskell in nearby Plymouth Grove in 1850: 'In this hot weather the windows are kept open, the whispering of leaves and perfume of flowers pervades the rooms.' The school was a Victorian edifice near a road that was now an endless source of interest to the boys as a haunt for prostitutes. It was not a great school. It was said it prepared boys to be policemen, salesmen or burglars.

It nevertheless boasted two teachers, Sam Hughes and John Lee, the headmaster, who were to change many people's lives, including John's. They followed in the proud tradition of intellectuals in Manchester, who tried to introduce the world of hard labour to the pleasure of the arts. In 1925 one brave soul twisted the mill-owners' arms to subsidise an influential exhibition. 'What on earth do you want with art in Manchester? Why can't you stick to your cotton spinning?' they replied. John Lee, the history teacher, was also determined that his boys should aspire to more than cotton spinning. John Monks, head of the TUC, developed his life-long passion for union battles under Lee's tutelage. Now, when anyone presumes Monks must have gone to the illustrious Manchester Grammar, he says: 'No, Ducie Tech, same as John Thaw,' which he maintains impresses them more.

Aside from teaching history, John Lee's passion was amateur

Courtesy of Beattie Meyrick

Dad made me laugh even at two months old. He also made my toes curl, more often with delight than embarrassment. My sister Billie is not so sure.

John at nine months old, enjoying the camera in a rather large knitted suit.

John less elegantly dressed, aged about four. The woman holding him is possibly one of his mother's relatives.

Me at about ten years old, posing my legs like Betty Grable in *Picturegoer* magazine.

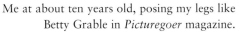

Above: Ivy Woodward and Enrico Hancock married in 1921. Dad's collar and Hitler moustache were not a good idea.

Left: My mother in an outfit she made herself, including the hat and gloves.

Dad in performance mode.

A more serious uniform: Dad in the ARP protecting the Home Front in the garden at Bexleyheath.

Auntie Beat, Grandma Thaw, John and his dad Jack, all in their Sunday best.

Grandma and Grandad Thaw on their golden wedding, 1958.

Uncle Charlie, Auntie Beat and Jack with his second wife, Mildred.

Uncle Charlie with Ray and John by the caravan at Ryll. John has obviously been eating too many chips.

John at RADA.

Vic Symonds gave him a home.

Tom Courtenay gave him friendship.

Jennifer Hilary gave him love.

ookery Nook at Oldham Theatre Royal, 1953. Judging by the set, not a high point of my
reer – Bryn Roberts and Iris Darbyshire are giving it their all but I look a bit sulky.

hn as Joxer in *Juno and the*
ycock at Liverpool Playhouse
1960. He was only eighteen
t a local reviewer noted that he
akes the character a little old
an out of Lowry'.

John, much less at home, as the fox hiding behind Barry J.
Gordon who is having a whale of a time as Brer Rabbit.
John left Liverpool Playhouse soon after.

Ellie Jane in 1964, resisting the request to 'smile, please'.

My wedding to Alec Ross in 1955. My mother made my frock in pink with a detachable sash so that after the wedding it could be adapted for use as a costume in rep.

Life is full of surprises for young Thaw.

John and Sally Alexander's elegant wedding, 1964.

Proud dad with Abigail in 1966, pre the disposable nappy era.

I dragged a reluctant Kenneth Williams off to support one of my many causes along with Albert Finney, Robert Morley, Kenneth Haigh and Johnny Worthy.

Nose to curious nose: with Bette Davis in the film of *The Anniversary*, 1967.

With Edward Woodward in *Rattle of a Simple Man*, a big success in the West End.

Over the top in the hit sitcom *The Rag Trade*, 1962.

'Don't mess with me.' John's first big break was in *The Younger Generation*.

This was taken during an interview with the *Guardian*. The brilliant Jane Bown caught me unawares between chirpy chats with the journalist. My mother had just died and Alec was ill with cancer.

dramatics. He produced the school play and pounced on John's obvious talent. His first role at Ducie Tech was a challenge to any young boy, but John's Mistress Quickly, wrapped in a huge white cloak, quelled the audience's misplaced giggles and held them spellbound.

Knowing he had something exceptional to work with, John Lee challenged John with ever more difficult roles. He introduced him to the classics, which John devoured from local library books. This careful honing of his talent culminated with the fiendishly demanding role of Shakespeare's Macbeth. So immersed was John in the manic Scot's world that when a luckless boy came on late and forgot his lines he nearly throttled him on stage, while filling in for him in perfect improvised iambic pentameter.

3 June

Arrived back from location filming to find John in kitchen looking wild-eyed and drawn. It shocked me – echoes of the drinking days – but I think it's because he has been coping on his own. I noticed his voice is still croaky from the singing and he said it had got worse. I feel a bit uneasy and we must look into it but he said it was worth it – he had enjoyed Peter Pan *so much.*

For light relief John was compere for the Burnage Community Theatre that went round old people's homes and local halls with their shows. While his brother Ray showed his defiance to the world by becoming the youngest cricket captain in Manchester and playing football for several teams, including the Manchester Under 15s, John sat on the edge of the playing field reading and learning lines. It is no wonder that he only achieved one O-level as the set books held no interest for him.

John mimicked the teachers' regional accents so accurately that they let him get away with it. Or maybe they were intimidated by this fierce lad. He was treated respectfully in the playground. His reputation was such that he ran a protection racket for a much-bullied lad called Bradshaw, in return for his sandwiches.

He was mindful of his dad's warning not to get caught, so another lad was forced to nick things on his behalf from a local shop. John became fat and unkempt. The boys' diet was not helped by the end of sweet rationing in 1953. Despite Beattie's watchful eye and the neighbours' solicitude there was no woman at home and frequently, because of his work, no father either. John was known as the boy with the grey vest and no underpants. His great discovery, with the help of John Lee, was that he could turn his back on all this by pretending to be someone else. In his early teens John had little time for girls, although he did languish after the beautiful Alison Liu, whose parents ran the Chinese laundry; he did not risk seeking love after his mother left. But something in him attracted it. He and Ray received much kindness from people – most of them with little but their compassion to give.

In the forties the grown-ups were still exhausted and dejected, despite the advent of the Welfare State, but the fifties saw a surge of energy amongst the young. The new pop music became central to their lives. To begin with, John and his brother and friends went to clubs in Manchester to hear Chris Barber, Jack Parnell, Ronnie Scott and the groovy Humphrey Lyttelton. Then they became excited by skiffle and Lonnie Donegan. Along came Bill Haley, Little Richard and the British contingent of Tommy Steele, Cliff Richard and Marty Wilde, who paved the way for the Beatles and the Stones. The age of the teenager had arrived. Before, young people had to be seen and not heard, but suddenly they were all-important and going wild. A seminal moment was Elvis Presley's appearance on *The Ed Sullivan Show* where he swivelled his hips as if he were 'sneering with his legs' and the grown-ups decided he should in future be shown only from the waist up. Young John thought him thrilling. An Elvis impersonation went into his act, slightly toned down for the old people's homes.

On the Belle Vue dance floor the old order fell apart. Sedate waltzes and quicksteps were replaced by jitterbug and jive. Girls were flung about in wild abandon. The iconic 1955 portrait of Marilyn Monroe, standing on a grille with the draught blowing her skirt up to reveal a glimpse of rather chaste knickers, was where it was at. On the tennis courts Gorgeous Gussie Moran showed her frilly ones. Young John enjoyed all this.

5 June
John still not made doctor's appointment. When I nagged him he did his usual 'Oh, never mind. Go on, show us your knickers.'

The entertainment world led the public into a revolution. Anything goes. The Goons were anarchic and incomprehensible to the older generation. Zaniness was unleashed: 'See you later, alligator. In a while, crocodile.' In his drainpipe trousers, huge suede shoes with crêpe soles, floppy jumper and cravat and sporting a long cigarette holder, a teenage John felt possibility in the air. He wanted money so that, like Liberace had in 1954, he could say to his critics, and maybe his mother: 'What you said hurt me very much. I cried all the way to the bank.'

Look Back in Anger opened in 1956 and when John read it, he recognised himself in Jimmy Porter. Film and theatre, although he had still only seen variety shows, were his obsessions. TV was not part of his ambition. In 1955 the BBC was joined by ITV but John was not one of the mere 340,000 in the country who owned a set. Olivier was his god. He spent hours listening to recordings of his performances and delighting in the idio-syncrasies of his delivery.

6 June
Went to see Dr Grimaldi about John's voice. Immediately sent him over to Harley Street to see a specialist. He said one vocal cord was frozen and 'something' was causing it. He ordered a chest x-ray. What the hell is it? I am pretending calm but I have a fearful foreboding.

Much as he wanted to act, he did not think it was a possi-bility. No one from his world went into the theatre. Instead, he left school at fifteen and tried other things. His brother was doing well as an apprentice plumber but John was positively dangerous with a soldering iron. He worked in the fruit market and nearly broke his back carrying sacks. He trained with a baker but was appalled at the thought of a lifetime putting jam in doughnuts. He passed the preliminary examination to be an electrician, but judging by his inability to change a light bulb without causing an explosion, lives were saved when he progressed no further.

Even though he had left school, his teachers rode to his rescue, believing that acting was the path John should pursue. His old headmaster, Sam Hughes, moved heaven and earth to wangle a grant from Manchester Council, should John succeed in getting into RADA. It seemed unlikely that a boy from a council flat in Burnage, with an accent you could cut with a knife, could enter those hallowed halls.

Finally John was summoned for an audition. The whole family got excited about it. Jack took a trip to the pawn shop to pay for some quick elocution lessons and buy him a new suit. His Auntie Beattie accompanied John into Manchester for the important purchase. She could not dissuade him from a complete teddy boy outfit, in which he thought he looked the bee's knees. His father expressed approval of it, despite grave misgivings, knowing how much bolstering his son needed to go to London for the first time and face all those toffs. 'Aye, lad, that's very good. Very smart.'

At six on the morning of the audition Uncle Charlie drove up to Daneholme Road in his white van. Jack got into the front to direct Charlie on the best route. Sandra and Beattie squashed up in the back to make room for Ray and John, taking care not to crease his suit. Four hours later John clambered out in Gower Street. Beattie brushed the cement dust off his trousers and he remoulded his duck's arse hairstyle in the wing mirror. His knees buckled under him as he passed between the stone figures of Drama and Comedy that flank the door of the Royal Academy of Dramatic Art. The others in the waiting room stared at him like he was something from another planet. He realised his suit was not like theirs. The fashion was obviously different down

south. He was tempted to leave. It was all a big mistake. But how could he face that lot waiting in the van? A cocky young man came out who'd obviously done well. 'All you need is confidence. Look like you're great and they'll believe you. Act it,' he told the assembled auditionees.

All right. It was now or never. He had to have this. He could act. He knew he could. So come on – act being confident.

In the audition room was a row of half a dozen people slouching on wooden chairs. John marched in, acting confidence for all he was worth. They all sat bolt upright. They looked impressed. Flabbergasted in fact. Good. He had chosen a speech from *Richard III* and he launched into his version, complete with humped back and a dramatic limp that owed as much to Grandfather Ablott as Olivier, as did the malevolence. He could hear his careful elocution slip into Mancunian now and then but he saw them nudge one another at his Olivier bits. Encouraged, he gave it all he'd got. They looked dumbfounded. When he finished they were silent. Then one of them just said, 'Thank you' and he said, 'You're welcome', and left. He told his family he thought he'd got away with it. He had. Mercifully, the panel had been shrewd enough to see the potential of the strange lad.

7 *June*

Grimaldi told us baldly – the best way really – it's cancer of the oesophagus with secondaries to the lung. He had already made an appointment with the best oncologist he knew – Dr Slevin. We were reeling. John probably doesn't realise it's the cancer Alec died of. We were incredibly calm and polite – even laughed a bit. Outside Grimaldi's door we clung to each other, then someone passed us and we were all polite again. Slevin, matter-of-fact, said he would have to have a line put into John's chest to take chemo plus a big dose by injection in a clinic once a month. Did he want to start today? John said he needed a weekend to steady himself. Dear God.

5

The Student

MY PROFESSIONAL LIFE HAS been a litany of mistiming. I have always been ahead of or behind my time. Only in old age have I caught up with myself. When I went to RADA in 1949 it was a finishing school for the rich, ruled over by a benign old buffer called Sir Kenneth Barnes. Nine years before the invasion of Finney, Courtenay and Thaw. I was too early.

8 June
Went to Tarlton. Such happy memories. The stubby trees we planted are an orchard now. The new building has mellowed. It's a lovely home. The visit seems to have made John very positive. The world Alec and I, then John and I, created has flourished. But I remember my poor skeletal Alec there and was full of fear but I did an amazing perform-ance of utter confidence in the treatment. Labour won the election. Tony's done it again. Clever bugger.

In my time the Academy moulded its students into the elegant actors required for the theatre and film of the period, for which I was not promising clay. TV, still in its embryo form, was not even considered. More important were the Radio Technique classes. My childhood encounters with drama were the *Saturday*

Night Theatre plays and *Children's Hour*, for which my family sat silently round our big brown wireless set. Radio was central to our lives. BBC English was the order of the day. Wilfred Pickles was allowed to use his northern accent for his variety show *Have a Go* but went posh when he read the news. Women weren't allowed to read the news at all. A BBC spokesman pontificated, 'People do not like momentous events such as war and disasters to be read by female voices.'

For most of the students of 1949, Received Pronunciation was no problem. All the Honourables and Lady Mucks spoke beautifully. Most looked beautiful too. I did not even try to compete, slopping around in baggy cords, ex-Navy polo neck sweater and duffle coat. The exquisite Eve Shand Kidd, huge blue eyes set in a piquant pixie face, caught me washing my face with soap. So horrified was she that she bought me a complete set of Cyclax cleansing products as used by the Queen. I eyed these beauties with envy in my soul. My early diaries, no, *all* my diaries are full of lamentations about my ugliness. An entry written when I was twelve reads: 'Please God let me look all right from the front.' Meaning the front of house.

I was acutely aware that the West End theatre welcomed only pretty women. There would have been no room then for the unconventional looks of a Juliet Stevenson, Fiona Shaw, Julie Walters or Zoë Wanamaker. They might have got character roles but not leads. I was unfashionably tall, with bad skin and an odd nose. I compared unfavourably to Joan Collins in the canteen queue. Diane Cilento looked a bit like me, but she was the pretty version. With natural white-blonde hair, green eyes and golden skin, she was what I would have looked like if my prayers had been answered. I once saw her in the bath and was overcome by her peachy loveliness. So presumably was Sean Connery, who later married her. In the sixties she played on film a part I created with huge success on stage, and it seemed absolutely right and proper. In my diary I wrote: 'News about Diane Cilento doing film of *Rattle of a Simple Man* in press. Felt rather left out and sad but don't blame them. How could I play it with this face?'

There were few men at the Academy. The death of so many in the war that had ended four years before, and the subsequent readjustment period needed by those returning to Civvie Street, meant women far outnumbered the male students. It was considered an odd profession for butch males. My first known encounter with a gay man was with Tony Beckley, at RADA on an ex-Navy grant. If there had been any homosexuals in Bexleyheath, they kept it to themselves. They had to or they could have been sent to prison. I didn't know what they were. My mother didn't till the day she died. She spent a lot of effort trying to find nice girls for my gay friends to settle down with.

What little fun I had at RADA was with Tony and his friend Charles Filipes, later Charles Laurence, the playwright. Tony treated the whole thing with merry contempt. Once, when late for an entrance as a servant in the marriage scene of *The Taming of the Shrew*, he gaily informed the audience that he had been buying a new hat for the wedding. He had a ball. He managed to inveigle himself into the Terence Rattigan party set – not difficult as he was devastatingly good-looking.

When being shown round Rattigan's opulent Brighton house,

champagne glass in hand, Tony broke the romantic spell by vomiting in the marble bath with golden taps. He regaled our little gang with tales of his glamorous escapades over coffee at Mr Olivelli's restaurant round the corner from RADA. Sometimes several of us spent an afternoon at Lyons Corner House on Tottenham Court Road, sharing a pot of tea for one and devouring bowls of sugar lumps while we applauded Ena Baga, entertaining on the electric organ. We reserved stools in the morning for a place in the queue for the gallery that evening. We worshipped at the shrines of Paul Scofield and Olivier. We discovered where Scofield went between matinees and his evening show and sat gazing in adoration as he sipped his tea. Tony and I were both in love with him. We dreamed of future stardom and vowed that when we were old we would retire to the actors' home, Denville Hall, and be outrageous till we died. All his life Tony achieved outrage *par excellence*. He acquired cult status as camp Tony in *The Italian Job* and is now buried between Tyrone Power and Marion Davies in Hollywood. A more fitting end than an old people's home for my dear, flamboyant friend.

15 June
The first operation John has ever had in his life to put a tube in his chest to put the chemo into his vein. I couldn't bear to see him laid out on the trolley but he smiled and was so sweet to all the people tending him. Eventually home with dozens of pills and potions.

I did my damnedest in classes to knock off my rough edges. I toiled at ballet and movement to control my ungainly height. A ginger-wigged man, Mr Harcourt-Davis, who taught make-up, regarded me as a challenge. He decided to go for an orchidaceous look, all slanting black eyeliner, white base and deep red lips. Startling but on the whole an improvement. I enjoyed Mr Froeschlen's fencing lessons. His cry of 'Down, down lower, and *sit*' to get us into the right stance is often repeated by RADA students of the period, especially in erotic situations. He praised my thrusts and parries and I knew I looked good in tights. During one lesson I noticed two of the dishiest ex-service students, Charles Ross and Peter Yates, who later became a film director, eyeing me intently. In the canteen they solemnly told me that after dedicated research they deemed my legs, from the knees up, the best at the Academy. That was probably the single most beneficial thing I learned at RADA – confidence in my thighs.

I had little in my voice after being subjected to the scrutiny of Miss King. Her cool, beautifully manicured hands stroked my jaw, rigid with effort, and gently lowered my shoulders from under my ears. She ignored the giggles of my fellow students as she tried to make me hear the difference between 'door' and 'dawer'. She enlisted the help of the great Clifford Turner, head of Voice Production. He suggested a tooth prop. This was an evil instrument shaped like a tiny dog's bone, that was held between the teeth in the centre of your mouth, with the object of opening up the vowels. I had it in my mouth for most of my time at RADA.

16 June
Not a good start. I mix up the pills and give him an over-dose of one. The clinic reassured me on the phone but John was pretty scathing about Sheila Nightingale.

My struggles with 'the tongue, the teeth and the lips', not to mention the ribs, the neck, the arms and the legs, did not make me an easy person to share digs with. There were four of us in the room at the Young Women's Christian Association in Archway. My RADA friend Stella sympathised with my cater-waulings but the two other girls, not being actors, were less happy, although they were content to share their clothes and food parcels from home. The rules were very strict. Doors were locked after nine o'clock. In the evenings I was in a cabaret show written by an American fellow student, Dick Vosburgh – clever mat-erial as befits the man who went on to be gag writer for many great comics including Groucho Marx and Bob Hope.

I enjoyed doing it. I also needed the money to augment my scholarship. I got in after hours through a window left open by my room-mates. When I was caught there were no second chances. Christian women were not expected to stay out late.

Stella left with me, and the two of us found a room in St John's Wood, which we shared with another RADA student called Gaynor. We took it in turns to sleep on the camp bed, the floor or the sofa. We cooked in a black frying pan that festered over the single gas ring. The landlord was a dodgy cove who employed us to sell his diamonds. We had to go into jewellery shops and pretend we had broken off an engagement and needed to sell our rings. I was his star turn. I shamelessly wove a tale of physical abuse and unwanted pregnancy that wrung tears out of jewellers from Hammersmith to Hackney. It was the best bit of acting I did while at RADA and provided a lot of our rancid chips.

Necessity drove me into many jobs, which usually ended in the sack. I worked at a milk bar in Edgware Road, but Tony took to inviting hordes of people to see me struggling with the froth machine in my large red-check hair bow that drooped over my face in the steam. The owner did not appreciate them filling the place and only buying one Banana Heaven with eight straws. Every Saturday I worked at the Archway Woolworth's. At Christmas-time I was put on the card counter. When I was handed a fistful of cards priced tuppence halfpenny, a penny farthing, threepence, three farthings, etc., I crouched behind the counter adding up on my fingers while the customers bayed for attention. The avenging supervisor demoted me to the toilet roll counter where one day I heard a perfectly projected, 'Sheila Hancock, what *are* you doing?' to which I elocuted back: 'Earning a crust, Mr Clifford Turner.'

I waited on tramps and derelicts in the British Restaurant in Oxford Street, including one regular who claimed he was Jesus and had holes in his hands and feet to prove it. I waited on the waiters at the Savoy in the staff kitchens, who vented their hatred of the clientele on us. The performers and staff of Bertram Mills' Circus were much more congenial. I was a showgirl and usherette and had to prod the lions with a stick as they ran through a tunnel into the ring, to make them roar, otherwise they would yawn all through the act after the hearty meal they were given before they went on.

One night we were told the Prime Minister was coming. The show had started when I noticed a lone man hiding in the shadows at my entrance. Mr Attlee refused to go in during an act and disturb everyone, saying he was happy to wait and have a little chat with me. Hard to imagine that happening with later prime ministers.

I grew very fond of the circus folk, admiring their camaraderie and vagabond life, and was tempted to stay, particularly when I became friendly with a man who did a motorcycle wall of death act in a contraption up in the roof of Olympia. One night his clown trousers caught in the wheel of his bike and I watched in horror as it spluttered to a halt. He floated down and died at my feet on the edge of the ring. I left soon after.

20 June
Bloody hell. The press office say a journalist is sniffing round about John. Advised to give a statement to get them off our backs. I resent this. It's like when I was ill. I don't want him to have to undergo this ordeal under the public spotlight but I drew up a short announcement. The press are usually pretty good if you are straight with them and they know I, and particularly John, have never sought publicity in a way that makes a plea for privacy hypocritical.

The nomadic circus life would have suited me. Having moved around all my childhood, I have never regarded one particular place as home. During my RADA holidays and early career I often took off and travelled. Ahead of the times again, I was a hippy before it was fashionable. In the late forties and early fifties, at every opportunity, I put a Union Jack on my knapsack, which in those days so soon after the liberation of Europe opened all doors, and hitchhiked, finding work where I could. I dug ditches in Holland to convert what had been a concentration camp into a holiday home for children. I washed up and waited on tables in Paris. Young wanderers congregated on the steps of the Sacré Coeur and sang songs to a guitar. People willingly gave us money and it didn't feel like begging. I slept rough in haystacks and barns or stayed in primitive hostels. In Paris I was delighted to discover a proper lavatory – I never enjoyed the holes in the ground – in the *Mona Lisa* gallery of the Louvre. As a result of my daily visits, I could write a paper on the beauty of La Gioconda. I stayed in Ibiza when there were only a few artists and dreamers there and sat at the feet of Robert Graves in Deya in Mallorca.

Despite these trips in the holidays, I worked hard at RADA. The biggest advantage of drama school training is the exposure to future employers and agents. But you need the right part to display your talents. In my final show I was allocated some old lady in a costume drama that has slipped from my memory. In those days there were dozens of prizes apart from the top Kendal and Vanbrugh awards. You could get one for merely walking across the stage with Grace and Charm. In 1951 I left RADA having achieved the near-impossible feat of winning nothing at all.

21 June
Filming Bedtime. *I got Andy Hamilton to tell the cast and crew about John's diagnosis, so they don't read it first in the paper. They were wonderful. We just carried on shooting in a businesslike way. One or two clasped my hand and gave me a hug – some of them have worked with John but we didn't discuss it, just went on trying to be funny. Christ!*

6

Another Student

JOHN ARRIVED AT RADA one year before the dawn of the swinging sixties. When he first got there it was stuck in a time warp. Even though Sir Kenneth Barnes had been replaced by John Fernald as principal, things had not changed a lot since I was there in 1951.

The Academy and the theatrical world were still trying to shut their ears to the rude hammerings on their doors. In 1955 the critics lambasted *Waiting for Godot* when it opened in London and in 1956 most were shocked by *Look Back in Anger*, in some cases merely because there was an ironing board on stage (although Kenneth Tynan declared in the *Observer* that he could not remain friends with anyone that didn't like it). Joan Littlewood, director of the revolutionary Theatre Workshop, riposted with *A Taste of Honey*. Shelagh Delaney, its writer, had seen a Rattigan play in John's home town of Manchester and hated its lack of relevance to life as she knew it. Littlewood said Delaney was 'the antithesis of London's angry young men. She knows what she is angry about.'

Olivier, John's idol, had dipped his toe in the New Wave playing Osborne's Archie Rice in *The Entertainer* at the Royal Court in 1957, but nicely spoken actors like Donald Sinden, Gielgud and Tony Britton were still the norm. RADA was doggedly preparing students for classical theatre for which Received Pronunciation was deemed essential. No one questioned yet why the majority of the people who received it didn't talk like that, particularly not the audiences whose knowledge of drama was through their new TV sets.

To the old guard at RADA, Marlon Brando's inarticulate performances were a temporary aberration and James Dean had died in his speeding car in 1955 in the nick of time – before he could subvert any more young actors into mumbling their lines. The famed voice supremo Clifford Turner had survived his struggles with me and continued to persuade students to concentrate on 'the tongue, the teeth and the lips'. John tried valiantly to take it all in. In one of his first lessons with the silver-haired, golden-voiced Turner each member of the class was forced to render the prologue to *Romeo and Juliet*. When his turn came John, in best-elocuted Burnage, got no further than 'too hhawoozoolds booth alayk en dugnuhtee' before Turner howled, 'Oh sit down, you're driving me mad.' Later, a much-used Thaw catchphrase, but pretty offputting at the time.

23 June
An avalanche of wonderful letters for John. We are not reading the papers but the girls say they are full of him. We caught the end of discussion on TV about his illness, saying there is only a 1 in 10 survival chance with oesophageal cancer, so we can't watch TV either. John doesn't even want to read the letters. He just wants to get on with the treatment and not think about it too much. Give it the Back Treatment. I show him the ones, quite a few, from people who have survived for twenty-odd years. His main concern is getting his voice back.

John withdrew into himself at RADA and snarled like a wounded animal. He made no attempt to make friends and no one dared to approach him. He went back alone every night to the YMCA, where he was living, to lick his wounded ego. His talent was admired in Manchester, here he was a joke. He missed his father's gruff love and his brother's devotion. Ray too was bereft. He cried for three days after his brother left, causing his Uncle Charlie to reprimand him: 'You've got your bladder be'ind yer eyes, that's wot's ter do with you.' Auntie Beat sent a biscuit tin of goodies to London every week and John ate little else. The choice of plays for the first end-of-term show didn't help. He was cast as landed gentry in Chekhov's *The Cherry Orchard*. The sound of the teacup rattling against the saucer in his shaking hands was the most memorable aspect of his first performance in front of the principal of the Academy. He was a failure and he went back to Manchester after his first term on the verge of a breakdown.

Back home he met up with his friend Harvey Bryant. Harvey reminded John that everyone had faith in him no matter what the lardy-arses down south thought, giving him the strength to drag himself back for a second term of purgatory and isolation.

The first person to battle through John's defences was Tom Courtenay. Acclimatised to London by having been at London University before RADA, he recognised the fear in the glowering boy and tried to talk to him in the canteen queue. All he got in response was a grunt. He persevered and eventually was rewarded with a few terse words. When death ended that friendship he said in a tribute to John in the RADA magazine, 'Were someone to ask me if I knew at RADA that John would become such a loved and famous actor, I would have to say I only knew there was something about him I liked, loved even.' Not many found him lovable to begin with.

25 June
Feel terrified. Sent copy of tabloid with the headline: Can Sheila's Love Save John?' Perlease.

Tom introduced John to others from similar backgrounds to himself. In the 1950s only a few bold souls from the working class thought of acting as a possible career, rather than the docks, mines or factories of their fathers. My Kent scholarship in 1949 had been one of the very first and it was still quite rare for local councils to give education grants towards drama school courses. At RADA Albert Finney paved the way just before him, although John was later to complain, 'Bloody Finney's dad was a bookie, and Tony Hopkins' a baker, they're not fuckin' working class.' John clung to a small group from the north. Tom was from Hull where his father worked in the fish docks. The gangling Geoffrey Whitehead was from Sheffield. His father had been killed in the war, so he was on an RAF benevolent grant which had also sent him to a minor public school. Michael Blackham, an enigmatic figure with black curly hair and wild eyes, whose father was a dance band leader, was from Leeds.

This intimidating gang would attend shows given by the finalists and 'rip the poor buggers to shreds'. 'Wankers!', 'Bloody rubbish!', 'What does he think he's *doing* up there?', 'Well, kid, if we can't do better than that . . .' They couldn't bear sentiment or flowery performances in drawing-room dramas, especially those in costume. John's pet hate then, as ever, was easy tears. They would tut-tut or stare silently as the cast bounded into the canteen after their shows. It was their churlish reaction to the bombardment of criticism they received from the tutors.

They fought a rearguard action against the eradication of their roots. A whole class on *A Winter's Tale* was spent trying to persuade the bolshie four that it was *shep*herdesses, not shepherd*esse*s. Tom and John's raw passion seemed to compel their arms to windmill and much time was spent pinning them to their sides at the expense of their bursting energy. Many of the tutors had been at RADA for years and had lost touch with the real world. Mr Froeschlen the fencing master was still there. He had a harder time, nine years on from me, persuading this awkward squad in saggy tights to go 'down, down lower, and *sit*.' The exception to their scorn was respected as a working actor. Peter Barkworth taught Technique and found all of them lamentably lacking in discipline. To John, much as he admired Barkworth's nimble trips and double-takes, it felt like a contrived approach. His sullen lack of co-operation drove Peter to threaten, 'You're unemployable.' He would have been in the Shaftesbury Avenue of the day, but not in the new drama that was fast approaching. A couple of the other teachers, Adam O'Riordan and Milo Sperber, discerned rough clay that could be eased gently into shape. John worked diligently on his voice and arms and comedy trips. He shed his teddy boy image for jeans and a grey sloppy joe sweater embellished with a red and white kerchief, but clung to his thick crêpe brothel-creepers. He smoked roll-ups and kept his head down but his eyes open.

There were a lot of beautiful girls at the Academy but the lads were shy of approaching them. Many were middle class or considered out of their reach. Sarah Miles fascinated them all, lovely and vague, with a large alarm clock tied round her midriff to cure her chronic lateness. One day John's eyes lighted on a tall, willowy blonde who joined the Academy a term after him.

She was standing bewildered in the canteen queue. Jennifer Hilary took John's breath away. He had not been so drawn to a girl since his schoolboy passion for Alison Liu. Her vulnerability – and his growing confidence – helped him to approach her. She was the first middle-class person he had ever been close to. He discovered that they were not all arrogant idiots, but could be as sensitive and scared as he. He visited her comfortable home and her parents welcomed him, revelling in his rough-diamond honesty. It was a salutary lesson. She too learned from him. He was better educated from library books than she'd been at her expensive school. John taught her a lot about literature, politics and the world. He fell in love with her and she became part of his charmed circle of friends.

27 June
A prison visit to Brixton. It's a ghastly place but they're trying to improve it against the threats of privatisation. The men were so sweet to me. Asking after John. Saying how much they loved his work, especially The Sweeney.

Now that John had a girlfriend, he found the restrictions of the YMCA irksome. He left and drifted around London, kipping at the home of anybody who'd have him. He managed to worm himself into some pretty glamorous places, such as Cheyne Gardens, and at one point lived with Terry Rigby, who was later to have a very successful career in America and the UK, in Soho. Here they held all-night card sessions and relieved the routine of RADA by attending workshops with Joan Littlewood at Stratford East. This rootless existence didn't help John's insecurity. Tom Courtenay came to his rescue again.

Tom was living in a large maisonette in Highbury. His landlords were Vic Symonds and Terry Bicknell. In the fifties and sixties Vic, a scenic designer, became successful on television, as did Terry, a cameraman who later married Rita Tushingham. Vic was doing a design job at the Tower Theatre, an amateur theatre in Islington where he had been told there was a lot of crumpet. There wasn't but, more interestingly, there was Tom.

Courtenay was struggling to get practical experience in a play at the Tower while studying at RADA, but loathed the effete director who kept picking on him. Vic befriended the lost soul and Tom moved into 9 Highbury Crescent. Soon after, Tom persuaded Terry to let John Thaw join them. Tom's warning, 'He's not really frightening, he needs a friend,' was slightly alarming. When John arrived, at first sight Vic felt he might indeed be full of violence. In fact, he was never any trouble. Occasionally, in his cups, he would snarl, 'That fucking butcher.' They assumed it was something to do with his mother. But even if he had it in for butchers, he was sweet with everyone else.

The house was full of media folk coming and going. Vic and Terry welcomed one and all. Slightly less welcome than some was a fellow student from RADA, Nicol Williamson, who on his occasional visits would be mournful and drink a lot of their gin.

Vic and Terry were quite happy to forget about the rent and provide the bulk of the food in return for their pleasure in watching this motley crew mature into their obvious potential. They realised all of them were 'potless' but Vic was sure that John would crack it. He was grimly determined. When *Room at the Top* came out in 1959, its hero Joe Lampton wanted 'an Aston Martin, three-guinea shirts and a girl with a Riviera suntan'. Yes, thought John, I want some of that. Vic had never met anyone with such fury, such fire. Tom, on the other hand, smouldered and sometimes seemed in danger of going out completely. He was morose and worried a lot of the time. He lived a life of enjoyable torment. Nevertheless Vic was sure that Tom, too, would make it. And Geoffrey and Jennifer. He was less sure about the wild-eyed Blackham.

Settled with his friends in his new pad, John allowed himself a bit of fun. None of them had much money and in any case clubs, apart from ones that played jazz, didn't interest them. They didn't drink a lot, not only because they couldn't afford it, but because of their typical young man's ongoing anxiety about their erections, which, judging by the visiting girls, was unfounded.

Cinema was an obsession. John delighted in spotting continuity mistakes. The boys and Jennifer visited the café of the ever-patient Mr Olivelli, who was still keeping a slate for impecunious students, as he had for Tony and me. They talked for hours over one coffee about their futures and the films and shows they had seen. They read library books voraciously and listened to records.

One lasting joy of the Highbury Crescent days was John's deepening appreciation of classical music. He had heard popular classics on *Family Favourites* on radio and the Halle at Belle Vue, but Tom listened to serious stuff and introduced John to it. He suggested the Sibelius Fifth Symphony to help John into the world of Webster's *Faust*, which they were working on. It blew John's mind. He progressed to Bach's unaccompanied cello music, which had John transfixed, lying for hours with earphones clamped on his head.

'Are you all right, John?'

'Mmmmmmm.'

On Sundays John, who knew how to cook, unlike Tom, who had a devoted mother who had done it for him, popped a joint and potatoes in the oven while they went to The Cock in Highbury for a drink. There they usually met Arthur Mullard, a cockney actor who looked like a wrestler. They were impressed because he was well known – a face. Arthur was happy to regale these young actors with theatrical anecdotes in return for a beer. On completing a season with the Royal Court he said, 'Good – done me art for this year', and returned thankfully to his sitcoms. They loved his down-to-earth approach.

28 June

Unknown to John, getting some second opinions on his case. He has such faith in his doctors he is not interested in looking elsewhere, but I feel I must explore every avenue. All seem to think the treatment right. He is bearing up to it amazingly. Poison is being pumped into him but apart from a few days in the middle of the cycle, which he calls his nadir, he carries on a normal life. He is a sturdy little northerner.

In the relaxed atmosphere of Highbury Crescent, John lightened up. He and Tom shared silly repetitive jokes and routines which gave them endless amusement.

Tom: 'Oh, that this too, too solid flesh would melt, Thaw.'

John: 'And dissolve itself into a dew?'

Another jest was speaking to each other as though they had no teeth. It probably started from a visit to see Pinter's *The Caretaker* in 1960, with which they were very taken, particularly by Donald Pleasence as the tramp. Their dialogue owed something to the radio comic Rob Wilton as well: 'Well, you schee, the ththing ish, Tchommy . . .'

They could keep it up for hours. The gag was still running in 2001 when Sir Thomas presented John, CBE, with his BAFTA fellowship.

John's trip home after one year at RADA was very different from after the first term. The Burnage flat was given a rare clean by Jack and Ray ready for his arrival, but when they opened the door, they were shocked. There stood a man with a goatee beard, cravat and long cigarette holder, and a posh accent.

'Is that you, John? What have they done to you?'

Presumably even RADA were not pleased with this transition stage, for his report said, 'He would be better if he could get the plum out of his mouth.' Harvey Bryant saw the difference in his friend and was slightly embarrassed by it. Harvey's new girlfriend had never met anything like this fellow who, at one point in the coffee bar where they met, leaped on to a chair and declaimed some verse. He mimicked a lot of actors they'd never heard of and used colourful language. They buried their heads in their hands, conscious of the rest of the clientele gawping, but John didn't seem to notice.

By their second and final year, Tom and John had become the shining hopes of RADA. They both triumphed in their RADA performance of *Faust*, in which John played Mephistopheles and Tom Faust.

The institution was at last aware that agents were now looking for actors to cast the New Wave movies, plays and TV. *Saturday Night and Sunday Morning* came out with Albert

Finney in 1960 and he also opened in *Billy Liar* in the theatre, both showing working-class England as it really is and using the genuine article to portray it. The laughable depictions of cockneys and eeh-bah-gums in the old English films were no longer acceptable.

Tom did a musical at RADA playing a Teddy boy, a performance that had agents begging for his services. John drew the short straw having to learn 400 lines of blank verse in Milton's *Paradise Lost*, but the pluses were that it was directed by the kindly James Roose-Evans and had Sarah Miles slithering around as a serpent. John, Geoffrey and Michael had a whale of a time, John relishing such defiant lines as 'Better to reign in Hell than to serve in Heaven'.

29 June
John entering Edward VII Hospital for kidney biopsy on another suspected cancer. Not best pleased with the Queen Mother's favourite hospital. When we arrived a dithering doctor asked John what he was in for. I told him tersely to read his notes. Then he said, 'Oh I see, biopsy of the right kidney.' No, you prat, the left. Then a nurse came in and twittered a lot when she saw John and asked for his autograph. I was incensed. The man is here for a life-or-death test, you silly mare. He's not Inspector Morse. He's John Thaw and he may be dying. I didn't say that of course but I did a lot of glaring. We agreed it would not rate very highly in the Rough Guide to Hospitals *we intend to write after this experience. We seem to have had visits to all of them one way or another.*

The conventional world still tried to tame them. A producer complained when Tom went to meet him wearing a donkey jacket. He was required by his agent to buy a respectable suit. Geoff, Mike and John accompanied him to Burton's Fifty Bob Tailors and tried not to mock the ill-fitting result: 'It looks the business, kid.' Tom was also ordered to get his rather charming uneven teeth straightened. Months of torture ensued. John was again supportive: 'You look fine, kid, and you'll soon learn to speak with them.'

Towards the end of their training John and Tom visited Stratford-upon-Avon with a student production of *Knights of the Burning Pestle*, or *Knights of the Burning Pisspots* as they called it. Peter O'Toole was giving his Shylock and Petruchio during the young Peter Hall's first season as director of the Royal Shakespeare Company. King of the rabble-rousers, O'Toole was delighted to meet these 'two little scamps, two scoundrels' outside the actors' favourite hostelry, The Dirty Duck. Never happy with state theatres and 'subsidised rubbish', Peter found the pub the only thing he liked about Stratford, and spent a good deal of time there, away from the 'biscuit factory'. He invited the two boys to the matinee and bunged them in the front row, thinking they would loathe such establishment fare, but as luck would have it, the lights failed and the afternoon was blissfully anarchic. Peggy Ashcroft struggled to play Katharine while Peter was driven to wild excesses by the boys' hoots of laughter.

Their student days were drawing to a close – apart from Jennifer who had another year to go. John and the rest of his gang had to prepare to face the real world. They had good show-case parts in their final term at RADA, so their careers were well launched. Geoffrey went off to get experience in various rep companies and then into television. Blackham, angry as ever, moaned about getting a role in a pot-boiler called *Come Blow Your Horn*. 'Well, you should know how to do that, kid.' Whilst the others kept in touch for a while after they left the Academy, Blackham disappeared. 'Whatever happened to Michael Blackham?' they asked one another. Tom, on the other hand, was very visible. Equipped with his new teeth and suit, he landed the lead in a major film, *The Loneliness of the Long-distance Runner*, in which John had a small part. Tom also won leading roles with the Old Vic and then took over from Albie in *Billy Liar*. The world was his oyster. John was never, for one moment, jealous but he called Tom 'Golden Bollocks'. His own were silver, at the very least, because he landed the two top RADA prizes, the Vanbrugh and the Liverpool Playhouse Prize, much coveted because it provided a year's contract with one of the country's leading companies.

30 June
Today I was actually making pacts with the devil, in the hopes there is one. What would I give to have John fit and well?

For me to die when he does? – Done.

For me to die in agony? – Done.

To lose all worldly wealth? – Done.

(Although I'm not too sure John would approve of that.)

Jack to be ill again? – No deal.

Any of my grandchildren or children to be harmed? – No deal.

My career to end? – Done.

And so on.

7

The Young Woman

YOUR FIRST JOB IN the profession indicates your career path. Kick off with Juliet at the Royal Shakespeare Company in Stratford and you are set fair for damehood. My first job after leaving RADA in 1951 was in twice-nightly repertory at the Theatre Royal, Oldham, playing in quick succession the leads in *Pick-up Girl*, *Reefer Girl* and *The Respectful Prostitute*. The last must have been a terrible shock to the management who, attracted by the title, did not realise it was an obscure play written by Jean-Paul Sartre. When I gave my mother some earrings bought from my first earnings she was grateful but urged me to try to find some 'nice' parts. I did my best.

3 July
The press have been wonderful since our statement asking for privacy but today at the post office two photographers started snapping at us. John was feeling peaky and just sighed but I was like a wild animal. Luckington has never seen such an unseemly display. The woman used her camera as a weapon, holding it at her face flashing it at me as I approached screaming. She muttered, 'I have to earn a living.'
'That's what the commandants in Nazi Germany said.'

A tad OTT perhaps. Offered to pay the man whatever he would earn for the photos. He actually blushed and said, 'Oh Sheila,' and slunk away. John was deeply embarrassed by my performance. As was everyone in the post office. Nobody mentioned it as I bought my stamps, but I bet it will be all round the village.

While teenage John was rocking round the clock in Manchester, I was doing the rounds of the agents wearing a smart rig-out made by my mother with obligatory hat and gloves for London. Day after day I traipsed up and down Charing Cross Road and Shaftesbury Avenue, where the agents hung out. Only one showed the slightest interest. Miriam Warner was the doyenne of tatty agents. She crouched in a filthy office in Cambridge Circus, her short, fat body enshrouded in shapeless velvet garments, with a squashy hat permanently concealing a suspected bald head. Occasionally she waddled through to the outer office and berated her staff and the waiting assembly for bleeding her dry. Regardless, her assistants, Pauline, a blonde ex-chorus girl, and Smithy, an ex-comic, both covered in cigarette ash, served tea and comfort to the footsore actors crouched round the spluttering gas fire in the fug of the outer office. Miriam sent me along to several general auditions known as cattle markets. A queue of actors forms outside a theatre and they gradually filter on to the stage. From the dark of the auditorium a voice yells, 'Next,' and that is your cue to walk off the other side and go away. Sometimes you are greeted with 'What's your name?' and, if you are lucky, 'OK, what are you going to do for us?' If you are extraordinarily lucky you get to finish your audition speech, but more usually it is cut short with 'Thank you, we'll let you know.' I never got beyond 'Next'. Eventually Miriam persuaded me to return to Oldham for a season. At least they wanted me and it would be good experience.

Doing a play a week had to teach you something. Mainly the ability to get away with it. In Oldham I learned and rehearsed one three-act play at the same time as playing the current one twice every night and three times on matinee days. The only direction there was time for was, 'Say the words and don't bump into the scenery.' The eminent critic Michael Billington thinks Harold Pinter's directorial approach of cutting the crap stemmed from his rep days. Pinter is quoted as saying, 'A rehearsal period which consists of philosophical discourse or political treatise doesn't get the curtain up at eight o'clock.'

I had neither time nor, as yet, inclination for political discourse but my social conscience was stirred by the conditions I found in Oldham. Kindly Smithy sent a note to the company manager Bryn Roberts: 'A little girl named Sheila Hancock will be joining the company for *On Monday Next*. Try to help her find digs.' What Bryn found was a room in just such a house as John had spent his childhood in. One outside loo between four houses, gaslight, black coke stove for cooking, no bathroom or hot water or heating. Every cobbled road seemed to have an illegal betting shop and a pub dedicated to serious drinking.

Ethel and Bert made me as welcome as their abject poverty permitted. Eventually I deciphered the Oldham accent and during the year I was there I grew deeply fond of them, especially Ethel. Bert's Saturday night ritual of getting viciously drunk and beating up his wife made him less easy to love. This was an accepted part of their marriage routine until one day I suggested bolting the door against him until he sobered up. He was a tiny man from a Lowry painting, and after a bit of shouting and banging slithered down the front door, out to the world. We lifted him on to the settee in the front parlour and left him to sleep it off. I think Ethel thought it was rather dull compared with their usual Saturday night.

When I saw the conditions under which he and Ethel worked at the local mill, I could understand, if not condone, Bert's impotent rage. They worked in day and night shifts. In the small hours of the morning a knocker-up rapped on the bedroom window with his pole. I was in bed learning my script by candlelight. The sound of the clogs clattered down the cobbles to the cotton mill at the bottom of the hill. Inside the mill the heat and steam were stifling and the din of the looms meant the workers either bellowed or communicated with their own sign language.

6 July

Bliss to be in France for a few days. We have mastered changing his chemo bag between us. He reads the directions and I do it, rubber gloves, sterile everything, drawing off blood, etc., etc. I pretend to be a nurse trying to seduce him. It's like a Carry On *film. I bought him a nice notebook to write his worries down. He can destroy it if he wants to but it will help to get it down on paper, I think. He says he will but I have my doubts. We barbecued sardines today, sat in the sun in a café in Saignon. He said, 'I keep forgetting I'm ill.' I fear I don't. It obsesses me, wondering about the future. I dread going back. But I don't let on.*

The workers in the mills and the local iron works were paid a pittance, as was I. Our staple diet was chips and mushy peas. Occasionally someone would bring a hotpot to the stage door because they thought I looked too thin. It was my first experience of the extraordinary fondness the public could offer me.

The audience in Oldham sat in the leaking, decaying theatre, sometimes with umbrellas up in the stalls, lapping up our escapist rubbish. My diary during that year's engagement has entries like: 'A horrid little piece, *My Wife's Lodger*. I spent my whole time writhing with shame and shrieking with laughter – it was so bloody.'

Again: '*Ma's Bit o' Brass*. A bloody awful perf. In a bloody awful play, bloody awfully done.'

'Terrible, terrible play, *Murder on the Nile*, I stink to high heaven in it. I'd like to do something violent to Agatha Christie.'

I played every age and type. Whenever the part demanded it, I did my best to bring some glamour to Oldham. My orchidaceous make-up was embellished with hot black, a block of wax melted and applied with matchsticks to elongate the lashes. We had to provide our own clothes for the shows. One homemade evening dress served several plays with the ingenious addition of a tulle overskirt, long gloves or a feather boa. To keep my spirits up, I treated myself once a week to a visit to the local bathhouse. It was a bleak place with concrete floors and chipped white tile walls. It echoed with the shouts of women doing their washing. The cubicles with the stained baths were not much used. The fierce woman who handed out a threadbare cloth and slab of carbolic soap was affronted by my rejection of them in favour of my own fluffy towel and Mornay pink lilac bath cubes, soap and talcum powder. It confirmed her opinion of the lardy-arses from the south.

At twenty I fell desperately in love with my much older, married leading man. Being a well-brought-up virgin, and fearful of hurting his long-suffering wife who was also in the company, it never went beyond a stolen kiss outside the pub after the show, and anguished playing of love scenes on stage. Ethel and her friends from the mill commiserated with me, sitting on the whitened front stoop, metal Dinkie curlers hidden in turbans, hands warmed on pint pots of tea. Their pungent views on men shocked and educated me.

After a year, with the confidence the Oldham audiences had given me, I decided to go back to London and try to get some more high-class work. That meant signing on twice a week for the dole. Chadwick Street in Pimlico was a branch of the Labour Exchange frequented almost entirely by actors, so it was quite a jolly experience. My parents could not get the hang of the new welfare system and were horrified that I seemed to be deliberately living off the state. A letter from my mother says: 'I hope you decide to earn some money, not keep *out of work*, be sensible and not too artistic for a while.' The puritan work ethic was deeply embedded in them. I persevered for a while in my quest for better-quality work, mistakenly relying on my only ally, Miriam. One day, just before Christmas, she summoned me to the office. I arrived in my best outfit, to be told excitedly that she had the perfect job for me: 'Wolf – skin provided'.

10 July
John was in sparkling form today. His mimicry is inspired. He makes me laugh so much. Walking through Apt he growled, 'This place is full of chien shit.' Sitting in the Grégoire Café he contemplated a drunken waiter who looked a bit like Alec Guinness playing Herbert Pocket and went into a long riff about the venerable knight visiting Apt to blow up the bridge in front of the café and, inflamed by the fornicating frogs in the river bed, leaping on a local barmaid, after a duel for her favours with Laurence Olivier who got lost in Apt on his way to Agincourt. His sad lovechild turned to drink, not knowing his father was a famous actor and it was our duty to tell him. I had to restrain him from doing so.

Even if I had had a decent agent I doubt if I would have found much better roles than pantomime wolf at that time. The West End was then ruled over by the management mafia of H. M. Tennent, run by Binkie Beaumont and John Perry, two witty gentlemen who presented plays with pretty people. After a few humiliating months of pounding the audition beat, I succumbed to my mother's plea, 'Really, darling, ambition is not worth all the anxiety you are causing yourself and others who love you and are your true friends.' I retired to the drudgery of weekly rep and tatty tours for another eight years of obscurity.

Miriam managed to wangle me into a set-up run by two sub-Binkie-type impresarios, Barry O'Brien and Michael Hamilton. Their companies were an improvement on Oldham, mainly playing seaside resorts like Bournemouth, Torquay, Ryde and Shanklin. Michael Hamilton was a plump, red-faced, pursed-lipped individual with a very short fuse. He liked my versatility as it saved money to have one girl who could cover leading lady, juvenile and character parts.

All went well until I joined one of his shows in Bath. The day I arrived I went into the pub near the Theatre Royal to meet the company. There, in the saloon bar, was a Greek god. Curly hair, brass-buttoned blazer, open-necked shirt with casually tied cravat and a debonair way with a cigarette, he was leaning languidly on the counter, holding court with smooth charm.

I didn't dare approach although I realised this was the highly regarded Barry O'Brien leading man, Alec Ross. I didn't think for a moment that he would cast his divine lopsided smile in my direction. But after one week's rehearsal and halfway through the playing week of our roles as lovers in *Duet for Two Hands*, he did. As with my first Greek god at school, Alan Coast, it was my acting that did the trick. That and the fact that by then he had probably exhausted the charms of the other female members of the cast, and probably most of Bath.

Alec was ten years older than me and his sophistication bowled me over. Back in London for a week out, he took me to the Salisbury pub in St Martin's Lane, seething with theatrical folk, all of whom he seemed to know. Jack's Club, Gerry's, the Buxton and the shady Kismet were full of out-of-hours heavy drinkers, among them Dylan Thomas, Louis MacNeice and Peter Finch. They were all his friends. I was gobsmacked. So was he, because, like a good working-class girl, I was saving myself for marriage, in compliance with my father's rule that there would definitely be 'none of that there 'ere'.

Michael Hamilton was unaware of my obstinate virginity. When we returned to do a season in Bournemouth, one night after the show he threw a tantrum about my relationship with Alec, ending with him trumpeting to everyone in the crowded theatre bar that I was an adequate actress – he could hardly deny that in front of the paying public – but I would never get anywhere with a nose like that. I was devastated and perplexed at the viciousness of his attack. Alec stood up for me, which made Michael bounce about with even more apoplectic rage. After he had stalked out, Alec comforted me but did not explain what was behind this unpleasant scene.

19 July
Greeted by a copper at Victoria who told us I had created a stir on EastEnders. *Shock, horror, incest. Oh, the English obsession with sex. Or rather the press. It was one drunken kiss from a rather sad old biddy, for heaven's sake. They seem not to have heard the much more shocking stuff about me beating my children with a stick. John exhausted after the journey. He didn't say a word about it on the way. He only tells me after the event – too late to help him.*

As a young actor with radiant good looks Alec had been languished over by Michael and the gay community, particularly at the BBC where he worked a lot. For a lad from Tottenham, the glamour of their social lives was beguiling. Unfortunately a young man called Kenneth Morgan, who was a lover of Terence Rattigan, became enamoured of Alec. He left Rattigan and moved into Alec's flat. What exactly was the nature of their relationship no one knows but it was fated to be unsatisfactory for Morgan. Always a disturbed young man, he killed himself when Alec was out one evening. Rattigan and many of his cronies blamed his death on Alec's attempts to befriend the youth. *The Deep Blue Sea* was written about this story, and it is said that the character of Freddie is based on what Rattigan knew or heard about Alec. In many ways it is an accurate portrait of a fatally attractive but feckless man who unwittingly commands devotion that cannot be as fervently returned.

Like Rattigan's Freddie, Alec was in the RAF during the war. Many young men who went through the ordeal of wartime service came out unable to cope with ordinary life. Six years of not knowing if they had a future, doing as they were ordered, and being regarded as heroes, was confusing for such young men. At eighteen Alec was a volunteer, as were all air crew, but he can have had no idea of what he was letting himself in for. He was a bomb aimer who could not bear bombing people. Lying flat in the nose of the plane watching the flak from gunfire coming towards him, he had to map-read and lead the pilot to the target and then release the bombs, often having to jump on them if the bomb doors got stuck. If the plane was attacked he also had to man a gun, something else he hated because you could see the whites of the eyes of the people you were trying to kill. He served in Africa, Italy and Egypt, covering hundreds of miles of hostile territory on each sortie, from which it was lucky if 50 per cent returned. Several times he crash-landed with bits of the plane missing, once in enemy territory. On one occasion a member of his crew caught fire in the plane and Alec cradled his smouldering body as he died on the flight back to base.

For two years he wooed me spasmodically. Sometimes in frustration he tried to break away by having a fling with someone else. The fearful rage these dalliances put me in started me on my career as a petition obsessive. In 1955 Ruth Ellis was condemned to death for shooting her lover who taunted her with his other affairs. Alec never did that, but I lusted after him to such an extent that he only had to look at another woman and I was consumed with jealousy. So when it was judged that for a woman jealousy was no grounds for murder, although it was often accepted as a reasonable motive for a man, and Ruth was ordered to be taken to a place of execution and there be hanged by the neck until she be dead, I was beside myself. I rushed around everywhere, stood on street corners collecting signatures for clemency and staggered up to the door of Number 10 Downing Street, as you could in those days, with the first of many petitions on various issues. Alas, I was ignored on this occasion, but her shocking hanging hastened the end of the death penalty.

Eventually poor Alec yielded to my conformist ideas and in 1955 he married me. My parents spent their savings on a nice wedding with a sit-down tea at the Embassy Ballroom in Welling near Bexleyheath. My father cried a lot in his speech and later our theatrical friends whooped it up with relatives from both sides. Alec was loath to leave such a good party, especially as he confessed he had done nothing about his side of the wedding arrangements – a honeymoon. We ended up traipsing around London looking for somewhere to stay. I lost my virginity in a gloomy room overlooking the dustbins in the back of the Strand Palace Hotel.

Alec and I started married life in a dark, two-roomed basement in Pimlico, which we shared with my girlfriend Jeanne to help out with the rent. The bathroom was also the kitchen, in which the bath became a table when covered with an old door. The colour and vivacity of the design in the Festival of Britain Exhibition in 1951 had made us aware of the drabness of the utility furniture and dull paints and wallpapers that we had grown up with. It took until the sixties for the new approach to filter through to the high street with the arrival of Habitat, but I did my best to be with it. I slapped on to the walls a very bright pink paint that I'd mixed myself with the help of red ink, and varnished the lino white to reflect what little light there was in our basement. An interesting texture was added by the dust and stray insects that landed on it during the drying process. My mother helped me to make covers to turn our bed into a sofa by day, with purple and mauve satin cases for the pillows. We were kept warm by a smelly paraffin stove.

The fifties were a strange interim decade. You could feel things changing, certainly amongst the young, but we did not quite have the courage to go with it. The reforming post-war Labour Government destroyed itself by the usual socialist infighting. The British public got nervous, and despite the huge benefits they had received from the changes brought about by Labour, put the toffs back in charge again. They had always felt bad about their treatment of Churchill, so back he came, aged seventy-seven, in 1951. When he resigned, aged eighty, Anthony Eden took over, followed by Macmillan. Members of the old school with a vengeance.

20 July

Poor old Jeffrey Archer, jailed for four years. Why are people taken in by these phonies? After I did Any Questions *with him years ago he sent me flowers and messages and I knew he was an upstart but he got a peerage and all sorts. The same as when I met Robert Maxwell. Everyone was kow-towing to him but with his dyed hair and silly eyebrows he was obviously a figure of fun. Why did anyone trust him? How do all these second-rate men pull the wool over people's eyes? But Archer didn't deserve four years in a hellhole for being a fantasist. It's society's revenge for being taken in.*

As the decade progressed our lives were getting brighter. I had learned to make a mean salad dressing in France, but was hampered in England by having to use a medicinal yellow olive oil from Boots. Then Cullens opened in Pimlico and stocked a beautiful French version. Only one brand and it sold out very quickly, but it was a sign of things to come.

I enjoyed the domesticity of caring for my home and husband. We acquired a kitten called Tarquin which I took on a lead to the nearest square, there being no earth in Claverton Street for feline toilet facilities. I took him to parties as well, affecting black velvet trousers and waistcoat to match his fur, worn with the new crippling stiletto heels. There were not many parties for us. When we were out of work, living on the dole, we could not afford the obligatory bottle to take with us, or to return the hospitality. Rationing had ended in 1954 but we hadn't the money for much food anyway. In 1957 Macmillan said that we had never had it so good, but it didn't apply to impecunious actors. In the same year I had a spell in hospital suffering from malnutrition.

When we were working we had no time for a social life except in digs with our fellow actors. This made for complicated love lives. Passionate affairs lasted the season and then everyone moved on. Propinquity, Alec and I put it down to. 'I think Bob's having a bit of propinquity with Sarah.' We were thrown together in an alien world. People were very suspicious of actors. We really were outsiders then. In a place like the Isle of Wight, where Alec and I did several summer seasons, the company's goings-on were legendary. Most towns had a Watch Committee composed of local dignitaries keeping an eye on people's behaviour. In Shanklin they kept constant vigil lest our embraces on stage became too explicit. The management had a letter of complaint that my shorts were too short for walking down the High Street. Husbands clutched their wives tighter when we went to social gatherings and our actors eyed up the local talent. One or two local husbands sent me naughty notes and surreptitious bunches of flowers. The son of a prominent local tradesman became flamboyantly gay, egged on by our juvenile character actor. A sombre note was struck when our dapper leading character man was arrested in a public lavatory in Portsmouth and committed suicide rather than face the inevitable sacking and disgrace. You had to be a star like John Gielgud to get away with it. When Sir John was expected back at rehearsal after his court appearance for a similar so-called crime, the indomitable Dame Sybil Thorndike rallied the company to keep silent and not mention a word about his case. When he walked in she was overcome with emotion and threw herself at him saying, 'Oh Johnny, you silly bugger.'

In the towns we played on tour, everything was closed by the time the curtain came down. If you speeded up the last act you might just manage a rushed drink before time was called in the nearest pub, but there was no hope of a meal except in the big cities where there might be an Indian restaurant open. Nightlife was non-existent. Crewe station on a Sunday was a bit of a treat. Only actors and fish travelled on Sundays and all our routes seemed to cross at Crewe. The buffet was kept open and stars mingled with the riff-raff. We exchanged gossip and cross-word clues and laughed over Tynan's latest vicious review. It was a hand-to-mouth existence but we had great fun. I enjoyed my work and the company of my fellow actors. Above all, I felt secure with my new husband. Even Michael Hamilton was pleased – he got us cheaper as a package than individually.

22 July
Tory leadership battle a joke. I long for them to produce someone I can hate like Thatcher. We need an opposition to fear. A new entry for the Rough Guide *– Harley Street Clinic for radiotherapy on top of his chemo. Lovely nurses, great oncologist Dr Leslie. John utterly stoic about it all. I filled him in on what to expect. He seemed not to turn a hair but after the session gripped my hand and said, 'I*

*don't know how you managed this all on your own. I'm
so sorry for that, my love.' I love him so.*

Another couple fell in love during a Barry O'Brien season.
Vivien Merchant, a withdrawn, sensitively beautiful actress,
became my rival for parts in the company. She had an enigmatic
quality that oozed sex appeal, so I got a lot of dreary plain parts
when we worked together. When David Barron joined us the
two were soon an item. He was a brooding presence and super-
cilious about the plays we did. It must have been torture to him
to utter that crass rubbish when his head was full of ideas very
soon to be performed under his own name of Harold Pinter. In
the Torquay season when we all went to the pub he was locked
away, writing in his digs. I thought he was a bit of a poseur
and nowhere near good enough for Vivien. When I saw *The
Birthday Party* in 1958 I was staggered by its rich originality.
Even though it was a flop, to my astonishment I discovered that
our mysterious friend was a great writer.

At the start of his career Harold's plays had more success on
TV and radio. The theatre was slower to accept him than the
growing TV audience. TV was now a significant element of
public life. The size of the audience had leaped ahead with the
broadcast of the Queen's Coronation in 1953. Two million
people had sets at the time. Then, in pubs, halls and other
people's homes, twenty million more saw the Coronation and
presumably rushed out to buy sets of their own. It was a major
event. Watching in a pub in Bournemouth, my favourite moment
was seeing the huge Queen Salote of Tonga waving from an
open carriage in the pouring rain. Seated opposite her was a
tiny man in uniform. Apparently, when asked who he was, Noël
Coward said, 'Her lunch.'

My mother's injunctions were now about taking care of my
husband rather than being artistic or ambitious. We kept our
Pimlico base but theatrical digs were our nomadic home. Signs
stating 'No blacks, no Irish, no dogs' would sometimes add 'no
actors' to their list. In 1955 many West Indians disembarked
from their boats dressed in their Sunday best in response to the

British request to fill gaps in the labour market. They were greeted by many with the xenophobia that seems to afflict our country. The Freedom Movement starting in America was beginning to enlighten and change us. Rosa Parks sitting in the white section of a segregated bus and Martin Luther King's 'I have a dream' speech were an inspiration. My mild protest was to tear down all the 'no blacks' signs that I could in the towns that we visited. We visited dozens. It always seemed to be winter when we toured. My sister gave me a cast-off beaver-lamb coat which Alec and I slept under in the freezing digs, spending all our spare daytime in the Turkish baths if the town had one. I felt as though I was caught on a treadmill, destined to remain in second-rate repertory and touring companies all my life.

When a friend of mine suggested a change of course I jumped at it. Eric Lloyd was stage manager of *Masquerade*, a concert party on the Isle of Wight starring Cyril Fletcher. They needed a soubrette and Cyril rashly took me on. Alec was at Shanklin Town Hall in the rep, ploughing through the usual Agatha Christies and dire comedies, whilst I did five changes of programme on the pier at Sandown. I danced, I sang, I fed Cyril in his act and played in the sketches. Most of my energy went into working out which item came next and what I should be wearing for it. I once shimmied on to the stage in a Carmen Miranda outfit and found myself singing 'My Old Man Said Follow the Van' in a cockney scena. It was my first experience of working with a comic and it stood me in good stead when I went to Bromley next to play in *Tons of Money* with Frankie Howerd. I was thrilled to be so near London where someone might see me. I was playing quite a good role but whenever I was in danger of getting a laugh, Frank would intervene with, 'No, don't laugh – poor soul – she went to the RADA, you know' (pronounced radar by Frank). 'No, perlease, perlease have some respect.' Nigel Hawthorne and I watched in awe as he jettisoned the script and went off into wild fantasies of his own. It was one of Frank's frequent periods in the theatrical wilderness and no one important came near us, but supporting this anguished man gave us a friend for life.

Alec and I stayed in the company at the New Theatre, Bromley, a converted swimming pool, and when I played the dual role in *Separate Tables* I wrote to all the good agents asking them to come and see me, as Miriam had retired. It was a double bill. In the first half, playing an ex-model, I put on the hot black and skintight dress and in the second, playing a dowdy frump, I took off my make-up and wore flat shoes and a shapeless frock. I worked hard on the two characterisations, using a different voice and physicality for them. On the first night when I came on transformed after the interval, my mother heard a woman cluck, 'Oh dear, hasn't she let herself go.'

One agent was sufficiently impressed by my performance to summon me to see him. He was John Redway, one of the very top, later to be John's agent. I was thrilled. At last. I walked into his sumptuous office and saw his face fall. He sat me under a lamp and moved my head from side to side. He said I would have to have plastic surgery. Obviously my prayer to look 'all right from the front' had worked, but close up I was a disappointment. I slunk back to Bromley and the comfort of Alec's love and his faith in my future, which never wavered. I played principal boy in panto, slapping the now fishnetted best legs from the knees up with aplomb. For two shows a day plus two matinees the salary was a dizzy £19 per week and Alec earned similar as Baron Hardup, so we ate well that Christmas.

20 August
Beautiful weather at Luckington. We went for a drive and had a picnic in a field. Made love in the sun, slightly hampered by me squashing his chemo tube, then sat in the grounds of Badminton House having tea from a Thermos reading the papers. I suggested we buy a couple of fold-up camp chairs and start sitting in lay-bys with our picnic. We really are becoming a couple of old farts. And it's lovely.

Tony Beckley dragged two of his friends down to see me in *Dick Whittington*. It was my first stroke of luck since leaving RADA nine years earlier. Disley Jones, a designer, and Eleanor Fazan, a director and choreographer, were producing a revue called *One to Another* with Beryl Reid. Known for her work in variety theatre, Beryl was taking a risk by doing a show with material by offbeat writers like N. F. Simpson, John Mortimer, and my acting colleague, Harold Pinter. Fiz and Dis took the risk of employing an unknown and I seized the opportunity to display the versatility I'd acquired during my arduous first years in the profession.

Harold's sketch had Beryl and me playing two old lady tramps discussing bread and cheese and pausing a lot. In rehearsal, both of us, used to quickfire comedy work, had been appalled by Pinter's insistence on the very long pauses being meticulously observed. In front of an audience he was proved right. They held their breath in the silence, then roared with laughter at the banality or repetition of the line that followed it. It was a huge success for Harold and a perfect sketch that still worked in 1997 when I played it with Dawn French.

The show brought me to important people's notice for the first time, but my next job, with the great director Joan Littlewood, was the one that changed the nature of my career. After leaving RADA in disgust, Joan worked in radio in Manchester. The BBC there was ruled by Alfie Bradley and Alice

Shapley. They were unashamedly revolutionary left-wingers so Joan was very much at home. She was an innovative broadcaster, one of the first to do interviews on location with ordinary people. Her questions were sometimes naïve, as when she asked a miner, 'Tell me, how long is your shaft?' She turned to the theatre and formed a brilliant team producing original work in Manchester. Her company, known as Theatre Workshop, then took over the Theatre Royal in London's Stratford East. The establishment began taking notice. *Fings Ain't What They Used to Be* and *Oh What a Lovely War* blasted the popular musicals of Ivor Novello out of the water, and her plays like Brendan Behan's *The Hostage* and Shelagh Delaney's *A Taste of Honey* were putting characters on stage which had never been seen there before. And actors. Joan liked real people. She liked clowns and characters. She rescued mavericks from oblivion and made them into stars, then was furious when they moved on to make more money.

22 August
Fabulous Prom. Young Chinese guy, Lang Lang, who no one had heard of. Rachmaninoff's Third, that old war horse, reborn by this youngster, he radiates joy at his genius. Beams at the orchestra, bounces on his stool and plays like an angel. The audience started indifferent and ended ecstatic. I leaped to my feet and yelped with delight. John tugged at my shirt. 'Yes, all right, calm down dear,' but he was thrilled too. A great star is born and we were there. Must get the recording. (I wonder if you'll hear me screaming.)

I managed to get an audition with Joan and stood on the stage in my best dress, giving her my St Joan speech. Loud laughter came from the stalls. Not what I had hoped for as, with tears in my eyes, I contemplated being burnt at the stake. A square-shaped woman leaped on to the stage, pulling a cap down over her brows, big eyes bulging. 'Stop, stop that rubbish! You're a clown, a lovely clown. Let's have some fun, bird.' Crouching round me, legs astride, bouncing up and down, she

led me into a wild improvisation. From that day on I
worshipped the woman. She released my creativity and made
me feel clever. She could be a cow because of her dedication
to creating exciting theatre – it was absolute and nothing was
allowed to impede it.

Joan gave me a small part in a musical by Wolf Mankowitz
called *Make Me an Offer*. The small part grew during improv-
isations in rehearsal and one day Joan needed something to cover
a scene change, so she ordered Monty Norman to write me a
song. 'It's Sort of Romantic' stopped the show on the first night.
I did an encore and still they cheered. Eventually, in true Theatre
Workshop tradition, I harangued the audience, explaining I
couldn't keep singing it over and over so would they please shut
up. I stole all the notices. It was my first experience of that sort
of success and it scared me. I thought audiences were expecting
so much that I would disappoint them. For several nights Joan
stood in the wings with me before my entrance, making me close
my eyes and imagine 'you're in a dark, dark forest and out there
is light and warmth and welcome. On you go, you lucky bird.'
And on I bounded with the help of a shove from Joan.

In the pubs and cafés of Angel Lane in Stratford East, Joan's company talked about politics and I listened. Joan and the people round her were a huge influence in forming my political conciousness. I felt at home with them. When I was fourteen I had joined the Young Communists' League, unbeknown to my parents, mainly because there were a few long-haired Greek gods in the membership. Stalin, the uprisings in Poland and Hungary and the building of the Berlin Wall had disillusioned me. The Workers' Revolutionary Party, very important for many people in the profession, did not appeal. My experience of the Blitz, the shock of Royan and the Fricker boy and above all the invention of the H-Bomb gave me, in common with many of my generation, a profound fear that underlay my whole existence. The Bomb overshadowed everything. We knew how close the human race was to annihilation. The Korean war in which two million died, the rattlings of the coming war in Vietnam, and later the Cuban Missile Crisis were powder kegs. It seemed to me the most important issue of our age.

When CND was formed in 1958, the idealism stirred up by Joan and her friends found an outlet. I sat in Grosvenor Square and marched and chanted and petitioned all over the place. In 1962 I made an LP with the folk singer and composer Sydney Carter, curiously named *Putting Out the Dustbins* considering it was all about CND and pacifism. As a filler I recorded a song of Sydney's about giving up smoking called 'My Last Cigarette' which to my chagrin and, I am sure, Sydney's was issued as a single and eclipsed the passionate political message of the rest of the LP. Love and peace were the aspect of the coming sixties that appealed to me more than the King's Road hype. To ban the Bomb didn't seem foolish, it seemed essential before it got into the hands of some maniac like Hitler. The arguments about the balance of power seemed not to take into account the rogue element in the human race. Not everyone is sensible enough to say this must never happen. It already had. Twice.

11 September

Horror. Driving to Oxford to chair a conference on the treatment of young people in prisons. Heard on the news that a plane had crashed into one of the Twin Towers in New York. Thought what an awful accident. Then there was a second. Couldn't comprehend what was going on. It didn't occur to me that it was deliberate. Turned on the TV in my room at the Randolph and the full dawning nightmare had me shaking and weeping. Phoned John and Jo and Matt in France. They knew nothing so I told them to turn on the telly. Went to the college to a session and everyone was stunned and disbelieving. Quite a few Quakers so we had a silent meeting. Words are useless anyway. The images of people floating down having jumped from the windows and what must be happening inside that hellhole are eating into my brain, I am appalled at the implications of what could follow. I fear the reaction of the Americans led by that idiot Bush. It is as shocking an occurrence as Hiroshima or Nagasaki and like them could change the world for ever.

My parents were terrified by my political goings-on. They were worried that I would jeopardise my growing success. Actors were expected to keep their opinions to themselves lest they offended sections of their audience. To stand up and be counted was new and dangerous behaviour in the theatre. Corin Redgrave and many others, including Vanessa, suffered professionally for boldly fighting for what they believed.

My ideal scenario was to change the world or maybe just one or two minds with my work. That was the crusade of the people working in the new television and newly emerging British film industry. The writers at the Royal Court Theatre, too, were intent on overturning the status quo. Joan's manifesto summed up her objectives:

The theatre must face up to the problems of its time; it cannot ignore the poverty and human suffering which increases every day. It cannot with sincerity close its eyes to the disasters of its time. If the theatre of today would reach the heights achieved 4,000 years ago in Greece and 400 years ago in Elizabethan England it must face up to such problems. To those who say that such affairs are not the concern of the theatre or that the theatre should confine itself to treading the paths of beauty and dignity we would say, read Shakespeare, Marlowe, Webster, Sophocles, Aeschylus, Aristophanes, Calderon, Molière, Lope de Vega, Schiller and the rest.

12 September
Not easy chairing a meeting when everyone is so distraught. I pointed out that we were powerless over the big consequences but here we had an opportunity to make some small gesture. We are dealing with young people caught up in violence and anger. The men that perpetrated these appalling acts were fuelled by a similar rage surely. We have got to try and understand why people do such things before we can stop it. Can't wait to get back to France to talk to John, Jo and Matt about it all. It's a time to cling together and value what is good and gentle.

In the next revue I appeared in was a young man who has since lived his life by a credo just like Joan's. In 1962 the renowned socialist director Ken Loach was Kenneth Williams' understudy in *One Over the Eight*. He may have been planning the revolution in the wings, or just praying for Kenneth's good health – only Kenneth could milk lines like 'Bleeoomin' great war clouds are leeoomin' on the horizon' for laughs. The chief joy of *One Over the Eight* for me was meeting and becoming friends with the writer of the show, Peter Cook, and Kenneth, the maverick star. We ran for some months, egged on by our dance captain Irving Davies' exhortation, 'Come on, darlings, eyes, teeth and tits,' in the West End of London, which the American *Time* magazine declared to be the most happening city on earth.

The swinging sixties were upon us. *Children's Hour* with Uncle Mac ended in 1961 in the same year as the contraceptive pill went on sale. We grew up with a vengeance. I went to the King's Road and bought my regulation Mary Quant miniskirt at Bazaar, one of the new boutiques full of sparkling new fashions. I got myself some Courrèges white boots to wear with it. They were a bugger to clean. In my late twenties I was a bit old for it all, but my Vidal Sassoon fringe came over my eyebrows and covered my forehead lines.

On the face of it, I was in there swinging with the best of them but somehow I didn't feel very dizzy. Neither did Kenneth Williams. One night after the show, when I gave him a lift back to his chaste flat on the back of my Lambretta, he waved his furled umbrella at Eros as we circled Piccadilly Circus, crying, 'Where is it? Where is it all happening? Where are all these orgies? Why haven't we been asked?'

8

The Young Man

REPERTORY THEATRE WAS STILL thriving in England in the late fifties and sixties, a lot of it featuring Sheila Hancock, most of it pretty tatty, but Liverpool had been one of the best. By the time John arrived in 1960 to start his one-year RADA contract, Willard Stoker, who ran the theatre, was old and tired, and the repertoire had become jaded. A local powerhouse called Maud Carpenter had a disproportionate say in the choices. When a Chekhov was suggested she wailed, '*The Seagull*? *The Seagull*? I'm havin' no more of them bird plays. When we did *The Wild Duck* we emptied the house.'

John's first play must have slipped past her guard, for she surely would not have liked Sean O'Casey's *Juno and the Paycock*. One of the local paper reviews hints that from the start John's style was at odds with the rest of the cast: 'The only performance which gets outside the bounds firmly established by thirty years of English acting is John Thaw's Joxer. He makes the character a little old man out of Lowry. Sprightly, shoulder-shrugging and sniffling little man whose only permanent terror is Juno.'

20 September
The world feels a much dodgier place. Going through the
Channel Tunnel was a bit scary. With terrorism you don't

know where it will strike unlike the wartime raids with nice sirens to get you ready to be killed. Lots of dire warnings of possible attacks, gas, smallpox, tanks at Heathrow, etc. But I am more concerned with my little personal drama. What is this new-sounding cough John has? Will they be able to operate? What will the next scan show? Bugger Osama bin Laden. What about John Thaw?

The attitude of his fellow rep actors appalled John. Tired out and often disillusioned, they struggled just to get the shows on, whereas in an interview to the local paper he said, 'You know, it rather horrifies me. I'm so single-minded about acting. I worry a good part to death, stay awake at night thinking about it.' He continued studying anything he could lay his hands on to learn his craft. The girls in the local library in Liverpool fought to stamp his books and overlooked his fines, having become fans of this bad boy of the local rep. He had an edge that disturbed and thrilled them. Alma Cullen, then one of the girls from the library, writes: 'He was part of the wave of actors, writers and directors – mostly from the North – that was then sweeping away so much dead wood from literature, theatre and film. It's hard now to convey the thrill of seeing, albeit from the sidelines, the strongholds of the privileged falling to tough invaders like John who didn't talk posh but confidently offered their work as the outward expression of a political vision. What an inspiration they were, even to the girls at the library.'

The girls in the library were the first of many women drawn to the mysterious centre that they felt they could understand and comfort given a chance.

John struggled to bring something to second-rate material, knowing that elsewhere exciting things were going on without him. At the Cavern, in the same city, the Beatles were causing a stir with a new sound and he was stuck doing old-fashioned plays in dated productions.

Jennifer came up to see him and, John, adrift again and away from all his friends, begged her to commit to him. She had not yet finished at RADA and marriage was the last thing she wanted.

They had night-long anguished talks, but could not resolve the issue of their conflicting ambitions. When John returned to London on visits to Vic in Highbury, he was often in tears about his dashed dreams of perfect love and companionship.

He was not completely friendless in Liverpool. While most of the actors found him a pain in the arse, with his moods and critical attitude, two men saw his worth and supported him. Freddie Farley had come over from Australia as a protégé of Frank Thring, a larger-than-life actor whose success was over-shadowed by his outrageous behaviour. The rampantly homo-sexual Thring went through with a grand wedding with all the trimmings, including Vivien Leigh as maid of honour, and as he sashayed down the aisle with his new wife on his arm, he spied a young man in the congregation and squealed, 'You're prettier than the bride, dear!' Freddie, in contrast, claimed he was asexual, 'an old virgin', but replaced this lack with genuine devotion to his friends. A learned man, he gently took John under his wing, directed his best performances and generally held his hand.

Freddie's compatriot and dearest companion, Barry J. Gordon, not only helped John but laid to rest another of his prejudices. With his belligerently male upbringing, it is understandable that John had no tolerance of homosexuals. Indeed, I was told by a gay friend that he had been mentally bullied by John and some of his friends at RADA. The victim was elegantly middle-class and it was before Jennifer infiltrated John's barrier of class hatred, so he was no doubt doubly heinous in John's eyes.

Regardless of John's prejudices, Barry offered his friendship. The approach he chose, as befitted his brash Aussie personality, was to be utterly open about his sexual orientation with John, as he was with everyone else – a brave move when most homo-sexuals in those days lived in dread of discovery.

Barry was the first openly gay man that John had ever got to know and, once Barry had assured him he had no designs on his body, John was surprised to discover that he could like and respect him. It is a measure of his trust that one day he asked Barry to accompany him from Liverpool on a trip to seek out his mother. She was working in a dingy pub isolated on a bomb site in an insalubrious part of Manchester. Barry sat discreetly in the corner, watching John perched on a barstool holding an awkward conversation with a bosomy blonde. She was a far cry from Jennifer Hilary.

The two men left the pub in silence. Eventually John blurted out, 'I'm glad I came, but I don't think I'll be bothering again.' Barry knew better than to probe further and the visit was never mentioned again. His tactful handling of this difficult youth was rewarded when one night in the wings, waiting with John for an entrance, Barry whispered that he was nervous. John looked him straight in the eye and said, 'You shouldn't be. You're unique.'

22 September

In Lincoln to raise money for a Quaker home for troubled boys. I looked out of my hotel room window when I woke and saw a cross in the sky. Like a vision. After a while I realised there was a heavy mist concealing the cathedral it was on, so it seemed to be floating. Very odd though. I hope it's a good omen or is it a signal of the agony of the Cross? It is certainly a suffering old world and I'm not exactly dancing with joy.

A little later, while still in Liverpool, John met Ken Parry. A rotund, Dickensian figure with no neck to speak of, he is known in the profession as Campari, partly because that was how J. G. Devlin, the Irish actor, pronounced his name, but mainly because he is blatantly and joyously the campest thing on two legs. Someone defined camp as the trait of trivialising the important and dramatising the frivolous and Ken is queen of the genre. He will declare, 'I'm a nasty washer-up', as if admitting to mass murder, whereas when he was diagnosed with a deadly illness, he threw a jolly 'suicide party'. He has fed, watered and pampered numerous young actors and actresses who call him 'Mother' whilst he calls them, regardless of sex, 'Alice'. Before he took John on as an 'Alice' he solemnly warned, in his posh

Wigan accent, 'You want to be careful what you say to me or if you befriend me – I'm an awful old poof.' John assured him that Freddie Farley and Barry J. Gordon 'had brought me up, so forget about all that'.

For many years Ken fussed over John like a mother hen, giving him a bed when he needed it, taking food up to Highbury or feeding him in his flat in Russell Square and, later, Islington. 'I've a beautiful home. I call it the Immaculate Conception, it's so clean.'

On one occasion, Ken went to Brighton to stay with a friend and Tom and John pestered him with phone calls about how hungry they were. Eventually he came home early to be greeted at Victoria station by the two herberts in dirty raincoats holding a bunch of dandelions. Once they caught him without his teeth; he swears their toothless jokes started from there.

Campari's advice to young actors was, 'Always do every job that is conceivably possible. Keep working.' John did his best to stick it out in Liverpool, but he was hating every minute. Auntie Beat went to a matinee of *Round the World in Eighty Days*. People were ambling in late after the interval, still drinking their tea. She was mortified when John came on for the second half and, seeing this, said, 'Stop. If they can't finish in time, neither can I,' and ordered a cringing assistant stage manager to bring on a mug of tea, which he drank slowly, sitting on the stage, before continuing with the action.

The final straw was a Christmas production of *Brer Rabbit*. Barry greatly enjoyed bouncing around as a frisky bunny, but John was far from happy in his furry fox hat. At one point, for some reason, they were jammed in a box together on the stage while children in the audience were being very rude, catcalling and running to the loo. Rising above the insults, the rabbit perkily washed his whiskers, while the fox cowered behind him quietly groaning, 'I can't put up with much more of this – this is fucking embarrassing.' Shortly after, he broke his contract and left the company.

It was a wise move. He had been spotted by people from Granada Television, but he still had his RADA-induced belief that theatre was the thing. In press interviews he talked of his preference for a live audience. He did a play at the Royal Court in which he was rather grumpy about the size of the part. Lindsay Anderson's comment to him, that there are no small parts, only small actors, became John's benchmark, but he didn't practise what he preached. When television offered him longer parts, the theatre lost its charm.

Now, back at Highbury Crescent, life was becoming exciting again. When Tom and John were filming *The Loneliness of the Long-distance Runner* they were picked up in a battered Rolls-Royce, chauffeured by Bert. He would ring with their time to be picked up the next day and on to the message pad would go, 'Bert rang'. Eventually, Bertrang became his name and the message read 'Bertrang rang'.

John dated several attractive girls but he still hankered after Jennifer. He played the field a bit, but with no great pleasure. Being deeply in love was more his style. Tom had an involvement with a delectable French actress who used to sigh, 'Oh, ze life', and when they rapped at the bathroom door would enchantingly call, 'Ahm in ze bas.' Both were added to their shared repertoire of sayings. John started to go to decent restaurants, and frequented Gerry's, a haunt for actors, and the more sleazy Jack's Club, favoured by the Joan Littlewood crowd and Alec Ross.

1 October
John had a breathing crisis. I was out. Jo drove him to the Harley Street Clinic in a panic. He couldn't breathe, was gasping and choking and then she realised he was also laughing. Had seen a restaurant on the Edgware Road with the name 'The Beirut Express' in neon lights. The man is extraordinary. They sorted him out at the clinic and all the while he was making them laugh about the incongruity of the café's name. He's so bloody brave.

John and the Highbury gang visited the Seven Stars Restaurant, part of the Lyons Corner House in Coventry Street. It was the most popular place for actors to go and let their hair down after the show, a huge room where you could help yourself to salads or have slices of juicy beef, accompanied by jacket potatoes with the chef's unique sour cream and chive dressing. The main attraction, however, was not the food but the clientele. Sir John Gielgud held court, scattering his famous faux pas to the delight of all: 'Oh, I thought you were that dreadful old bore, Ernest Milton.' It was. John considered the Kenneth Williams and Sheila Hancock table overly theatrical and raucous. Campari knew them all. One night Tom and John were falling about with laughter and, when challenged, did an impersonation of him greeting everyone in the restaurant with royal hand gestures and silently mouthed, 'Hello, how *are* you?'

To Alan Plater, one of Tom's friends from Hull, the inmates at Highbury Crescent seemed the height of sophistication. That said, he was bemused when he showed them the model of a Jaguar he had bought for his son and they were happy spending hours pushing it round the floor making 'Vroom, vroom' noises. Alan was to become one of the leading new TV writers. A grammar school boy like so many of them, he had seen the film *Saturday Night and Sunday Morning* and it had set his brain on fire to realise he was not the only one to feel like that. Very soon everyone was flattening their vowels and drop-ping their 'h's and claiming to be common; in fact Alan suspected that there were workshops on the subject, but he and his ilk were the real thing. Writers were given their head on television. If they were good they just had to produce an idea on a scrap of paper and they were commissioned. The only stricture was that they were not allowed to say 'fuck' or show explicit sex. These restrictions proved no obstacle to truthful drama like *Cathy Come Home* in 1966 which opened everyone's eyes to the problem of homelessness. Before Thatcher's children took over, with their obsession with ratings and budgets, a programme could be any length, no fitting in a slot between adverts. Say what you've got to say and then stop was the order of the day. The preoccupation was with quality and the audiences lapped it up. The thought of dumbing down never entered the writers' heads. They respected their audience. These guys – and they were nearly all men – wanted to change society.

7 October
Oh God, here we go. We are bombing Afghanistan. Grow up, you stupid bastards. This is a new kind of war. You don't beat terrorism by killing people and making more people hate you.

When the opportunity arose, Alan suggested John for a role in one of his plays. At their first meeting, Alan had found him a bit intimidating, but there was something about John that made Alan want to earn his respect. It seemed important to do so. Granada had already heard of John's work at Liverpool rep and were delighted to employ him. When Alan watched him work in the studio, he realised that there was a quality that, if you just pointed a camera at it, was very exciting. Over a drink one day, John asked him how to play one of his roles. Alan had no idea how to direct actors so he said, 'Climb inside and say the words.' Probably the best note he ever had.

John had found his métier. From the start, he was completely at home in front of the camera. Authors wanted him for their plays and the plays were ground-breaking and thrilling. He worked for all the top writers emerging in TV. This was where it was at. In spite of the upsurge of production of good British films, by the likes of Schlesinger, Richardson, Lindsay Anderson and Karel Reisz, cinemas were closing. The country was enraptured by the telly and ordinary people were becoming the stuff of drama. *Coronation Street* had a huge following. The old order changeth, and up there with the changes, loving every minute of it, was the twenty-year-old John Thaw.

Alan received a summons from the great John Hopkins to write for *Z-Cars*. It was a Papal blessing for a writer. Based on an idea of Troy Kennedy-Martin, with writers like Troy, Hopkins, Alan Prior and John McGrath, and directors of the calibre of Ken Loach, James McTaggart, Shaun Sutton and Herbert Wise, *Z-Cars* had changed the face of police series. Gone was dear old Jack Warner plodding the beat and in his place were cars and witty, quick-talking coppers. Alan had the idea of introducing a bent cop, a shocking idea for TV in those days, and what's more, he wanted it to be one of the regulars. This was deemed impossible, but he was told to write in a new character for a few episodes and then bend him. Thus, in 1962, John played his first TV copper. Not only that, but he met John McGrath and Troy Kennedy-Martin and his brother Ian who were to influence his career in the future, as well as becoming good friends.

In the same year, Granada chose John for a new series called *The Younger Generation*. A small team of young actors did a series of plays, at first on stage in the Stable Theatre in Manchester, then on screen. It was a great opportunity which John grabbed with both hands. An article in the press summed it up thus:

They are the lucky ones. They have grown up in a young actor's paradise, a time when the men seemed to be old at forty and screenplays were full of teenage villains and twenty-year-old heroes. A time too when distinctive accents – which

ten years ago might have banned an actor from success –
came to be accepted, exploited and finally worshipped. These
seven men must bless the day ten years ago when ITV came
on the air. Then they were in their teens, most of them still
at school, tomorrow they could be idols. They are the young
lions of TV.

Despite his growing success as a 'young lion' of TV, John did
not completely desert the theatre. He fitted in a couple more
plays at the Royal Court in Sloane Square and *Women Beware
Women* at the avant-garde Arts Theatre. He also continued to
study other actors' performances closely, particularly those of
his hero, Olivier. He visited Chichester where the embryo
National Theatre was performing *Uncle Vanya*. John wandered
backstage to find a crisis unfolding. The Russian musicians had
lost their way and the curtain was due to rise. He cowered in
a corner and saw his idol, Sir Laurence Olivier, Knight of the
Realm, burst into the dressing room of Sybil Thorndike, eighty-
seven, venerable Dame of the British Empire, and proclaim: 'Shit,
baby, we've lost the band.'

Shortly after, in 1962, John got his dream job. Not only did
he get a very good part in a West End play, *Semi-detached*, by
David Turner, but the star was Laurence Olivier. Unbelievably,
he was also called upon to understudy him. It was strange that
a twenty-year-old New Wave, ultra-naturalistic actor should
worship such a member of the establishment, but John relished
Olivier's flamboyance. He recognised a great actor who could
mesmerise an audience and felt privileged to be working with
him. He greedily vacuumed up any advice. When Oliver said,
'Do as I do, baby, amaze yourself at your own daring,' he did
his best to comply. For the rest of his life.

21 October
*John in Luckington. Me to London on my own for a
meeting. First time on my own for some time. Even when
he is in hospital I stay with him in a camp bed in his room.
Alone, I let go and sobbed with fear and frustration. I*

*would do anything to make him better. If there only was
a devil I could sell my soul to I would gladly let him have
the poor tattered thing. Anything, anything to have him fit
and well.*

Olivier had a curious relationship with his audience. They
adored him, but John would watch him spying on them through
the curtain before the show, revving himself up by muttering,
'Fuck pigs.' Maybe it was because the role was not one of his
triumphs. He was off ill for several nights and a terrified John
had to go on for him. The groan when it was announced over
the tannoy that Olivier was going to be replaced by a little-known
whipper-snapper changed to cheers at the end. Truth was, that
even though too young for the part, John was more suitable for
the role of a working-class man, and it was generally acknow-
ledged that he was better in the role. Heady stuff for a relative
beginner. Olivier was endlessly generous to him, as he was many
years later when John beat him to a Best Film Actor award. On
that occasion John was so embarrassed that he almost refused
to go on to the platform and collect his statuette.

After the fiery dedication of his television work, it was fun,
in *Semi-detached*, to be directed by the louche Tony Richardson.
Egged on by James Bolam to wear make-up, John appeared on
stage at dress rehearsal smeared inexpertly with theatrical Five
and Nine panstick, 'slap', as it is somewhat sadistically known.
He was greeted by one of Richardson's shoulder-heaving laughs.
The director's nasal, lock-jawed voice drawled: 'I mean – I mean
– John Thaw, what have you got on your face? You look like
Ivor Novello playing a Red Indian.'

Assistant stage manager on the production was a young
woman called Sally Alexander. She had been at RADA a year
below John and, like so many of the girls, had worshipped him
from a distance. When she walked into the rehearsal room on
the first day and saw the leather-jacketed, bejeaned vision she
had so fancied, she was overjoyed. A middle-class girl, attractive, long-legged, intelligent but shy, she was just John's cup of
tea, and very soon she was putting in appearances at Highbury

Crescent. He was still raw from his loss of Jennifer, but over time he began to trust Sally and eventually to love her. His career was on the up and up. He felt secure enough to contemplate marriage more sensibly. Whereas a couple of years earlier he had said, 'If ever it becomes clear that I'm not going to make it, I'll give it up,' now he was confident of the future. A bewitched woman journalist reported: '"What I want," he said, fixing me with eyes like twin aquamarines set between sideburns, "is to be respected. People are going to think of John Thaw as an actor who played good parts often and well."'

The nineteen-year-old Sally respected his talent, was in awe of it, and wanted to help him. Again he was welcomed into a wealthy family with great warmth. When they got engaged John took her to Manchester to meet his family. Although she loved his relations she had never seen such poverty as the flat in Daneholme Road that he had grown up in. There was almost nothing in the room – rudimentary furniture, no flowers, no ornaments, just an HP Sauce bottle on the table. It opened her eyes to a way of life she had never encountered before.

They had a lavish wedding with the reception in Sally's father's house in the Home Counties. There was a marquee in the garden and champagne round the pool. Tom was best man and John's motley group of friends were bowled over by the glamour of it all. Vic Symonds, Michael Blackham and Ken Parry were impressed but worried about the John they knew embracing the hated bourgeoisie. Auntie Beattie, Charlie and the family travelled down to Berkshire in the van. Beattie forgot her hat and they had to stop off at C & A in Oxford to buy another. They splashed out on lunch at a posh restaurant where the waiters frightened Beattie to death by flambéing her steak. They had never known anything like it. Beattie proclaimed it 'the day we lived'. Uncle Charlie had to take Ray out of the church because he predictably sobbed his heart out. He was even more heartbroken when, shortly afterwards, he bade John and his father goodbye and emigrated to Australia.

John's friend from RADA, Nicol Williamson, behaved, as was his wont, disgracefully at the wedding reception. Auntie Beat and the family watched aghast as he leaped into the pool in his underpants, took them off and squeezed them dry into the champagne glasses waiting to be served. Since his student days, he had become even more of a melodramatic madman after a few – no, a lot – of bevvies. In the year of John's marriage, 1964, he proved himself a superlative actor in John Osborne's *Inadmissible Evidence*, and was considered likely to follow in Olivier's footsteps. John admired him profoundly and they were devoted friends. Drink could make Nicol cruel and dangerous but entertainingly outrageous. He took to walking off the stage if he didn't feel like performing, and during a dress rehearsal of *Macbeth* in Stratford, the revered director Trevor Nunn, who can go on a bit, was dithering about the most effective way to kill one of the Macduff children, when from the stalls Nicol drawled, 'Why don't they take him into the wings and you can bore him to death?'

7 November
Beautiful autumn weather. Old fart mode again. A picnic with Thermos and papers in the car at Badminton Park. One of those conversations you can only have if you have been together for aeons.
Along the lines of:
There's a bit here about . . .
Yes, I saw it.
Was he married to your friend . . . ?
No, that was . . . er you know . . .
Oh yes . . . er . . . er mudger.
We met him when you were at the RS –
No I was at the National with –
No you weren't, that was before.
I tell you – what was his name?
Began with a P.
No it didn't.
An odd name.
It'll come to me in a minute.
Had a funny voice.

Er . . .
Oh bugger, I'll get it in a minute.
M – N – P –
Oh, I give up. He was a rotten actor anyway.

John and Nicol were part of a group of idealists, left-wing and passionate, who worked together on a wonderful film called *The Bofors Gun*, directed by Jack Gold, who had come from documentary and news and didn't know how to direct actors, but knew how real people behaved. His only note ever was: 'I don't believe it,' which they all understood. (In his later career, after a superlative take John would often mutter, 'That was almost believable'.) Jack went on to an illustrious career in movies after his beautiful telly feature about Quentin Crisp, *The Naked Civil Servant*, but being a man of huge integrity, he chose committed work over making a fortune in Hollywood. The film was produced by Tony Garnett, and written by his *Z-Cars* pal, John McGrath. In the cast were Ian Holm, David Warner, Nicol and John, all of whom later had battles with demons of various sorts, but at the time they were young, hopeful and brilliant.

Every now and then over the years, Nicol rampaged back into our lives for a while, but – whatever happened to Nicol Williamson? The last time John came across him was in Harley Street, when Nicol walked straight past him. John was convinced Nicol had seen him. Ken Parry waited for Nicol to come out of a stage door in New York, only to be pushed aside like Falstaff by Prince Hal with a curt 'My public is waiting.' Nicol was in London when John died and it was in all the papers. He had lunch with one of their mutual friends, but never mentioned John's death. A brilliant, self-destructive nutter, much loved by John.

It was not only Nicol that John drifted apart from. He lost touch with most of the other people who had been so impor-tant to him in those early years. Some, like Ian Kennedy-Martin, were hurt by his neglect. Others – Ken Parry, Barry J. Gordon, Jennifer, Vic, Geoffrey and Tom – accepted that it was part of the business. Propinquity. Close and affectionate and then move

So What about Love?, 1969: the play on which John and I first met.

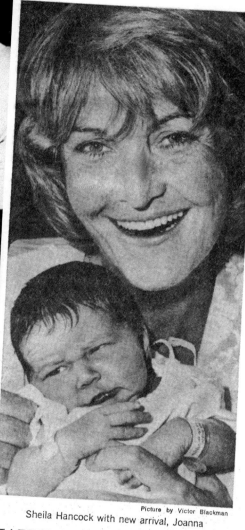

Picture by Victor Blackman

Sheila Hancock with new arrival, Joanna

HAPPY DAYS ARE HERE AGAIN FOR SHEILA

By Brenda Holton

ACTRESS Sheila Hancock, aged 38, whose life has not always been as joyful as her stage and TV performances, was the picture of happiness yesterday as she showed off her new baby, Joanna Suzy.

Miss Hancock, who married actor John Thaw last year, gave birth to 8lb. 2oz. Joanna at Queen Charlotte's Hospital, Hammersmith, at the weekend. She already has a nine-year-old daughter by her first husband, actor Alec Ross. They were married for 16 years until he died three years ago of cancer.

Recently Sheila appeared in a TV appeal programme, speaking in aid of the home where Mr. Ross was cared for during his illness. Now she says : " The sadness has gone."

And with baby Joanna joining the family the happy days seem here to stay.

FremantleMedia

You're nicked!: John and Dennis Waterman on set in *The Sweeney*.

FremantleMedia

Off set, in the pub after work.

Keeping up with the day's news. John was a newspaper addict.

The Teeny Sweeney interrupts filming.

Jo has her daddy's eyes.

Garfield Morgan, John and Dennis cornered by fans whilst trying to film.

Joanna wants his attention as well.

John was very moved when his brother Ray flew in from Brisbane to surprise him on *This is You Life*, 1981.

John and Dennis's rapport was worked into the script of *The Sweeney*.

One of John's proudest moments was appearing on the *Morecambe and Wise Show*.

Rehearsing with Angela Lansbury and Dame Peggy
Ashcroft for Edward Albee's *All Over* at the RSC.
A big success.

As Tamora in *Titus Andronicus* (Mrs Goth) with
Hugh Quashie, Roger Allam and Colin Tarrant.
An epic failure.

The Two of Us by Michael Frayn. We look serious enough in this rehearsal but during
performance we were convulsed with giggles. Working together was not a good idea.

With Robert Hardy as Churchill, John was uncannily true-to-life as Bomber Harris.

Cardinal Wolsely in Shakespeare's Henry VIII with the RSC: 'A working man in the court of kings.'

Joe Cocks

As Sir Toby Belch in *Twelfth Night* at Stratford.

Joe Cocks

John enjoying rehearsal of *Pygmalion* with Peter O'Toole, Jack Watling and Joyce Carey. John is wearing his Doolittle boots to help get the character, O'Toole is trying not to corpse.

Embarrassing Ellie Jane.

Behaving with more decorum, collecting my OBE in 1974.

The Morse team: Kevin Whately, Colin Dexter, Kenny McBain and John.

on. Over the years they heard about one another on the grapevine. All except Michael Blackham.

But in 2003 Geoffrey was walking by Camden Lock when he saw a familiar figure coming towards him. Recognisable even beneath a long black beard and shoulder-length hair, dressed in flowing robes obviously worn by a religious cult of some sort, was their friend of old. He was still enraged, ranting as they had when rubbishing their fellow students' performances: 'They're all wankers, kid, they've got it coming. The end of the world, fire and bloody brimstone. It's all coming to an end, kid. That'll show the fuckers.' *Plus ça change, plus c'est la même chose.*

11 November
Very low and frightened. The world is a mess. Wonderful disillusioned quote from Albert Camus on the Spanish Civil War seems to fit: 'Men learnt that we can be right and still be beaten, that force can vanquish spirit, that there are times when courage is not its own reward.'

John's domestic life was transformed from his Highbury days; Ken Parry was rendered redundant by Sally: 'When they got married my job was done.' Sally was making their Notting Hill home comfortable, and when their baby, Abigail, was born, they enjoyed a period of great happiness. John adored his daughter and was happy changing nappies and helping in the house. He was patient, gentle and loving with the child. When his old friends came round to carouse there was now a baby upstairs, and it could be awkward. Sometimes Sally felt left out when they talked about their ambitions for she had none. If she did ever mention pursuing her acting career, John would say, 'I'm the actor in the house.' On rare occasions when he was out of work he became morose and unapproachable and she didn't know how to help him. At other times his love was overwhelming. She was only twenty-two, with no experience of this kind of volatile temperament.

Not long after they were married, John's *Z-Cars* friend, Ian Kennedy-Martin, came up with an idea for him to play the lead in a military police series, *Redcap*. John Bryce and Lloyd Shirley, the producers, nurtured him in the role and this, his first big series, was a success. People started to recognise him in the streets and he found it difficult to cope with.

John began to realise that his future would be mainly in the medium of television. An interview appeared, showing a certain arrogant defensiveness, 'I asked John Thaw if he ever doubted he would be a successful actor. He just said, "No. Unlike some actors I have no ambition to play Hamlet or Romeo. What bores they were. Didn't even get the girl in the end. I prefer meatier roles."'

Sally thought that he should pursue his theatre career and he accused her of being an intellectual snob, only interested in reviews in the *Sunday Times* from Harold Hobson. She wanted him to do more jobs like the one at the Traverse Theatre in Edinburgh in *La Musica* by Marguerite Duras. (A later colleague, Oliver Ford-Davies, saw John in the production and, when he worked in *Kavanagh*, blackmailed him with the threat, 'If you're not careful I'll tell the film crew you're very good in avant-garde French drama.') But John earned virtually nothing in Edinburgh whereas he could make good money now on television. He berated Sally for having no idea what it was like to be poor. She became alienated by his rage. Eventually, she turned to someone else who was kind to her. It was a meaningless relationship, but it destroyed what was left of their three-year-old marriage. Walk away. Turn your back. As with his mother, John did not question why this had happened. He, like Sally, was devastated, but too hurt and inexperienced to put it right.

18 November
Molly Mae's birthday. Lovely party at Abs and Nigel's. All Sally's family there. I left John to talk to her for a long time. It must be awful for her to know how ill he is but not be part of his life. Although thankfully they are now good friends. Life is too short, God knows, to hold grudges. How can people who have been married and have kids together manage to walk away and never contact one another? It's beyond me. To be that close and then just say I'm never going to see that person again. But then I'm hopeless at goodbyes. I'm an awful clinger.

Like Jennifer, Sally came out of her relationship with John wiser and stronger. He opened her eyes to the inequalities in society and the importance of politics, even threatening to lock her in the lavatory if she didn't vote for Wilson in 1964. Very soon she pulled her life together, went to university and became a much-respected socialist feminist historian. And of course they had their beautiful daughter Abigail.

After the break-up of his marriage John first fled to stay with Nicol and then moved in with Ken Parry. He went back to his bachelor existence, bitterly disappointed. He hated seeing his beloved daughter only occasionally. Sitting glumly in a launderette with Jimmy Bolam, watching their washing go round, he muttered, 'Look at us, Stars on bloody Sunday.' Ken drew the line at doing his ironing, wailing, 'I'm only an amateur poof, dear, I may be a mother but I can't iron, I just can't do it.' John always liked a neatly ironed shirt so he invested in an ironing board. When he became moody Ken would confront him with, 'Now listen up, Mr Piss Quick, you behave,' and remind him 'You have the privilege of going to your bedroom if you're depressed. I never inflict discipline on anyone.' He proved a rather better mother than Dorothy Thaw, keeping his sex life apart: 'Not one of them ever saw me with a man.' All John's energy became focussed on his acting and he was getting very good at it, but he didn't know how to achieve his dream of perfect love and a safe family life. Ian Kennedy-Martin and his wife Barbara befriended him at this time and he observed how happy they were. He wanted some of that.

John was doing telly in Manchester when his agent called to say that one of his wild friends, Victor Henry, had gone AWOL before starting rehearsals on a West End comedy called *So What About Love?* Victor was another brilliant young actor set on a path to destruction. Not long after, his car hit a lamp-post, leaving him in a coma for three years before he died. Arnold Wesker, who had a difficult time with him, said: 'Victor came from Yorkshire, one of that generation of working-class actors who strutted cockily through the profession scorning everyone middle or upper class and dismissing with contempt anything such as intellect or genuine emotion with which they couldn't cope . . . He had wit and was possessed of a kind of passion albeit contaminated by that most insidious of all psychological states – the inferiority complex.'

Some of that description makes it clear why John's name came up to replace Victor. John, obviously, was different. He came from Lancashire.

Michael White, the producer, and Herbert Wise, the director, wanted him to take over the lead but Sheila Hancock, the star, was insisting on meeting him before it could become an official offer. John's initial reaction was to say, 'Piss off.' Some bloody sitcom queen, loud mouth from the Seven Stars, vetting an actor with a track record of non-stop success seemed a liberty. But they were willing to pay his fare from Manchester and he could see his mates. Besides, Beattie and Dad thought she was lovely on the telly.

Sheila Hancock was late and he was livid at being kept waiting. Eventually she burst in with a flurry of 'Darlings, I'm so sorry,' and dropped shopping bags everywhere. She was wearing a full-length red fox fur coat over a miniskirt up to her arse. He was buggered if he was going to kow-tow to her. She drew up a chair and sat down too close to him; he hated people invading his space. She crossed her legs and out of the corner of his eye, he glimpsed her knickers.

28 November
John went to a reception at Buckingham Palace. He had a blood transfusion to pep him up. Then had to go up a huge flight of stairs in front of the cameras. The Queen asked very fondly how he was.

9

The Woman

IN 1962 TOM STOPPARD wrote of me, 'Sheila Hancock fits into the new clutch of toughened individualists now ousting the tradition of sweet young things who once conquered all with a wistful lift of a false eyelash.' So there, Snow White. I *think* it was a compliment when Stoppard went on to liken me to 'a tired chrysanthemum, who could put on a cruel blue look that could freeze a hummingbird to an oven door'.

When that was written I was playing the lead in a hit show in the West End, thanks to a young impresario called Michael Codron who was challenging the old guard with new plays and new actors. While John was heralded as a 'young lion' of TV, I was breaking new ground in the theatre. Michael cast Edward Woodward and me in a virtual two-hander play written by Charles Dyer, who like Pinter had been a fellow actor in rep. It was designed by Vic Symonds, but he never invited me home to Highbury. None of us was the usual West End fare. The play was called *Rattle of a Simple Man*. At last my name was up in lights above the title. The first night was a triumph and, of course, my father wept with joy. After the champagne, at one o'clock in the morning, we read the rave reviews. It should have been the glamorous night of my dreams. Instead it ended with Tony and his friend Barry helping Alec and me push my Morris

Minor, which had replaced the Lambretta, up the Charing Cross Road, when it refused to start.

Having achieved the success of my childhood ambitions, I was working far too hard to enjoy any of Kenneth's orgies, even if I'd known where they were. As well as my theatre work, I was doing the TV sitcoms that John was so snooty about. An innovative BBC producer called Dennis Main Wilson, affection-ately known as Dennis Main Drain, had seen me in revue. He was a wiry, scarecrow of a man with brown mouth and fingers from his habitual smoking. A wild enthusiast, he would often literally fall off his chair laughing at rehearsals. His antennae detected much talent for the BBC. He was behind many of their biggest successes, from *The Goons* on radio through to *Steptoe, Hancock, Till Death Do Us Part*, and numerous other classics. He discovered many artistes, often from the theatre, of which he was an avid fan. This was where he saw Ben Elton, Stephen Fry and Hugh Laurie. He put Kenneth Williams into *Hancock's Half-Hour* after seeing him play the Dauphin in *St Joan*. After seeing me in *One Over the Eight*, he suggested me for a new sitcom that took place in the unpromising setting of a clothing factory. *The Rag Trade*, written by Ronnie Wolfe and Ronnie Chesney, was an instant success.

It was the first show in which women got most of the laughs. We were a motley crew. Tiny Esma Cannon, fluttering with confusion, doing a lot of falling into boxes. Myself as Carole, flirty and daft, frequently running around in my undies as the factory model. Also draped around the sewing machines were Wanda Ventham, Ann Beach, Barbara Windsor and many other colourful lasses. Miriam Karlin, as our union leader, started a national catchphrase when, every episode, she blew her whistle and shouted, 'Everybody out!' A succession of sitcoms followed; they might not have furthered my desire to change the world, but they raised my public profile. I specialised in dizzy blondes regarded as kooky, which was then considered an attractive thing for a woman to be. The titles *Mr Digby, Darling, The Bed-Sit Girl* and *Now Take My Wife*, show that *The Female Eunuch* had not yet been written.

If we girls were stuck in a rut, the boys were charging through taboo barriers in comedy. It was said of the Oxbridge *Beyond the Fringe* boys, who changed the course of revue, 'They don't know the meaning of good taste.' That was what a lot of us found refreshing but also disturbing. In 1963 cricket got rid of the snooty gentlemen players, and the Great Train Robbers were admired for cocking a snook at authority – the old values were being vigorously shaken. Sacred cows were shot at in the theatre and on telly. In *That Was The Week That Was* our leaders were mocked. In 1963 the Profumo scandal exposed the murky goings-on of the gentry. They were shown to be sleazy liars. Or spies. The establishment had been home to public schoolboys and Oxbridge graduates Philby, Burgess, Maclean and later Blunt, who now proved to be traitors, or idealists according to your point of view.

4 December
The US has withdrawn from anti-ballistic missile treaty. Well, that's helpful of them. Elizabeth Fry on the banknotes. Is it the first woman? Certainly the first Quaker. A gutsy lady. I knew all about her prison work but I didn't know she had eleven children. How did they do it, these women? Same as Mary Livingstone who trekked all over the place with David, setting up schools, planning his trips whilst dropping babies all over the place. Mind you, she ended up in a lunatic asylum.

In 1968 stage censorship was abolished. It had become very foolish and had to go. On the night after Princess Margaret's marriage to Antony Armstrong-Jones, I changed the lyrics of my song in *Make Me an Offer* to: 'It's sort of romantic, like Margaret and Tone.' We received a stern reprimand from the Lord Chamberlain's office. The trial of *Lady Chatterley's Lover* in 1960 was a farce. The prosecution counsel, Mervyn Griffiths-Jones complained of 'bouts of sexual intercourse with the emphasis always on the pleasure and the satisfaction of sensuality'. That was exactly what everyone, apart from poor Mervyn, was after in the sixties, with the liberation of the pill. His case was lost when he asked, 'Is it a book you would wish your wife or your servant to read?'

There was a backlash to all this new-found freedom. I did a television play in 1964, with Thora Hird, called *Say Nothing*, in which there were some off-screen huffing and puffing noises depicting sexual intercourse. There was a leader in the *Express* the next day and dozens of letters leading to Mary Whitehouse forming her campaign of cleaning up the media.

For my parents it was difficult to adjust. For me too. I was torn between the uninhibited new world opening up and the more restricted structure of my upbringing. Exciting things were happening for me, which I had to play down for fear of upsetting Alec, for whom work was thin on the ground. *Rattle of a Simple Man* was the hot ticket in town. The story of a football fan visiting a prostitute during a trip to London for a match was considered daring for the West End. There was a lot of talk about me undressing on stage; considered particularly risqué was the removal of my make-up. I got a lot of press coverage. Many big stars came backstage to praise me, although Joan Littlewood was so bored she left in the interval. Famous people asked me out to the Savoy Grill, Le Caprice or The Ivy, and I found it hard to resist, but felt obliged to go straight home. I could have been the toast of the town, instead I was in my kitchen, having my toast with baked beans.

When I returned home after the show to find Alec out with his mates, sometimes till the small hours, sometimes all night, I felt resentful. Nor was I best pleased when I found our home full of his carousing friends. The poor man could not win. They were entertaining company though, including Patrick Magee, rollicking Irish actor, Ruskin Spear, Royal Academician and rabble-rouser, Johnny Briggs, young, perky, up-and-coming actor, and Alan Lake, passionate gypsy, who later married Diana Dors and shot himself when she died. On one occasion I too let loose. I did a charity appearance with Peter O'Toole one afternoon. He invited me back to his dressing room where he was holding court during the run of the rather melancholy Brecht saga, *Baal*, in which he was appearing. As a tediously earnest young actress I was struck by what a lark he seemed to be having with his friends. For a couple of hours I joined them. I staggered back to my theatre and, according to a bewildered Teddy Woodward the next day, spoke most of the right lines, but not necessarily in the right order and never from the plotted position. It was the only time I ever went on stage very, very drunk,

Like my dad, Alec was jovial when drunk. I understood why he did it and felt guilty about it; he had to stand idly by while his young wife's career blossomed. The war had interrupted his career and now his looks and style were out of fashion. Rumour had it too that Rattigan's vengeful cronies had impeded his progress. I had gone through years of tat and poverty and now longed to enjoy a bit of the high life, but Alec had no wish to trail along as my shadow. It was a dilemma.

5 December

John woke in the night. Couldn't breathe. 'Help me.' Jo was staying the night, thank God, and phoned 999 while I held him. Lovely ambulance men who didn't turn a hair when they saw who it was, just wonderfully efficient. Charing Cross Casualty whisked him in and got things under control. Jo and I shaking with fear. So here we are in another hospital. Ray Whiting convicted of Sarah Payne murder. That poor woman. How does she bear it? One's mind would forever be polluted with images of what happened. She looks frenzied when she appears on TV. And some people believe in a merciful God. Well, he's not very good at his job, that's all I can say.

My mother was worried lest I was neglecting my private life and she was right. I had to make up my mind where my priorities lay. For women then there was often a choice between career and marriage. When it was mooted that I should go to New York in *Rattle* I opted for my marriage and declined, much to the amazement of David Merrick, the high-powered American producer. No one turns down New York. To have a baby? Oh, for Gaad's sake. For all our sakes I did. Melanie Jane, Ellie Jane

– or Smelly Drain to Frankie Howerd – was born on 15 July 1964. My best production to that date without any doubt.

Alec and I were now living in a better class of basement in St Peter's Square in Hammersmith. It was a lovely area where all the kids could play in the square's garden. Lots of actors and artists lived there and the flat was much more cheerful than the one in Pimlico despite the all-pervasive smell of dirty nappies in a bucket of Napisan – this was before the days of disposables. We were quite content, but our window-cleaner Charlie Jackson was not. He thought the two rooms were too small for the three of us. One day he shouted through the window that the little cottage next to him was up for sale. It was run down and had no bathroom or proper kitchen but plenty of potential. We had never thought of buying property. Actors did not saddle them-selves with mortgages. We were rogues and vagabonds. Charlie twisted my arm, marched me to the council offices and fixed up a mortgage and conversion loan. Thanks to him we put our nervous feet on the property ladder. Alec and Ellie Jane and I moved rather belatedly into our first real home. I had settled for family life with the obligatory loans and tea-drinking builders.

No one was more delighted with the baby than my father. My parents had retired and lived in a caravan called 'Half-Hour' after their namesake Tony Hancock's radio programme. It was on a site near Eastbourne, where Dad loved to show off his grandchild. In 1965 he demonstrated his excitement that we were coming on a visit the next day by doing a high-kick routine in the bar. He collapsed and died of a heart attack. It was a classy end. Both funny and sad, like him. Although I was thirty-two with a family of my own, I was devastated. This joyous man who wept and laughed with delight at my achievements was gone, so who would I try to please now? If anything exciting happened to me, my first reaction was always to tell my father. He was brave and good – the salt of the earth, as he would say. My mother wept his loss only once in front of me, and then made the best of a wretched job and came to live near me in London to help out with Ellie Jane. The thought of looking after only herself did not occur to her.

6 December
Charing Cross. Doctor here very pessimistic. Let him die,
was the theme. Fuck off. Then Slevin arrived at midnight
in a dinner jacket, with his wife in evening dress, and calmed
us down. Positive as ever. He needs an op and Slevin will
find someone to do it. No one at Charing Cross can appar-
ently. Or will, maybe. It's too risky. Sleeping on a camp
bed in his room. His breathing is bad, but he is still laughing
and joking with everyone. They adore him. Not because of
who he is, but what he is.

An opportunity for a complete change of scene came with a
trip to New York to play Kath in Joe Orton's *Entertaining Mr
Sloane*. Alec, Ellie Jane and my mother came too. My mother
cooked roast beef and Yorkshire pudding for Joe and he walked
around Broadway with us, pushing Ellie Jane in her pushchair.
Some of the other things he got up to in New York might have
surprised my mum. It was a good job his social life – not to
mention his sex life – was a success, for the play was not.

In the ritual public reading of reviews at the party after the
first night it did not bode well when the first one started: 'Throw
this British cesspool back in the Atlantic.' The others were in
similar vein. Joe loved it. Shocking people was his favourite
pastime. However, Tennessee Williams, Tallulah Bankhead and
other lovely decadent souls became devotees. I was given a Tony
nomination, presumably to make up for the vitriol heaped on
our heads by the critics. My mother, surprisingly, thought it was
rather a nice play. The sexual complexities seemed to go right
over her head. She said I reminded her of someone she worked
with at Mitchells and the mind boggled at the thought of such
an Ortonesque monster putting cash in the overhead carrier and
exchanging pleasantries with the residents of Erith.

My mother made my burgeoning career possible. Without her
babysitting I could not have offered the world my definitive
portrayal of Senna, wife of Hengist Pod, inventor of the square
wheel, in *Carry on Cleo*. I fear I did not always appreciate her
or realise how bereft and sad she must have felt without her

beloved Rick. She certainly would never tell me. Stiff upper lip, pull yourself together, laugh and the world laughs with you, weep and you weep alone. Weep alone I'm sure she did and I'm ashamed that I was too busy to notice or care.

9 December
Off to the Brompton. Another entry in the Rough Guide. *A Mr Goldstraw is prepared to put a tube into his trachea to help his breathing. The bastard thing has spread to his windpipe. He told John straight but he just didn't seem to take it on board. After he left, having given us this dire news John said, 'I like him. He looks like Albie Finney.' He does too.*

On top of my continual television work I did plays at the Royal Court. In 1964 I turned down a part in their production of *Inadmissible Evidence*, so I didn't meet Nicol Williamson and his best friend, John Thaw. I did do *The Soldier's Fortune* at the Court with Arthur Lowe. The young men who ran the place were apt to rehearse all night if necessary, so great was their enthusiasm. Arthur would flummox them by declaring, dead on

five o'clock: 'That's it. We've all got homes to go to, you know. Goodnight.' He would have no truck with impros or political discussions and went on to give a superlative performance.

I too could tire of endless analysis. When I did a play by Edward Albee at the RSC with Peggy Ashcroft and Angela Lansbury, Peter Hall sighed that I was like a small child splashing around in the pool while everyone else was learning to swim.

My career was a fearful hotch-potch of the serious and the trivial. No one was guiding me to plan it and I had to take everything on offer to earn enough to support us all. My rep experience had covered such a wide range of parts and styles that it was difficult to pin me down. I confused managements but I kept working. In fact I was working far too hard, trying to be a wife and mother as well. And marching and petitioning and canvassing. There was much to protest about. There was the Vietnam War and the Six Day War in Israel. The wall had gone up in Belfast. In 1969 the sixties gaiety was soured by the hideous murder of Sharon Tate and her friends by drug-crazed hippies. Their leader, Charles Manson, called himself Jesus, and his band of devoted disciples called themselves the Family. It was a savage travesty of our moral base lines. My concern about the state of the world was deepened by my devotion to my child. Like my parents had for me, I wanted a safe world for her. And nice little frocks from Biba of course.

At four years old, Ellie Jane was already fashion-conscious. I was getting ready to take her to buy her first school uniform when my agent phoned to say that Victor Henry, the brilliant young actor who was going to play opposite me in *So What About Love?* had done a runner. The director and the producer were keen on replacing him with a young man I knew nothing about. I'd caught him in a military police series and he seemed all right but I'd hated him and everyone else, including Olivier, in *Semi-detached*. I said we needed a bigger name as I didn't want to shoulder the burden of drawing an audience on my own. They said they had tried to find someone and nobody was available. Would I at least meet him? I explained that I was rehearsing a telly series and was snatching a couple of hours off to buy my kid's school uniform but I'd give them ten minutes.

In the window of Biba's beautiful new store in Kensington High Street Ellie Jane espied some red velvet pumps with diamanté buckles. When I dragged her into Barkers, explaining that black lace-ups were better for school, she threw one of her tantrums. She lay on the floor of the shoe department, eating the carpet and wailing that she wanted the pretty shoes. '*All* my friends wear red shoes to school. *All* my friends' mummies let *them* have diamond buckles.'

People gave us a wide berth, clucking disapprovingly at my lack of control. One or two shouted, 'Everybody out!' I walked away and came back a few minutes later. She was still screaming. Eventually I dumped her on my mother and, shaking and drained, clutching my bags of uniform and food for supper, I got a taxi to the producer Michael White's office in Duke Street.

In the cab I threw down a Purple Heart. I managed my workload only with the help of the fashionable uppers and downers. Hyped up, I rushed in, apologising profusely. I hated being late. Michael and Herbie told me not to worry. Sitting hunched deep in an armchair was a surly young man who said nothing. His head, resting on his hand, barely turned my way when I said 'Hello.' He flicked his eyes in my direction and grunted. He didn't get up. OK, you rude little bugger. It had been a difficult day. I was glad that I was wearing my full-length fox fur; it gave me confidence. I was even more glad that I had vetoed my new up-to-the-minute maxi skirt and stuck to a mini. OK, my son, I'll make you bloody well look at me. I moved a chair close to him, sat down, and fixed him with a look. Crossing the best pair of legs at RADA from the knee up, I said, 'So you're John Thaw are you? Well!—'

24 December
Our 28th Wedding Anniversary. After all the strife and turmoil we have reached this complete union. I cannot, I will not believe it will end.
    Anniversary card from John.
    '*My darling Sheila,*

What would I have done without you? You truly are the love of my life. I am so proud that you stuck with me when things were awful for you – so proud to be your husband, lover and friend and so proud to be the father of such wonderful and caring girls. I think it's 28 years, but I pray there'll be a few more so that I can make up for this dreadful year. If this year has taught me anything it's that my love for you is so deep and profound that I don't have the words to describe it. I must have done something right in my sixty years to be blessed with a great woman – for that's what you are. I shed a tear this morning because I still can't believe (I suppose) that you love me as you do but I know this – I love you every bit as much.
Your husband
John.
PS The cover of this card shows how I feel most of the time.

10

So What About Love?

THE FIRST WEEK OF rehearsal of *So What About Love?* was an unmitigated disaster. I always approach a new role convinced that I cannot play it and on the few occasions that John Thaw looked up from his script, his expression of contempt implied that he agreed. If I suggested a piece of comedy business in the scenes with him his silence made me feel like the cheap end-of-the-pier comedienne I feared I was. When Herbert Wise endeavoured to discuss the play, Anne Bell and Peter Blythe made intelligent contributions. John Thaw sighed and grunted. The three of us agreed with Herbie that it was a slight piece that with invention and a light approach on our part could raise a few laughs. The brooding, dark presence of the leading man in the rehearsal room was not what we had in mind. At the end of the first week I told Herbie privately that I thought John Thaw was a mistake and he should seriously think of recasting. Herbie assured me he was a good actor. Yes, but had he done comedy? No, not much, but he's funny offstage. Funny peculiar, yes. I pointed out that very few of the men I knew who were hilarious onstage were a barrel of laughs off. Indeed most, like Frankie Howerd, Kenneth Williams and Tony Hancock, verged on the tragic. Anyway, this guy had not exactly had us falling about in rehearsal.

25 December
Lovely family day. John was divine. We laughed about some
of the awful Christmases we've had. When he went to bed
the girls and I clung to each other, none of us daring to
say out loud what's in our minds.

The following Monday the atmosphere was tense. I had spent
the weekend being reassured by Alec and my mother and was
determined not to be cowed by this little upstart. In the coffee
break some costumes arrived from my friend the designer John
Bate for Herbie's approval. The fitter got me into one stunning
evening dress. We loved it but there was a snag. I had to get into
it alone onstage as part of the action. The dress did up with a
zip from my bottom to the back of my neck, making it impossible to do it myself. It did, however, have a large ornate ring as
a handle. I had an inspiration. John being the nearest person to
me in the rehearsal room, I told him to unzip the dress. He did,
rather shakily I was gratified to notice. I then mimed increasingly
frantic writhing attempts to reach the zip, culminating in putting
the ring over the door handle and doing a ballet plié, thus pulling
it up behind me. It was as yet a bit messy, but it worked. John
laughed and laughed. It was a wonderful laugh. It transformed
him. His shoulders heaved, his eyes watered. He wiped them,
squeaking 'Oh God, oh dear, oh dear.' Just like my father.
   'It's not that funny, is it?'
   'It is, it's brilliant, it's so daft, kid.'
   Kid? I was nine years older than him.
   I glowed at his approval. It was all the more welcome for
being hard-earned. The zip business went into the show and
subsequently got a round of applause every night. Emboldened,
I suggested some ideas to him in our scenes, pointing out that
the script needed all the help it could get. The respectful attitude towards writers in Sloane Square had not equipped him
for the crack-papering approach that *Ma's Bit o' Brass* in
Blackpool had me. But Herbie was right. He was very funny
offstage. In a wry, self-deprecating way. He began to make me
laugh a lot.

27 December
John says he feels the T-tube but it's OK. I've had a new
mattress put on our brass bed and he's thrilled with it. Says
he feels wonderfully comfy. Christ, with a bloody great tube
in his windpipe, how could he say that? Anyone else would
be distraught. I beg him to relax and let me love and care
for him, not to keep struggling, but it's not his way.

Being such a small company, the four of us had many a larky
supper together and often shared digs on our pre-London tour.
John had a two-seater MG and I a two-seater Morgan, so if we
went for a trip during the day, we could only take one other,
and more and more it became John and I. We enjoyed each
other's company. I realised, as Peter O'Toole said later, that 'his
features simply fell into a kind of brood in spite of him, he could
be thinking of pigeon racing, anything.' He had not been
despising me in rehearsal. Quite the opposite. He had been over-
awed by the expertise of the three of us and did not dare open
his mouth. Indeed, that first weekend he had nearly walked out
but could tell I was nervous and did not want to let me down.
Could tell I was nervous? Could see through my bluster? Not
many people did that.
  He told me little about himself, but two incidents were
revealing. The first happened when we were playing Manchester.
We normally went out after the show to a club-restaurant, one
of the few places open late in those days. One night he tersely
said he was not coming. The next day, whereas he normally
popped into my dressing room before the show to say hello, we
did not meet until our first scene and then with none of the
usual jokes in the wings. He was about to leave after the show,
without saying goodbye, when I confronted him in the corridor
and asked why he was being so rude. At first he denied he was
behaving oddly, but when I persisted he told me that some bloody
aunt of his had left a message saying his mother would like to
see him. After a lot of probing I discovered why this was
disturbing to him. His mother had deserted him, he felt nothing
for her and had absolutely no desire to see her. I was shocked

by his cold dismissal. How could anyone feel like this about their mother?

31 December
Ray over from Australia. It's so painful for him to see his adored brother ill. John finding it difficult to communicate with him. Ray keeps asking questions that John doesn't want to answer.

I suggested it might help him to deal with it if he saw her, and came out with a lot of other half-baked psychological clap-trap. It gave me a self-righteous satisfaction when he agreed to go and meet her, but that night he curtly told me he had done as I said, had still not liked her, and never wanted to see her again. I realised that if we were to carry on working together amiably I could not pursue the subject further.

The second strange thing happened in Oxford. There was a very distinctive female laugh in the audience one night. I was liking it as she seemed to get the few subtler laughs in the play. It threw John into a frenzy of rage. I extracted from him that it was his ex-wife with whom he had just gone through an acrimonious divorce. No details were forthcoming or sought. I had learned to let well alone. The two incidents showed an unforgiving side to his nature that I did not find attractive. In fact it frightened me in its violence. He was not someone to tangle with. I was glad it was none of my business. There was a fear and insecurity in him that I recognised and understood, but I could only just about cope with my own.

So we drove light-heartedly over the moors, visited galleries and enjoyed food and wine together. One day in the MG he put on a tape of the Sibelius Fifth Symphony and I was astounded that this trendy guy in hipster velvet flares, silk shirt open to reveal a medallion, should be so besotted with the same fuddy-duddy classical music as I. He said he loved Elgar, then a deeply unfashionable composer. I had never met anyone so full of surprises. Nothing about him could be taken at face value. I was sorry when the companionable tour ended and we faced the reality of London.

3 January 2002
John's 60th birthday. We should be in Barcelona. The girls
bought us a family trip for his present, but he's not well
enough. So we will go in April, please God – who isn't there.

Any idea of West End theatre being glamorous in 1969 was
dispelled as you entered the stage door of the Criterion Theatre.

The first hazard was climbing over the recumbent drug addicts
who used the stage door entry to inject the heroin prescription
they got from the all-night Boots in Piccadilly Circus. Once
inside, you descended to a gloomy catacomb where only the
mice were healthy on their diet of theatrical greasepaint, which
they shared with the cockroaches. There were no windows, so
the outside world was banished once you'd descended into hell.
We actors had to resort to oxygen inhalers on matinee days to
keep us bubblingly energetic for our merry romp. Unfortunately
Harold Hobson, the drama critic of the *Sunday Times*, was
depressed by his journey to the theatre. Part of his review was
about the squalor of Piccadilly Circus, and he seemed to blame
our little play for the state of the nation. He was furious with

the first-night audience for enjoying it. 'A drawing-room comedy for guttersnipes' set the tone of the review.

The characters' dalliances appalled him, as did our performances. When Sally had wanted a Hobson review for John she cannot have foreseen it would start, 'I awaited with dread his every entrance.' It then went on to detail how much 'a pretty, witty actress' who accompanied the critic had hated John's performance. Hobson must have had a miserable evening, for there was no respite when I was on, as I was 'neither pleasing to the eye nor endurable to the ear'.

I was destroyed by his vitriol, although I did laugh at a typically high-camp letter from Kenneth Williams: 'Poor old Hobson seems to be in dementia and it's reported that she's actually dressing up as the Pope and delivering her stuff to the paper ex cathedra.'

10 January
Read an article about me in Time Out *full of lovely things. What a bloody irony. Russian Bride, one of my best performances ever, so I'm told, all sorts of good career things happening, and I don't give a sod. It means nothing. John stumbled and fell outside the clinic. Face bleeding, dazed, clinging to me. 'Sorry pet, it's my stupid foot. Hopalong Cassidy.' Taken in on a wheelchair. I parked the car, pelted back and there he was laughing and joking about it with the nurses and Jo.*

John was bemused that I was so upset. He gave Hobson the Back Treatment. For him a glass was half full and all the other reviews had been very good. But it is not easy to prance on stage the day after a review like that and convince people you are really enchanting and funny, whatever one venerable critic thinks. John just said, 'Fuck 'im' and set about finding out who the 'pretty, witty actress' was so that he could wreak vengeance. In her later career she never did a *Morse* or a *Sweeney*, that's for sure. The situation was made doubly embarrassing when Hobson, who was an honourable man, was persuaded by his fellow critics that he had maybe got things out of proportion, so he came back to re-review the play. The opening paragraph of his second appraisal was along the lines of 'I was right about Beckett, I was right about Pinter, but I was wrong about Leonard Webb.' Our unpretentious author was likened to Anouilh and I was accredited with *abattage*. As Hobson adored all things French and now, it seemed, me, I knew it couldn't be anything to do with slaughtering animals, as Tony Beckley gleefully maintained. Tony thought it dull when it turned out to mean 'dynamism', but was pleased that he could henceforth call me Hobson's Choice.

We settled in for a successful run. I was preoccupied with my family again, and John with his friends. During rehearsal he had been crashing with his pal Nicol and had now moved in with Ken Parry, and was also being fed and watered by Barbara and Ian Kennedy-Martin. It was a peripatetic existence. We saw less of each other, but on matinee days between the shows when the sun shone, we went to nearby St James's Park and sat in deckchairs listening to the band playing on the grandstand. Or we had tea at Fortnum and Mason, quibbling over which was the best blend or the most tasty ice-cream sundae.

16 January
The treatment is ravaging John but he still managed a walk
in Regent's Park. It looked glorious even in winter. I wrote
a letter to the gardeners thanking them. They probably never
hear how much comfort their work gives. We had tea at
the Langham. We do like a nice tea. When we got home
he wept with weakness, but he insists on doing these things.

For me, life was good. I was in a successful play with a congenial cast. My little house in London had been transformed by one of my Theatre Workshop pals, Harry Green, later to become well known for do-it-yourself programmes on television. Ken described going to a party at my house in a letter to Joe Orton: 'What a posh place she has moved to! It's all Scandinavia and patio-Spanish. V. mod, I must say. I got terribly sloshed.'

Alec and I had bought a derelict cottage in Tarlton in Gloucestershire, which Harry was converting to provide a country escape. Maybe because I'd had no settled base as a child, creating homes became a passion. When I bought the cottage, the Cotswold stone tile roof was collapsing and there was a rotting cat and piles of dead flies inside. As each fee came in it went to a new roof, staircase or windows. The cottage was set in an acre of wilderness; Alec and I planted trees and shrubs and formed paths as I had with Daddy in Bexleyheath. It is satisfying to make gardens, which will be there for other families long after your death. My friends Brian Sack and Frances Coulson had a wonderful garden round their exquisite hotel by Ullswater in the Lake District. One day I was wandering round it, feeling a bit low, when, as I walked on the camomile lawn, for no reason my spirits soared and I felt delight. I saw no apparition and heard no voice, but I knew there was a woman with me. I questioned Frances, who told me that a hundred years ago a woman had indeed designed and lovingly laid out all the little nooks and crannies, pools, plants and statues.

My mother enjoyed our homes and loved her granddaughter. We clashed over the importance of clean white socks and nice table manners, but she was an invaluable support. Not for me all the worry of nannies and au pairs. In working-class tradition I had my mum to help out. It all seemed too good to be true. It was. I accompanied my mother to the doctor when she complained of a pain in her side. As she re-dressed herself behind the screen, the doctor silently shook her head at me. She turned out to have a form of cancer called Hodgkin's disease and the prognosis was bad.

That night I told my mates at the theatre. I could hardly get through the show, so preoccupied was I with what lay ahead. The next day John called in for his usual pre-show visit. He asked me to sit on the shabby armchair and put on a pair of earphones. He clicked on the cassette player and left the room.

When you're weary
Feeling small
When tears are in your eyes
I'll dry them all. I'm on your side
When times get rough
And friends just can't be found
Like a bridge over troubled water I will lay me down
Like a bridge over troubled water I will lay me down.

I was deeply touched by his sweetness. Yet again this young man had realised I was less able to cope than everyone thought. For several more months I continued to do my daffy performance while dealing with horror at home. I was relieved when the show drew to an end, although it had been fun to do. I would certainly miss the companionship of the cast.

17 January
Recorded Just a Minute *in Hastings. I thought it would be hard to be funny, but as always it was therapeutic to forget myself and, high on adrenaline, become a performer again. Mind you, after the show I fell apart and actually crashed my car. That's all I bloody need.*

One night in the last week of the run, John asked me to drop by for a drink on the way home. He had bought a flat in Troy Court in Kensington High Street and was very proud of it. He said he had something to discuss with me before the show closed. I thought he wanted advice about his career as I knew by now he respected my opinion. He sat on the other side of the room with a drink in his hand. The ice was clinking against the glass. The traffic hummed outside. Inside our idle chat subsided and we sat in silence, looking at one another. At last he said casually: 'The thing is . . . I have a bit of a problem.'

Long pause.

'Well, what is it?'

A puzzled laugh. 'Well, you see, I'm afraid I've fallen in love with you. It's a nuisance.'

Gobsmacked silence.

'And the bugger is, I know this is for the rest of my life. You needn't say anything. I just wanted you to know, that's all. 'Nother drink?'

It never occurs to me that I can be an object of love. It didn't with Alec. I take a lot of persuading. This friend, as I thought of him, nonchalantly declaring his love was not convincing. I was embarrassed. Romances on tour and during shows are par for the course but were not really my style. When I recovered my wind I rattled on about propinquity and how, when the show ended, so would his infatuation. He sat, white-faced, on the other side of the room and I could see I had got it wrong. He just said quietly, 'I don't play games. I love you.'

I discovered later he had already told several of his friends, including Ken Parry and his ex-wife Sally. I was the last to know. I explained to him as gently as I could that I did not play games either. I hadn't meant to lead him on. He must not think of this as another rejection, I was just not available.

I got into my car and sat for some time in shock. It had not dawned on me, and I would not let it now, that I too loved him. I did not do that sort of thing. I had been married for seventeen years and something fresh and exciting was tempting, but Alec and I had a pretty good set-up in which our five-year-old daughter was secure and happy. Besides, Alec needed me, John did not.

18 January
Took Ray to Heathrow. John didn't see him off. He sat in the car in the car park. Ray clung to me, crying. Those two little boys . . .

11

When the Journey Was Rough

AFTER *SO WHAT ABOUT LOVE?* we both went our different ways.
I was glad to see John's career flourish. Having honed his comedy
technique during the run of the play, he went straight into a
classy TV comedy series *Thick as Thieves* by Ian La Frenais and
Dick Clement. He and Bob Hoskins played two ex-convicts vying
for the love of the same woman, played by Pat Ashton. He
continued to do theatre work as well as his telly, with a success
in a play at the Edinburgh Festival and another at the Royal
Court, but his private life was unsettled. After his sons had left
home, John's father had remarried, to a delightful woman,
Mildred, and lived comfortably with her in Marple, a posh
suburb of Manchester, where John felt less able to arrive without
warning if he needed his father. His brother was now settled in
a good job with Ford in Brisbane; the refuge of Daneholme
Road, however rough and ready, was gone, and even though he
had his flat at Troy Court, he was on his own. He had a few
girlfriends but none meant a lot to him and he treated them
badly, often brutally walking away from a relationship without
giving a reason.

When the play closed, I too went back to sitcom land in a
top-rating series called *Mr Digby, Darling*. It was about a firm
manufacturing rat poison in which I doted on my boss, played

by my old *Rag Trade* mate Peter Jones. Incomparable laugh-getters. I also did some plays in the theatre. I submerged myself in work and family and the nitty-gritty of everyday living. The experience with John had already shaken me, then three traumatic events hit me that radically changed my philosophy of life, insofar as I had one.

Since my convent childhood I had been deeply religious. Indoctrination about hellfire is not easy to shake off. When I was a child my father and I would visit different churches every Sunday in a quest for the perfect sermon, the best choir, the friendliest congregation. We never quite decided on a denomination, but heads turned in visited churches as my father lustily joined in hymns, usually offering a descant or harmony. Occasionally we would have delicious giggles, crouching under the brown pew on hairy hassocks while worshippers around us leaped up and down in accordance with the ritual. We tried to fathom what was going on with the goblets and vestments round the altar and Dad's outrageous whispered theories about priests not being able to make up their minds what frock to wear and gasping for a drink had me convulsed. Despite his irreverence, he had a simple belief in an all-loving God. He just didn't know the best way to express it. Whenever I was on tour or in repertory I was uneasy if I could not attend at least one Sunday service.

My mother's illness became increasingly distressing. I prayed as hard as I could for her deliverance, at least from pain. In the event, what relief she had was from the ministrations of my friend Dilys Laye, a born carer, who supported me in nursing her. There seemed little help from on high. I tried to see a divine plan in her suffering, but it was hard to equate the indignities inflicted on this good woman, of incontinence pads and violent vomiting, with a merciful God. My father had the luxury of being a volatile delight only because my mother was the rock of the family. Like most women of her generation, her happiness was seeing other people happy. Her single-mindedness about what was 'right' and 'not right' could irk, but it was a useful yardstick to measure whether revolt or conformity was appropriate.

19 January
The Euro has been launched in France, but we hang on to the pound and resolutely drive on the wrong side of the road. I feel so European I cannot identify in any way with this strange obsession about a bit of paper with the Queen's head on. John's tube pipe taken out. Radiotherapy has shrunk the tumour. He now has a hole in his throat which he delights in making farting noises with.

I was consumed with guilt at how I had taken my mother for granted since my father died, and tried to make up for it in her last months. I lavished as much love on her as she would allow. She bore the suffering with her usual stiff upper lip, spending what little respite she had from the pain setting things in order for her death. Dilys and I had given her an injection and she seemed peaceful but suddenly sat up and, clear as a bell, said, 'Now wait a minute, Rick, I have things to do.' Busy till the end, but on the way to her beloved Enrico. I believed that implicitly. I kissed her as she died, realising I had never done so before. She had kissed me on the forehead as a child when she said, 'Goodnight, sleep tight, hope the fleas don't bite,' but I didn't kiss her back. People didn't kiss their mothers where I came from. I wished I had. I knelt by her body and thanked God for her deliverance, whatever that meant.

The next day I was recording an episode of *Mr Digby, Darling*. I told no one of her death lest it should make it difficult to deliver all the rat jokes. After the recording in front of the studio audience, I crept behind the set and sat on the floor and wept. A passing stagehand crouched beside me and said, 'Come on, Sheila love – it wasn't that bad.' When I told him why I was crying it was a relief to cuddle him and laugh together. I had a message of condolence from John.

I had barely steadied myself after my mother's death when the second blow struck. Alec was diagnosed with cancer of the oesophagus. If, as a result of John's declaration, I had any doubts about my marriage, they disappeared as soon as the specialist delivered his verdict. My father, mother and now Alec, the three people who loved me unconditionally however badly I behaved. There was hope that Alec could have a new life-saving opera-tion. That proved impossible. He was given weeks to live. Having had little outside help, apart from Dilys, in nursing my mother, I was relieved when he was referred to St Christopher's Hospice. With the help of their palliative care in the home, Alec lived another nine months. He sweetly bore my only slightly improved nursing. During a particularly nasty procedure he said, 'You are an angel.'

In apology for past hurts, I said, 'I always meant to be an angel.'

He said, 'Yes, a militant angel.'

I felt ashamed, but he said it with such tenderness I supposed he had forgiven me for the bullying it implied.

20 January
Brian Sack from Sharrow Bay Hotel is dead. That place has been a solace throughout my life. Now he and Frances

are both gone. Oh dear, everything is slipping away. The old standards are changing too. Awful pictures of prisoners shackled and covered with hoods shuffling around a prison in Guantanamo Bay, where they have no rights under the Geneva Convention, according to the Americans. This is us behaving like that, not some despotic alien power.

Alec was a lovely man. Feckless, but with graceful charm. He did not appear to realise how unfair his life had been. He greeted the blows with a lopsided, wry smile. And now, at forty-nine, he was dead. My Christian forbearance left me. I was very angry. One year after kneeling at my mother's deathbed, I stood by his. As I stared at his emaciated body that had so gently loved mine, I said aloud, as in prayer, 'There is no God.'

I felt no lightning strike me, no hellfire consume me, just profound relief flooding me. No need to ask, 'Why suffering – why this?' It just happened. We are human. We are born, we make mistakes, we sometimes suffer and are sometimes happy. We die. No one else is involved. It's up to us. I entertained no thoughts of a future life. It would have been comforting to think of meeting again, but until somebody scientifically proved me wrong, I would not waste my energy on hoping. It made my sorrow more harrowing but at least it was real.

As with my mother's death, a misunderstanding soon had me rocking with unseemly laughter. It was a heartless requirement of the state that you go in person to register a death. My good friend Tony Beckley agreed to accompany me. He loved Alec and was as shattered as I by his death. We both looked drained and dishevelled as we slumped in a gloomy room waiting for the arrival of the registrar of births, deaths and marriages. He breezed in, chortling with delight, 'And are you the happy couple?'

Wrong – in more ways than he could possibly imagine. He was visibly shocked when we told him, through tears of laughter, that we had come to register a death. Perhaps when the happy couple arrived, they greeted their marriage with floods of tears.

I was trying to adjust to being a single mother of a seven-year-old daughter, with all my crutches taken away, when the third challenge arrived. I read *The Female Eunuch*. In 1971, when I was aged thirty-eight, it threw my whole approach to life into question. At Ely Place Convent I had accepted the rightness of priests coming in to perform the holy rituals while the nuns kept quiet and watched; I was indoctrinated to believe that men were superior to women. My mother's genuine fear of my stepping beyond the safety of home had made my ambition for myself and a career seem unnatural. My father's belief, albeit later shaken, in the infallibility of leaders never questioned for a moment that they were all men. Up until *The Female Eunuch*, my search for and wish to please Greek gods had dominated my life. The book, together with my loss of faith, demanded a rethink.

So flummoxed was I that I joined one of the women's groups that sprang up and then formed one of my own, with three actress friends, that meets to this day. These meetings were sacrosanct. If one of the male of the species asked us out it was no longer understood that that took precedence over a date with a girlfriend. Not any more. Women mattered. They must stand on their own two feet and not look for a man to lean on, emotionally or materially. I had little choice at the time, so it made sound sense. I was enraged when I contemplated how men and we ourselves had colluded in forcing women to take a back seat in every area of life. I threw aside my angel wings and became a militant feminist. I spoke up, rather muddle-headedly, wherever I could, becoming the first woman to win the Best After-Dinner Speaker of the Year. In 2002, I won the Women in Film Award for the Most Outspoken Woman, proving that I have bored on for thirty-odd years.

22 January
Very scary State of the Union address by Bush about the axis of evil: Iraq, Iran and North Korea. What is he building up to? He probably, understandably, feels he has to wreak revenge for the American people for September 11th. Please God he is restrained by calmer voices.

Germaine has a lot to answer for. Sally, John's ex-wife, was more active than I was. She ended up in a police cell, having thrown flour at Bob Hope during a Miss World contest and stubbed her fag out on a policeman's hand. When she was arrested she phoned John, and he supported her but must have wondered, when he also read some of my polemic in the newspapers, why he fell in love with such troublesome women. My new credo scuppered my comedy career with the BBC. Analysing my well-meaning sitcom roles, I realised all of them conformed to the comforting stereotype of dizzy blonde desperate for a man. At a grand BBC party, I loudly demanded to be taken more seriously by the powers that be, in those days mainly retired admirals and certainly all white, male and middle class. I nagged them to distraction, so to shut me up, they gave me a series, to go out very late at night, called *But Seriously – It's Sheila Hancock*. I devised it with Barry Took, and we used clever clogs from university to write it, including John Cleese, Peter Cook and Graham Chapman. In one sketch, by Ken Hoare, I portrayed a malevolent landlady, mad with prejudice against everyone: Jews, Irish, black, pink, fat people, thin people. It was deemed from on high that it would shock people and spoil my image. I fought every inch of the way and did it. It was a success, I was proved right, but it was ten years before I worked for the BBC again.

With women like Jennifer Saunders, Dawn French and Victoria Wood leading the way and writing their own material, there's nothing now that women can't say or do, but in those days we were only allowed to be funny as long as we stayed charming and didn't rock the men's boat. In *Seriously* I had a guest star to chat with each week. One of them was Germaine Greer. I have met many eminent people. All our prime ministers since the sixties (I always preferred their wives), other important politicians, barristers, most of the royals, writers, surgeons, you name 'em, I've come across 'em. Of them all, Germaine has never disappointed. She has remained true to herself, even to the extent of admitting she is wrong, an invaluable virtue. She took – and still takes – ill-thought-out, vicious criticism and rises above it all with wisdom and strength.

To fill the void in my life I got involved with more and more causes, some worthy, some daft. My new humanist approach demanded I relinquish hope of divine intervention and do it myself. My messiah complex, as John later called it. Drug addicts, the bereaved, the dying, Vietnam, cats, the homeless, Vietnamese homeless cats only had to look balefully in my direction and I was in there fighting. My reaction to the picture of a naked Vietnamese child running down a road with her little friends, her back aflame with napalm, or to the man kneeling while another shot him in the head, presented no great philosophical dilemma to me: I knew why it happened. People, especially men, for they were usually the perpetrators, were shit. Especially people who thought they had a monopoly on what was right. It didn't occur to me that I myself might be included in that category. Bloody Sunday, when demonstrators were shot at in Ireland, and the massacre of Israelis at the Olympic Games merely confirmed my abhorrence of religious fanaticism. I had a whale of a time, hating people and institutions. The problem was, what could I love? I smothered Ellie Jane. Though so young, she was made to feel solely responsible for my happiness. I had a couple of affairs that left me feeling cheap, as both men were married. I loved the idea of promiscuity but was hopeless at doing it. My conditioning was stronger than Germaine's logic. I needed a man.

3 February
He is fading. I want to pull him back. Force him to stay. I want to scream don't leave me you bastard, but I pretend and smile and smile and smile.

12

It Took You

I CANNOT REMEMBER A glad reunion with John. I vaguely recollect a meal at a Chinese restaurant with a lot of gazing into each other's eyes, and walking round the Serpentine holding hands, but not much else. I suppose I was still dazed from the shock of the events of my life and the total change in my circumstances. John was quoted later as saying, 'Sheila Hancock is all mature woman. I wanted her and I was determined to get her.' He was just gradually there, presumably not by accident. He laid siege and I was only too willing to surrender. He later claimed I jumped on him, which is probably true, but he was there waiting for me to pounce. It did not feel like a betrayal of Alec, relatively soon after his death. His loss propelled my need for comfort and passion. His affection gone, a vacuum was left in my life. I was powerless anyway. Our mutual consuming need exploded in each other's arms.

14 February
Slevin tells me the end is near. I tell him to tell John, he says
he has tried but some people choose not to know. That is
their right. The modern belief that we all should be told
everything doesn't work for everyone. He advised me to keep
John in the clinic as there could be disastrous complications

*that I can't handle. When I saw him in that bleak room I
knew he had to go home. I'll take the risk. The palliative
care man is utterly honest with John but still he says when
he leaves, 'Well, that all sounded very positive, didn't it, kid?'
I arm myself with drugs and information, phone Macmillan
Nurses, Dr Heathcock in Luckington, trying to cover all
eventualities and we – Jo, John and I – head for Luckington.
It's Valentine's Day.*

John maintained that the age difference worked in our favour.
A man's sexual potency is reckoned to be at its highest between
seventeen and twenty-six years old, while a woman's is between
thirty-five and forty-two. So at thirty and thirty-nine, he would
have to make an effort whilst I had a few years in hand. He
certainly showed no signs of being past his peak. He bought a
beautiful brass bed for his flat in Troy Court, to celebrate our
love. He got purple satin sheets that seemed the height of sensuality. We did tend to slip off them and they were beasts to iron
but he enjoyed a bit of ironing. The bed had belonged to Ivor
Novello, doyen of sentimental musical comedies with titles like
Glamorous Night, The Dancing Years and *Perchance to Dream.*
One night, John woke convinced someone was strangling him.
Doubtless it was Ivor, aghast at our heterosexual goings-on.
Many years later, we bought a grand piano that belonged to
Siegfried Sassoon, lover of Ivor. We liked to think of them being
linked again through us.

John was touchingly romantic. After one row, he drove all ninety-
eight miles from London to my house in Tarlton, left a single rose
on the doorstep and drove straight back without knocking at the
door. Another row had a less happy conclusion. I bought him a
beautiful ring. I gave it to him, sitting in his MG in a country lane.
He was delighted. Then I took it back and said he would have it
for good when he stopped smoking. He berated me for treating
him like a child and imposing rules. In a temper, I threw the ring
out of the window and he roared off. Next day, having made up,
we crawled around on our hands and knees looking for the ring,
but eventually left it for the non-smoking rabbits and squirrels.

We had fun together. Fun had been in short supply in my life. He wined and dined me like an old-fashioned beau. Although I was a much higher earner than him, he always insisted on picking up the bill – a novelty for me. He was excited one night about taking me on a treat. He had booked at what was then the most highly rated, and highly priced, restaurant in London, Le Gavroche. He retold endlessly how I spent the whole meal complaining about the rotten table we had been given, and what it was costing. I was not used to being gracious with men. But he said he preferred my honesty to girlie guile. On one occasion I was flirting with someone else, I suppose to make him jealous, and he grabbed my shoulders so hard they bruised saying, 'Don't. Don't play games with me. Don't ever play games.'

17 February
Luckington looks lovely. Extraordinarily warm. Spring already. The daphne is in bloom, the perfume drifting through the window. John spent the morning choosing the colours and extras for his new Jag and discussing whether he should sign up for another year with Carlton. My heart is breaking.

We were more at home in the less grand bistros in the King's Road in Chelsea like The Casserole. A favourite was Daisy's, where Jose Feliciano tapes became our theme songs, 'Light My Fire' and 'I'll Be Your Baby Tonight' having special resonance. John called me his 'Uptown Girl', which I wasn't, and I christened him my 'Little Northern Peasant', which he was. As I hit forty, my biological clock was ticking loudly and I decided that I wanted another baby before it was too late. We were not married or even living together, but that was all right. The new modern Sheila didn't want all that conventional set-up. I conceived almost at once and when I told John he was beside himself with joy. So were our two daughters. Ellie Jane was delighted that this groovy, funny guy who had a constant supply of Mars Bars had entered her life and she had a new ready-made sister and another on the way. Abigail and Ellie Jane had settled into a happy relationship. They kept dropping hints about becoming *proper* sisters. Sixties permissiveness notwithstanding, John and I were not really comfortable with the half-in, half-out nature of our relationship. It didn't work for us. In our backgrounds, you got married and created a home together, so that's what we decided to do.

We chose Christmas Eve for our wedding as I was appearing in *Absurd Person Singular*, appropriately back at the Criterion Theatre, and would have one day off for a honeymoon, on Christmas Day. It was a very different occasion from both of our first weddings. We kept it quiet to avoid the press, not realising that the Cirencester Registry Office was opposite the local paper's office. I wore a long suede jacket given to me by Tony Beckley just before he died – I wanted him there in spirit – and a rather nasty suede hat. I did not look my best. John wore a trendy suit and the girls thought he looked dashing. He was every bit the Prince Charming coming to rescue Ellie Jane from her mother's grief. He and the two now official sisters leaped around gleefully.

They had a whale of a time. Me, less so, as I was suffering from chronic morning sickness. The only other people present were Maureen, our help, and a neighbour at Tarlton we scarcely knew, who acted as best man. After a hasty, but happy, lunch we drove back for the evening show. On the way, the radio announced that Sheila Hancock had got married that day. In London, the newspaper placards announced: 'Sheila weds in secret.' On the covers were huge photographs of me and little tiny ones of the young actor I had married. John swallowed this billing rather better than he did the following year's entry in *Who's Who*, which under his name said: 'See Sheila Hancock'. All that was soon to change.

The first years of our marriage were a time of ecstatic happiness. We really did feel our lives had been leading up to this union. We rejoiced in the coincidences linking our childhood and early experiences, and were intrigued by the differences.

That old cliché, 'We were meant for each other', was true, though not in a sedate way. From the start it was tempestuous and exciting, but underlying everything then and for ever was the certainty, which John had known before me, that this was for the rest of our lives.

19 February

'I feel I'm on holiday, kid.' The steroids seem to have put him on a high. 'I've turned a corner, I'm sure of it.' Asked me if I liked it now in the country. I told him I'll always be a city girl but I love anywhere with you. We went round the 'estate'. 'It's ours, I tell you – we've cracked it.' Saw someone in the field. Pretend loading of gun, country gent voice, 'I say, bugger orf my land.' He's eating well, looks great, full of energy compared with recent weeks. I think he's really happy. My guts are wrenching. I love him, I love him, I love him. I can't believe what's happening. I long to pour my heart out to him, for him to comfort me, for us to talk about it. But that is pure self-indulgence on my part. His whole behaviour makes it clear he wants business as usual. The Back Treatment comes into its own. What could we say more than we have already? How would it be for him if he knew he might choke to death? I'll deal with it for him. He will be all right.

The press bombarded us with questions about the age difference. It's the stock question they always churn out. For us, it was meaningless. I had married one man ten years older than me, and now my new husband was nine years younger. So? If anything, the answer was the reverse of what they expected. My frequent whine during our marriage when John was dragging his feet, or in his case tripping over them, was, 'You're too old for me.' In an interview with Sally Brompton she reported that 'He is the brown ale of the partnership and she is the champagne.' Over the years this somehow became 'You're stale beer to my champagne.' Kevin Whately said, 'Sparks always flew when they were together. A great double act.' Things were never boring. I sold my little house in Hammersmith and he his flat and we bought a place in Chiswick big enough to house our instant family. With the birth of Joanna in 1974 and John's adoption of Ellie Jane in 1975, and Abigail's frequent visits, we had three daughters to accommodate plus Maureen, later replaced by Mary, to help out in place of my mother. John would open the back door and yell to the world, 'Help me, help me, I'm surrounded by women.' On less harassed occasions he would waltz round with the baby in his arms singing, 'Isn't she lovely?'

20 February
Another beautiful day. On our own, relishing each other. He wanted a Lancashire Hot Pot so I cooked one with him giving instructions. We went round the garden. He was leaning on me until he saw Jane, working in the garden, and then he pushed me away and walked on his own. Wanted to inspect the new wall, noticed a tree missing, smelt his beloved daphne, glowed with pleasure. He stared long and hard at everything. Was he getting the energy to move on or drinking everything in for fear of losing it? He watched TV and he made his usual funny snide comments. The family arrived late and he went to bed happily. Ellie took him up his hot chocolate. He says it takes the place of alcohol – he's addicted. I gave him his pills and methadone, his 'cough mixture', as he calls it. He's very calm and happy.

One of the joys of my marriage to John was the family that came with him. Especially Grandad. After John and Ray left home Jack became a social worker. He had no formal training but his experience in dealing with difficult lads was invaluable. He was tough but caring. With little girls, especially ours, he was useless. He was putty in their hands. If they misbehaved, the habitual reaction was a laugh and 'Eeeee, ye little bogger.' He was enchanted by them. They could do no wrong. Nor could he for them. They laughed at his northern vernacular when he called them 'pretty pigs' or 'yer mardyarse'. His passionate hatred of Manchester United was the only area they could not mock. He meant it. He would sit alone, watching them on the telly, spitting 'Bastards' if they scored a goal. His mealtime grace was 'Right, let the dog see the rabbit' and his 'Go on then, just a little' was the cue to pile his plate high with a second helping. He introduced the girls to Eccles cakes, Archer's pies and pickled walnuts but their attempts to get him to taste garlic or any other foreign muck was greeted by an implacable 'Oh noo, not for me.' Any lack of love as he toiled to bring up his lads was recompensed by that showered on him by Jo, Abigail and Ellie Jane. The romps, the tickles, the cuddles were non-stop. He was their contact with the roots that John and I had moved away from. We were in a classless limbo, not really middle class, no longer working class, but Grandad was. He was the genuine article.

Despite his shouldering of his sudden responsibilities, John had puzzling moments of childlike naivety. He didn't seem to know how to behave. When we were moving he showed me a bundle of letters from a past girlfriend and asked, 'What should I do with these? Is it all right to throw them away?' I realised how little his childhood had prepared him for the niceties of life. He wanted so much to get it right but he hadn't been taught the rules. If you told him they weren't important he would protest that only people who knew them said that.

A similar dilemma was presented by the death of his mother in 1974. Only this time he defied convention on the right thing and declined to visit her during her final illness. His implacable rejection was not up for discussion. He did not go to her funeral either. Later he gave me some rings of hers, with the offhand comment – always a sign of deep emotion for John – 'You'd better have 'em. You won't leave me, will you?'

In those halcyon days I couldn't imagine that I ever would.

21 February

About 5.00 a.m. he woke, not able to breathe. I was kneeling on the bed with my body supporting his back. His weight was toppling me. I said to the girls, 'Help me, I can't take his weight,' and I felt this gasping, struggling, dear sweet man try to go forward to relieve me. His last panted words were not epic, comic in fact, in their denial: 'I'll be all right, you didn't give me enough cough mixture, pet,' but his last gesture was that of the selfless man he was. He went into a deep sleep. We sat in his room for the next hours, talking to him, hoping he could hear how much we adored him. The girls left me alone with him and I lay on the bed – our beautiful brass bed – and held him in my arms. Then I called the girls. With the sound of his grandchildren playing in the garden he drifted away. Thank God none of the horrors I'd been warned about happened and his death was full of grace. He died so elegantly. He did it with style. He looked beautiful. Like a Roman statue.

'Noblest of men woo't die?
Hast thou no care of me, shall I abide
In this dull world, which in thy absence is
No better than a sty?'

13

It Took Two of Us

AFTER THE PEACE AND love of the sixties, the seventies were full of violence. Maybe it was always there but television was showing it to us in detail. Marshall McLuhan said, 'TV brought the reality of war into the comfort of the living room. Vietnam was lost in the living rooms of America, not on the battlefields of Vietnam.' We saw the results of the My Lai massacre in which GIs inexplicably slaughtered 347 Vietnamese villagers. The Americans saw their men slaughtered in a pointless war. In England, the IRA and the Loyalists were bombing all and sundry. The Yom Kippur war raged in Israel. Arafat ominously threatened the United Nations in New York, 'Do not let the olive branch fall from my hand.' Crazed American citizens had killed three good guys: John and Bobby Kennedy and Martin Luther King. The US landed themselves with the corrupt, foul-mouthed gangster Nixon as president. In the sedate Mall in London someone took a pot shot at Princess Anne in an attempt to kidnap her. Similarly, the Queen was attacked at the Trooping the Colour. Respect for authority was declining fast. The aristocracy were despicable figures of fun. Milords Jellicoe and Lambton cavorted with prostitutes, Lord Lucan killed his nanny having mistaken her for his wife and then disappeared, protected by his gambling cronies. In literature, Solzhenitsyn revealed the horror of the Russian gulags. In films, the violence was reflected in *A Clockwork Orange* and *One Flew over the Cuckoo's Nest*. British TV was still relatively restrained, yet audiences were not in the mood for pretty entertainment.

22 February
My birthday. I found his contract for another year with Carlton, signed, on the piano. We are all distraught. Me numb. Busy, busy, busy, anything to stop thinking. Beautiful bunch of flowers from Highgrove and lovely, handwritten letter from Prince Charles. He is a sweet man. Apparently huge reaction to John's death. He would be astounded. I don't want to think. More Shakespeare keeps coming to my mind. Lear on the death of Cordelia. Or is it the Fool?

'No, no, no life,
Why should a dog, a horse, a rat, have life,
And thou no breath at all? Thou'lt come no more,
Never, never, never, never, never!'

That's it exactly.

Lloyd Shirley, George Taylor and Ted Childs came up with a proposition for a pilot leading to a series based on the police Flying Squad that was more in tune with the times. John's great friend Ian Kennedy-Martin had thought of it, and considered him ideal casting for the rough, tough leading role of Regan. John was hesitant to do another police series after his supporting role in *Z-Cars* and the lead in *Redcap*, but he could see this was different, and Ian and Ted were so persuasive that he chose to take a chance on the pilot show of *Regan* written by Ian, rather than another series of *Thick as Thieves* that had been mooted by Clement and Le Frenais. Ian and Dick turned that show into *Porridge*, starring Ronnie Barker, with spectacular success, so everyone was happy.

Ted Childs, the producer of *Regan*, remained John's mentor for the rest of his life, coming up with most of his best projects, sometimes writing or directing them himself. A quietly spoken man with a smooth line in mockery of himself and the world, he is dedicated to television. Like most of the best, his roots were in documentaries and he is always ahead of the game in his ideas. He could see it was time for a change in police series. When the show erupted into the drawing rooms of Britain in 1974, there were strong protests at its violence, especially from dear old Mary Whitehouse and her warriors, but Ted was more in touch with the real world than they. *Regan* was a success and a spin-off series was commissioned, called *The Sweeney* – from Sweeney Todd, rhyming slang for Flying Squad. This division of the police are a hard-hitting lot, who race about in cars, wearing civilian clothes and operating at the coalface of crime. The opening shot of the series set the mood. Regan slams a man up against a wall and snarls, 'We're the Sweeney, son, so if you don't want a kicking . . .'

Ted assembled an impressive team for the show. Tom Clegg and Terry Green were two of the brilliant directors, and scriptwriters included Trevor Preston, Roger Marshall, Ranald Grahame and Ian's brother Troy Kennedy-Martin of *Z-Cars* fame, the writer of the all-time TV classic *Edge of Darkness* and the film *The Italian Job*. They were based at Colet Court, a disused school building in Hammersmith where they operated with little interference from the bosses and accountants which abound nowadays. There was not even a script editor to tamper with the scripts until later on they were joined by Chris Burt, who was on their wavelength anyway and would continue to work with John in various capacities for the rest of his life. Dennis Waterman was the inspired casting for John's sidekick. He was streetwise and larky, on and off the screen. Dennis, who once said, 'My family are all boxers, except my mum, who's an Alsatian,' had a similar childhood to John.

The writers built on Dennis and John's friendship to bring a quirky, natural humour to the script. In one episode, they were leaning against a wall after nicking some villains and were asked to fill in with something. John took out a packet of cigarettes, at which Dennis said, 'Can I have a cigarette?'

John: 'I've only got one.'

Dennis: 'I only want one.'

Each episode was shot in ten days, so with fights and stunts there was a lot to get in. 'A kick, bollock and scramble.' If things got tense during filming, John would leap on a desk to do a cod tap dance and sing what became his theme song:

> The sun has got his hat on,
> Hip hip hip hooray,
> The sun has got his hat on and is coming out to play.

The day after John accompanied me to Buckingham Palace to receive my OBE in 1974, the crew awaited the arrival of his car. They filmed it coming on to the lot, with someone recording a commentary *à la* royal broadcasts: 'There is a car coming into view now. I think it's him. Yes, yes, it's him.'

As John got out they unrolled a red carpet. Stifling his laughter, John gave a V-sign version of the royal hand wave and everyone stood to attention singing an anthem-like version of 'The Sun Has Got His Hat On'. This clip was played at the end-of-picture party. Their inclination to burst into song and dance inspired Troy to write a scene in a pub with John and Dennis performing a wonderful drunken routine.

I'm not quite sure what gave Troy the idea of giving Regan a liking for sleeping with ladies naked but for a steel Nazi helmet.

So once more, Silver Bollocks was in pace with the times. A copper who snarled, 'Shut it' and, 'Put your trousers on, you're nicked,' 'We're the Sweeney and we haven't had our dinner yet, so be careful,' became a folk hero. *The Sweeney* was anarchic and anti-authoritarian. The policemen were as devious and violent as the crooks. They mocked and disobeyed their superiors, usually in the guise of the superintendent portrayed by Garfield Morgan. They were especially cynical about the law. 'You nail a villain and some ponced-up, pinstriped barrister screws you up like an old fag packet on a point of procedure and then pops off for a game of squash and a glass of Madeira.

He takes home thirty grand a year, and we can just about afford ten days in Eastbourne and a secondhand car.'

Some high-ranking police officers objected to the portrayal of the Flying Squad as such rogues, but the rank and file loved it. There was outrage at the bad language, although by today's standards it was pretty mild. Four-letter words being out of bounds, the writers got round the restrictions with colourful phrases like, 'I'm utterly and abjectly pissed off,' which in John's inimitable style sounded pretty rude. One man who accosted him obviously thought so when he said, 'There's too much fucking swearing in that fucking programme of yours. I've got a little kid at home and I don't want him sitting in front of the TV listening to that fucking language every fucking night. He's only fucking eleven.' When there were complaints about the effect of the violence on young children, Ted Childs retorted that most of the series' fans were over sixty. 'If our critics are right, shopping precincts would be full of marauding, gun-toting senior citizens, beating the rest of us over our heads with their pension books.'

The Sweeney was shot on film, edited to make it fast and furious. There were some exciting car chases, often done in the old playground round the back of Colet Court. The violence was leavened with humour. For one chase all the cars went backwards. The boys did their own stunts. They mucked in with the crew, working like a co-operative. They had no caravans, so nowhere to change costumes. They had to use the backs of cars and pub toilets, and sometimes crouched behind a wall in the street, which could be awkward when fans descended on them. They got a chair each at the end of the second series. 'We've cracked it, kid.' There was little time to sit down, however, so tight was the schedule. John learned to conserve his energy. One shot showed him and another policeman arriving after a long chase. The other actor, an earnest young man, used his Method training and ran round the block in preparation. John assessed the size and length of the shot and when the panting Brando-aspirant arrived, stepped in to join him at the last minute. At rushes the next day, John's acted exhaustion looked much more real, with the added bonus that, unlike his wheezing fellow actor, you could hear what he was saying.

24 February
He was my whole life. Everything was in reference to him. Without him I don't exist. I can't bear this crippling pain. I can't write it down. No words. My mind and body are paralysed.

'His life was gentle, and the elements
So mix'd in him that Nature might stand up
And say to all the world, "This was a man!"'

The Bible's useless, I am searching my Shakespeare for comfort.

Filming the shows involved long hours of gruelling physical work, not to mention the mental exhaustion of learning lines every night. They needed to unwind at the end of the day. Their hostelry of choice, as strangely it had been with Alec, was a grubby pub in Hammersmith, near the studio, called The Red Cow. John was not really a pub man but he needed a drink and he enjoyed the company.

Not always, however. Nobody was interested in serious debate after a hard day's slog. During the election of 1976, John was pontificating on how they should vote. Dennis goaded him, 'Why do all you people with big motors vote Labour?' and turned his attention back to the performance of the seedy stripper writhing around on the pub floor. During the dance a discarded cigarette stuck to her buttock. Political discussion was further hampered when Dennis challenged everyone to bet on how long it would take to drop off. John was incensed: 'You bloody stupid sods. I'm discussing the future of the country and you're worried about a fag end on a girl's arse.'

As the viewing audience grew to nineteen million, it became less easy for John to go to The Red Cow or anywhere else in public. *Redcap* had turned him into an 'I know that face, who are you?' kind of actor. Or the more existential, 'Are you anyone?' (Better than one I later received: 'Weren't you Sheila Hancock?') Now, however, there was no mistaking him. Or rather, they did completely mistake him. They prodded and pulled at and tried to provoke someone they thought was an aggressive in-your-face kind of guy. The man that cringed from their familiarity was a guarded person, who turned his back on trouble. The aggression was there, but firmly suppressed except when he was being Regan. It was one of several images imposed on John, which stemmed from the characters he portrayed rather than his own nature.

I was used to public recognition from *The Rag Trade*, although on nothing like the scale John found himself suddenly plunged into. When he was challenged by men in The Red Cow, usually showing off in front of their girlfriends, and didn't respond, things could turn ugly. I knew how volatile the public's reaction could be. I told John about a time, when Alec was ill, when I had done a show in Gloucester and had to change trains at Swindon. I was slumped on a seat on the railway platform, contemplating the latest dire bulletin on Alec's condition. A porter yelled across from the opposite platform, 'Cheer up, Sheila, come on, give us a laugh.' I was able to raise no more than a feeble smile, incapable of merry badinage. Having laid himself on the line as a friend of the stars, the porter felt insulted by my lack of response in front of his mates and a few other waiting passengers. Very soon his chirpiness had turned to insults in which he was joined by some of the others. 'Well, I don't think you're very funny anyway. Who does she think she is? Stuck-up cow.' And on and on.

John began to get piles of mail from fans and was bewildered by their devotion to a stranger. One in particular presented a problem. He received twenty-page letters and long rambling tapes from a woman called Eileen. They got more and more odd, culminating in her accusing him of fathering her child, presumably by post, and informing the police, her local MP, the Prime Minister and the Queen of the happy event. She changed her name by deed poll to Thaw and took to journeying to

London and lying in wait for him. He always avoided her. When he starred in Tom Stoppard's *Night and Day* in 1978, I suggested that if she came to see the play, he should invite her backstage and talk kindly to her, showing that he was not Jack Regan, with whom she was in love, but an ordinary bloke. The visit failed. Somehow she slipped past the stage doorman and was lurking behind the door of his dressing room when he came offstage. She was tiny and wearing a red mac. He leaped out of his skin when he saw what he thought was the homicidal dwarf from the film *Don't Look Now*. She continued to haunt him for many years, as well as threatening my life. Then, suddenly, the communications stopped dead with no explanation. She lived in Hyde and was always talking about visiting her doctor. Dr Shipman, the mass murderer, was based in Hyde.

On the whole, John tried his best not to disappoint his fans. On one occasion he played a whole charity football match with a broken arm rather than let Regan be stretchered off. He fended off female embraces as politely as possible. When approached in a supermarket he was known to say to autograph hunters, 'Sorry, no,' and if they persisted he would snap, 'Fuck off.' If I remonstrated with him, pointing out that he was dependent on the public so should at least be polite, he would explain his reluctance: 'I don't want to have to be Mr Nice Guy all the time. I do my job, now leave me alone.' Eventually he stopped going to public places unless he had to.

25 February

Rushed cremation to avoid the press. Sad little nothing cere-mony. Strauss's last song sung by his beloved Schwarzkopf, a bit of the Elgar Cello Concerto, some Charlie Parker and silence. Flowers and leaves from the garden to put on his coffin. Just the family. No priest, no palaver. We will do more later. Then home to lunch with the people who work at the house. Suddenly desperate to be alone so I asked the family to go back to London and leave me. When they'd gone, I howled like an animal, prowling round, looking for traces of him. I can still smell him but he has absolutely gone. Utter despair at his absence, his total absence. I feel as though a whole part of me has been hacked away, leaving a bleeding gaping wound. I sit, lie on the floor, crouch, trying to stop the physical pain of it. I weep and weep and weep. I can't do anything without him. Watch TV, have a cup of tea, cook, it is all linked with him. I'm talking to him as if he were there, but he's not, he's so not.

The children could not hide away. Joanna was too young to be riled at being called the Teeny Sweeney, but Abigail and Ellie Jane found the limelight disconcerting. They were not allowed to watch the show as it was too late and, I thought, too violent for nine- and ten-year-olds. It could be disturbing to see your dad beating people to a pulp, not to mention hopping into bed with nubile women who were definitely not their mum. This put them at a disadvantage when kids in the playground discussed the finer points of last night's punch-up or hummed the theme tune at them in the corridors. Harry South's music contributed hugely to the success of the show as, later, did Barrington Phelong's *Morse* theme. It was a show everyone talked about next morning in the bus queue and, whilst giving the girls street cred, it was confusing to equate the man slaving over the Sunday roast with the title of Thinking Woman's Crumpet. Unusually for such a popular show it was a critical success; more importantly to John, it was admired by his peers. John was the first to win the highly esteemed BAFTA Best Actor award, normally reserved for weighty drama and venerable actors, for a prime-time series.

The awards mounted up for the programme and John. It was a mixed blessing. He was honoured but his sweaty hand would cling to mine as we walked up the red carpet between baying photographers and fans. The brevity of his terrified acceptance speeches was welcomed in the endless evenings, if sometimes appearing a little graceless. The most enjoyable accolade Dennis and John received was to be invited on to the *Morecambe and Wise Christmas Show*. In return they persuaded the two comics to appear in an episode of *The Sweeney*. A great deal of liquor was imbibed, before, after and during the filming. The script was peppered with inspired ad-libs from Eric, and Ted Childs had difficulty in bringing them to order. He frequently arrived on set to find everyone 'rolling about laughing with their legs in the air, having a lovely party but not doing a lot of work'. When eventually John reeled home he would recount Eric's latest *bons mots* with glee, and the more he fell about with laughter, the less I was amused.

Stuck at home with a small baby and a difficult ten-year-old, I was having nowhere near as much fun. In addition, having just finished converting one new home, John had heard that a Victorian Gothic house at the end of the road, with a garden backing on to the river, was up for sale. He insisted on a visit. We were shown round by an old lady who had lived there for years without doing anything to the house. There was no heating, gas lighting, and the kitchen was a cracked sink and rusty cooker in the basement. Original features, they called them. But there were also stained-glass windows, marble fireplaces and a Victorian summerhouse with the Thames lapping at its windows. John leaned against the stone wall at the bottom of the garden, the river behind him, and uttered quietly the phrase I came to dread: 'I wan' it.' By this time Mrs Fitzwalter was enchanted by John's passion for the house, which extended to mowing the overgrown lawn for her. She rejected all the rich Arabs and pop stars fighting for it and was prepared to wait till we had raised the asking price, which she lowered for us. So, once more, I was plunged into the nightmare of builders not turning up and then going bankrupt, exquisite original tiled floors collapsing with dry rot, and cats being trapped under floorboards. Despite our odd childhoods, both of us had grown up with the belief, still prevalent in the seventies, that a woman's place really is in the home and the man is the official hunter-gatherer. Trouble was, I too was hunting and gathering as well as earth-mothering, and I'd read *The Female Eunuch*.

Then there was the jealousy. While I was cow-like feeding my baby, at work he was leaping between the sheets with lithe beauties with no stretch marks. I could not believe they did not lust after him as I did. John, for his part, was shocked that I should doubt the loyalty of a man who doesn't play games.

As I was working at night in a theatre play and John during the day on television, we saw little of each other. John was working a sixteen-hour day so he was exhausted. In three short years he had gone from being a bachelor, seeing his one child at weekends, doing the odd bit of telly, to becoming a husband and father with two homes, three children and worldwide renown. It was no wonder that he needed a few drinks to help him on the way. Just like my father and Alec. Aware that the drinks had become more than a few, on my advice he decided to go to a health farm to recuperate, starting with a fast. There he obviously ruminated on my moans: 'Just a little note to tell you I feel very weak and can't get it together, I have a terrible headache and I love you very much. I was talking to Roy [a masseur] about your *This Is Your Life* and felt very proud to be part of that life. I'm very proud of the love you give me, the trouble you go through for me, and proud of the children you gave me. In short you are the most beautiful woman – person – in the world, kid. Help me, help me, mangé, mangé.' I liked the pc use of 'person'.

26 February
Woke up after a few hours' sleep and realised it was still true. Girls phoned to say they are coming to get me, but I am not fit to face anyone. Thousands of letters. I know these people are actually hurting, but oh God what I'm feeling is beyond comfort. Nothing helps. Especially that 'Death is nothing at all' bollocks. Oh really? And no, he isn't in the sodding next room. The thoughtful strangers say it will help me but it makes me roar with rage. OK, you say I'll meet him again. Prove it. I would like to believe it, God would I like to. If I thought it was true I'd kill myself and meet him now. I have absolutely no sense of his presence. He is utterly gone and I can't bear it.

One aspect of his success John relished was the increased wealth it brought. His childhood had given him a dread of poverty. Yet for both of us there was ambivalence in our attitude to our new-found affluence; relish tinged with guilt. But John needed tangible proof of his success – a big motor, a big house. He loved giving presents. He showered me with jewellery and the kids with toys. I only had to admire something and he would say, 'You wan' it, kid?', be it a saucepan, a Picasso in the Tate or the Eiffel Tower. It was a way of demonstrating his love and he lapped up our pleasure. He was bad at receiving presents, often not undoing his Christmas gifts from one year to the next. It was as though he felt unworthy of them. The one thing he bought for himself was radios. He could never resist a new model. Especially for the bathroom. If he turned on the radio loud enough, he could stay there for ages, not hearing our calls. If he did, his reply was, 'Ahm in ze bas' and we would know we'd lost him for another hour.

We splashed out on a swimming pool, which gave him endless pleasure. Not to swim in. He rarely ventured into the water and, when he did, the shuddering and howling were heard throughout Chiswick. His chief joy was cleaning it. He had a mechanical cleaner that he christened Fred. He passed many a happy morning chuckling as it scurried round the bottom of the pool, cracking its plastic tail. Jo refused to go into the pool for several

days after he warned her that it ate little girls. Other than that, he would scoop off the leaves with a net and then clamber clumsily on to a big plastic lilo on which he would float blissfully, imbibing a large one sitting on a lilo of its own. 'Oh yes, this is ze life, I tell you.'

Our luck was not shared by the rest of the country. The miners and teachers were building up to major strikes and people were being made redundant as unemployment rose. Heath had gone to the country hoping for a vote of confidence on his 'Who Rules Britain' ticket, only to be defeated by Wilson whose comment on victory was, 'All I can say is my prayers.' The atmosphere was not helped by a series of horrific murders carried out by a mysterious Yorkshire Ripper. It seemed a good time to go abroad.

John's brother Ray was feeling homesick in Brisbane, so when we were offered a tour of Michael Frayn's play *The Two of Us* in Australia, it was an opportunity to take the whole family on a visit. The first night in Melbourne could not be counted as a triumph. The last act of the piece required us to play many parts, changing costume in the wings and rushing on miraculously transformed. It was meant to be funny, but was not to the rather stuffy people of Melbourne, which in architecture and atmosphere felt like Cheltenham. There was scarcely a titter. One of the last lines commenting on the party we were depicting was, 'I think that went well, don't you?' Sweating and wilting, John collapsed into giggles, I followed suit and the curtain descended in confusion. We decided it was not wise for The Two of Us to work together.

Our journey home too had its down side. We took Ellie Jane with us to Bali, and then India. Bali in the seventies was not such a popular tourist destination as it is now. Our trip was organised by that great traveller, Derek Nimmo, and we were staying with a Balinese antique dealer, Jimmy Pandi. We dined under the stars, swam in the warm sea and visited remote villages full of beautiful people. So unused were they to foreigners that they crowded round us, particularly fascinated by blonde, blue-eyed Ellie Jane. There were dark tales of purges of Communists and corruption in high places, but it seemed a blissfully happy place. By contrast, the poverty we saw in India made it impossible for us really to enjoy its magnificence. The Taj Mahal is beautiful beyond expectation, seeming to float on air, but we found it difficult to see through the beggars. One day when I was entering into the spirit of the place and bartering with a merchant over the price of a bracelet, John leaned on the stall and wailed, 'Oh, I can't wait to see Doris at the Express Dairy.' He shut himself in the hotel and ordered a bottle of vodka and a bottle of whisky. So amazed were they at this lavish order of exorbitantly priced drinks that it arrived with thirty glasses and a bowl of peanuts. John hid away in the hotel with his booze and refused to go out any more. Ellie and I braved the huge bats and rabid dogs of Udaipur alone. It is a philistine reaction to an obviously fascinating country, but we were riddled with guilt to be flashing cameras and other signs of wealth about whilst others needed to beg to eat.

27 February
Propped up my face with make-up and took four-year-old Lola as protection to face the world in Marks and Spencer. People kept clutching my hand and saying kind things. I bit the sides of my mouth to stop crying. Lola was strangely silent, sitting on my trolley. She listened to all these comments and looked at me struggling and suddenly in a sing-song voice with a sort of mock-Jewish shrug she said at the checkout, 'Now look, Grandad's dead, he won't come back, but you're very old so you'll be dead soon too.' It was obviously a garbled version of Ellie's attempt to explain things to her. It was the first time I've laughed, so of course she went on and on: 'Grandad won't want that coffee because he's dead,' 'Grandad likes cream cake but he won't want them now because he's gone for ever.' At least she's coming to terms with it.

In 1978, when we returned to England, Margaret Thatcher was being heavily promoted as a possible prime minister. I had met her in 1975 as a fellow panellist on *Any Questions*. At that time she was being groomed for the leadership of the Tory Party and her posse of supporters came with her, including Airey Neave, who was later killed by a car bomb in the House of Commons car park. I had no one advising me but I held my own against her on the programme, and even scored a few points. On our return from Australia, I played Miss Hannigan, in charge of the orphanage in the musical *Annie*, at the Victoria Palace. One night the tannoy demanded that we wait on stage after the curtain call to greet Mrs Thatcher, the newly appointed Leader of the Opposition. I did not think she would remember me or care if I told the stage manager I had to get home and relieve my babysitter. I was in my bra and pants and a very grubby kimono when there was a knock at my dressing-room door. The lacquered blonde smiled sweetly into my greasy, make-up-less face and purred in her studiedly soft voice 'I didn't want to miss you.' 'Vantage, Thatcher. A few years later, John and I visited Number 10 for a party and she welcomed the guests in front of the press photographers. As I put out my hand she grasped it and hurled me across her to clear the shot for the far more beguiling picture of the Prime Minister with Inspector Morse.

In 1979, when she was elected the first female prime minister, it was a triumph for feminism. On her election as leader of her party she had said, 'I beat four chaps, now let's get down to work,' so we hoped she would give some credit to the campaigning women without whom her position would have been out of the question a few years previously. For her victory speech she chose to ooze a prayer of St Francis of Assisi, which up until then I had rather liked.

> Lord make me an instrument of your peace,
> Where there is hatred let me sow love
> Where there is injury pardon
> Where there is doubt faith
> Where there is despair hope
> Where there is darkness light
> Where there is sadness joy.

The previous year, after fifty-three episodes and two features films, John had decided to quit *The Sweeney* while it was still a huge success. The last speech spoken by Jack Regan started with, 'I'm thoroughly pissed off with this lot' and ended, 'You can stuff it' – rather more in the mood of the country than Maggie's unctuous prayer.

28 February
Daunted by all the planning. The ashes ceremony at home for close friends and then, sometime, a memorial service. It is expected. He has become a sort of icon for people. He would be utterly bemused and probably pretty cynical about the reaction to his death. People didn't really know him, and what most of them are mourning is Morse, or Kavanagh, or Jack Regan. People want someone to look up to. He always played fundamentally decent, if troubled, men. But he was *decent as it happens. He was worthy of their respect but not for the reasons that most of them have imposed on him.*

14

It Takes Care

WE HAD WHAT WAS known as the Winter of Discontent in 1979. Strikes had become violent, rubbish was uncollected and bodies unburied. Maggie endeavoured to bring about a glorious summer by balancing the books as her shopkeeper father had taught her. Her main objectives were less public spending, lower taxes and control of the unions. How she achieved them had a lasting effect on our country. Our hopes of her boldly advancing the feminist cause were soon dashed; the Sexual Discrimination and Equal Pay Act in 1975 had nothing to do with her. Nevertheless, women were making progress in the seventies and eighties. They were allowed on to the floor of the Stock Exchange for the first time, and in 1977 Angela Rippon was permitted to read international news on the BBC. ITN followed suit with Anna Ford the following year, and, even more daring, in 1981 a black woman, Moira Stuart, was allowed to announce serious matters to the nation. She still receives hate mail more than twenty years later.

In the eighties the Thaws conformed to Maggie's belief of the importance of the family unit. Take care of you and yours and society will take care of itself. There's no such thing as society, only individuals. We joined the Me Generation. Our family was all right. We were having a very good time. Not being involved in a demanding series, John was around more. He cooked Sunday lunches, on one occasion varying the regulation roast with an attempt at Peking duck – lunch was served at 6 p.m., preceded by a lot of blow-drying of the scraggy bird with hairdryers and a fair amount of bad language, but we were duly appreciative of his efforts. Barbecues were less of a success. Richard Briers was usually his co-cook and they always miscalculated how long it took to light the barbecue and get the coke glowing. They used everything from paraffin to gin to encourage the fire, and we dreaded their burnt sausages with petrol sauce. My Christmas parties were not hugely popular with them. The games I organised drove John and Richard to cower in the basement with a bottle of gin – or two. My treasure hunt with clever clues laid round the house and garden usually descended into open warfare. Thaws Junior and Senior used spying and violence in the battle to pick up clues. On one occasion one of my cunning ruses took them to the phone box in the street where they had to phone home and pick up the next riddle on the answer-phone. They were in the middle of a pitched battle to prevent each other using the phone when Lucy Briers arrived wailing that she had no coins. John sweetly paused to give her his, then continued to do battle with his father. The neighbours nearly called the police.

On the professional front, John was disappointed that a series called *Mitch* about a crime reporter was left on the shelf for two years, so that when it was aired its topical material was dated. He swore he would never work for that company again, and didn't. I landed a coveted role in the most expensive musical ever staged at that date. When I was cast as Mrs Lovett in Stephen Sondheim's *Sweeney Todd*, to be performed at the vast Drury Lane Theatre in 1980, I was daunted but, egged on by Steve and Hal Prince, did well in rehearsal, absorbing the complex lyrics and music. At the first band call, when the rest of the cast were cheering excitedly as the complex, sensational score was revealed, I became rigid with fear. I had always suffered from stage fright, starting in my repertory days when every Monday night I had faced audiences

gave John a custom-made script cover from Asprey with space for photos. The ones he chose
to have with him at work were:

Top left: The new family: Abigail, Ellie Jane and the two of us in Gloucestershire.
Top right: Mildred, Joanna, me, Ellie Jane and Grandad celebrating Grandad's birthday.
Above left: Me ('Lovely Bum'), Kate Binchy and Hugh Paddick in the dressing-room at the
King's Head pub theatre.
Above right: This is the photo I carried with me: John at Sharrow Bay Hotel. On the back it
says; 'To my darling "Treasure", with all my love, John.'

Grandad in the garden at Tarlton with two of the 'little boggers'.

5 December 1973, a less glamorous second wedding for us both, with the two new sisters, Ellie Jane and Abigail.

Ellie Jane delighted to acquire another new sister in the space of a year. I'm in the dead foxes I was wearing the day I met John.

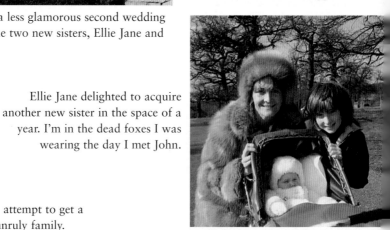

Below: John's futile attempt to get a good photo of his unruly family.

My version of *The Sweeney*: with Dennis Quilley in *Sweeney Todd*.

One of my favourite photos of my sexy husband, taken around 1975.

Directing with Tom Stoppard at the National. I too resorted to fags when stressed.

John and Dennis were working a sixteen-hour day on *The Sweeney* and it showed.

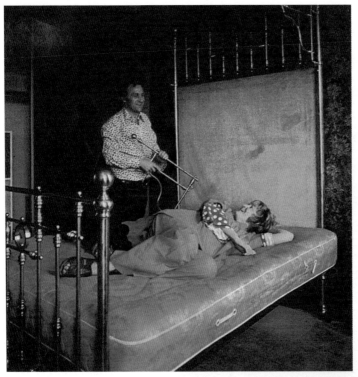

Putting up our beautiful brass bed in our new home, me heavily pregnant.

'It's mine I tell you': John presiding over the new house in Grove Park with its gas lighting and coke stove, Ellie Jane freezing to death with a blanket over her legs.

It took us years to convert the house – here I am taking a break for a drink at the bottom of the garden to escape the builders.

My first house in Hammersmith with my Morgan parked outside.

The Victorian Gothic splendour of our family home in Chiswick.

John's beloved 'Lucky' (Luckington).

The hamlet in France with the villagers playing boules.

'I'm a pedallo and I don't care': John on Lake Garda.

John and Richard Briers cooking another five-hour barbeque.

John suffering from 'marble foot-rot' after a day in Rome trailing after me and my guidebook.

Our favourite pastime, picnicking in Brighton, April 1985.

Finding it difficult to communicate.

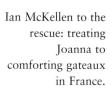

John was not good at Christmas, but he did try.

An unsuccessful holiday in Paris.

Ian McKellen to the rescue: treating Joanna to comforting gateaux in France.

'The kind of work required to help John out of his life-long depressive misery is long and arduous,' Udi Eichler wrote to me.

Ellie Jane's Christmas present of a cartoon for her father inadvertently summed up the disaffection in our family. Even the cat was prostrate.

with only a sketchy knowledge of my words and moves in the current play. I had a firm conviction, usually proved right in rep, that first nights were synonymous with disaster. It was many years before a hypnotist replaced this engrained negative thinking with something more helpful. But at the *Sweeney Todd* band call all my usual convictions of inadequacy rendered me sick with terror. Only my family were aware of this, because it would not do for the cast, or the management or, God forbid, the press to know that the leading lady was seriously planning to do a bunk. I would have done, had it not been for John's hands grasping mine night after night and steadying me.

1 March
Vivid dream about John last night. It was so real. I was by the fridge and John came into the kitchen carrying a box and said, 'Put the stuff for Lucky in here.' I was doing so when suddenly I remembered he was supposed to be dead. I grabbed his hands, felt their chunky strength and said, 'It's you.' He smiled radiantly. I said, 'You've come back.' He still glowed. I hugged him. I could feel exactly how that felt. I smelt him. I caressed his hair, felt its silkiness. I kept saying, 'Please stay. Don't go. Please please stay.' He just looked at me with that wry, loving, private smile.

John had beautiful hands, small, round and always immaculate. Not manicured, but clean and neat. Next to my bony ones, his were almost feminine. They often spoke for him. If he could not find the words to express his love, his caresses demonstrated it. When I came home from rehearsal he did not know what to say to help me because this sort of destructive dread of performing was alien to him, but he took my shaking hands firmly in both of his, looked me in the eye and said with absolute conviction, 'You can do it, kid.' So I did. I got through the run of the show with his help, but my stage fright prevented me from acting for a whole year.

Instead I turned to directing at the Cambridge Arts Theatre. After a year of that I was tempted by an offer to act again in

Stratford-upon-Avon, with the Royal Shakespeare Company. It meant a disruption of our family life, but to begin with John was happy to accept that. In 1981, at forty-eight, I had never appeared in a Shakespeare play and I embraced the Bard with a naïve enthusiasm. I was the only member of the company who had not been to university and read all the right Shakespearean scholars, so my contributions at rehearsals were more 'Oh my God, isn't it wonderful?' and 'That's so bloody true' than a Jan Kott thesis. It was not easy juggling a family and the demands of the company but we just about managed.

Then John, too, was invited to Stratford to play Sir Toby Belch in *Twelfth Night*, Cardinal Wolsey in *Henry VIII* and Nick in Saroyan's *Time of Your Life*. In one episode of the ill-fated *Mitch* he had worked with Oliver Ford-Davies. Admiring the power of John's acting, Oliver suggested that he should do more theatre. Six months later, standing in the wings of the Memorial Theatre, Stratford-upon-Avon, buckling under a sweaty wig and heavy regalia, Cardinal Wolsey turned to the Bishop of Winchester and snarled, 'It's all your fucking fault.' John's attitude puzzled the Young Turks at the RSC. He didn't join in the earnest discussions on text. In one scene Howard Davies, who directed him in *Henry VIII*, wanted him to break down in tears and admitted he didn't know how to help John reach that emotional peak. John just looked at him as if he were a moron, and played the scene. The tears flowed then and every night of the run. Richard Attenborough had a similar experience when directing him as Fred Karno in the movie *Chaplin*. He had to do a difficult drunk scene and Dear Dear Dickie, as John affectionately called him, wondered if he would like a nip of whisky to help him. John's gentle reply was, 'That's very thoughtful, Dickie, but I thought I might tackle it through acting.'

2 March
Full of fear. I keep panicking. Perhaps I didn't allow him to die properly. Maybe I should have forced him to face it. Ellie is worried about that too. We all went for a walk in Richmond Park but we are all so spent. Grief is exhausting.

John was simply a born actor. The reason he was sometimes ungracious when people complimented him was because he could just do it, it was a gift, and it did not seem to warrant praise. As a child he had learned to cope on his own and, as an actor, he could develop his characters on his own. Many actors, especially young ones, expect the director to tell them what to do. This is foolish because many directors are rubbish, gaining their reputations through good casting and having a brilliant designer come up with a concept that gives the critics something to write about. Paradoxically, though he slaved away at his scripts at home, John was also adaptable to other actors' performances, which is why they all loved working with him. He liked fluidity. He hated the sort of actor who, if John unexpectedly came into the scene riding an elephant, would still give the same performance. Despite his God-given intuitive talent, John loved being directed if it was by someone he respected, and would complain that most people just let him get on with it. That was because they knew he would.

He was naturally observant. He had a photographic memory of places and persons, their manner and appearance. He could mimic anyone perfectly within minutes of meeting them. He then deepened this portrait by incorporating his own feelings. Despite his retiring demeanour, he seethed with emotions that he could call into play. Like me, he felt at a disadvantage in the rehearsal room with all the 'clever clogs'. Canny as always, he used this in his portrayal of Wolsey. Howard Davies says: 'He was a working man in the court of kings, and there was something about John that was the same in his working life. When Cardinal Wolsey's fall from grace happened in *Henry VIII* he was able to tap into something about class difference, about the pain of being displaced in a world that didn't recognise you, and didn't follow you and in the end support you.'

As always, John was unaware of just how much the company did support him. He kept himself to himself offstage and left after one year, refusing to accompany the shows to the Barbican in London. Terry Hands's plea that the London critics should get a second look at his performances was met with, 'I don't give a fuck for the London critics.' But he did. He was irked that despite the general verdict of the cognoscenti that he was giving superb performances, some of the desperate-for-copy critics made disparaging references to *The Sweeney* and TV actors. He too was discovering that once those guys have put you in a pigeonhole, usually in the first role they see you in, they won't let you out. John claimed that one of the reasons he was leaving was that he was uncomfortable at the RSC because it was institutionalised, though Terry reasonably averred that so was a long television series. But in TV, John was in a world he understood and, more importantly, he was top of the pile. At the RSC his already fragile identity was swamped – and what's more, he was paid a pittance for working his arse off.

He could have made a lot of money in films but, despite a brilliant performance as the vile police chief Kruger in Atten-borough's *Cry Freedom*, which brought offers from Hollywood, he chose to stay a big fish in a small pool, or so it seemed to others. John did not consider TV inferior. To him, the Holly-wood movie schedule, as opposed to the speed of TV filming, was as protracted and boring as the repetition of a theatre job. There is no doubt, as his performances at the RSC and later at the National and Manchester Exchange showed, he was a fine stage actor, and that, had he focussed on theatre, he would have been more lauded by the 'posh wankers', as he called them. He did have an ambition to play Lear one day – though he was worried whether he could carry the dead Cordelia in the last scene without tripping up: 'Never, never, never, oops, sorry.'

In 1993, when he was doing *Absence of War* at the National, John was irritated by the ten weeks of rehearsal: 'We could get this bloody thing on the road in three weeks.' Oliver Ford-Davies, with whom he was working again, felt his reluctance to contribute to the rehearsal process hampered him. Richard Eyre thought John did not like to be seen to be working too hard lest it looked like showing off. Oliver plucked up courage to discuss one scene with John and Richard that he felt could be more profoundly realised. John just smirked and made Oliver feel uncomfortable. Then they ran the scene and John did, brilliantly, exactly what Oliver had intended. The question is, would he have done so without the discussion? Had he not been so inhibited and inhibiting to others, could his work have been even richer? Howard Davies again: 'There was something in his shyness that didn't believe his own talent. Both endearing and attractive, it gave him humility, but it tugged at his feet and held him back. Very regrettable.'

3 March
Dealing with all the mail very slowly. The hundreds of letters are kind and loving. Full of sorrow for the man they felt they knew. What he would have been most proud of are the letters from his peers, praising his extraordinary ability as an actor. It seems the whole profession valued him and recognised that he was a fine actor. He would have like that. And been amazed.

After bailing out of the RSC, John was a bit depressed about where his career was going, but he did a job that cheered him up no end. Peter O'Toole's days of excessive drinking were over by 1984, but when John played Doolittle to his Professor Higgins in *Pygmalion* Peter still had a jolly good time on stage. In front of the audience he would frequently chortle with delight at his fellow actors' performances. He thought John's Doolittle was a perfect Shavian performance, capturing Shaw's sympathy for the downtrodden, that was the stuff that turned people into Marxists. There was one particular line, the delivery of which O'Toole cherished at rehearsal. When Higgins challenged Doolittle about going to a pub, he loved the way John barked the reply: 'Why shouldn't I?' in fierce defiance rather than whining reproach. Unfortunately it should have got a laugh, but never did. It became an obsession for them all. John tried every possible inflection, those on stage tried different reactions. Nothing. Eventually that line came to dominate the whole scene. You could see John preparing for it pages before. The more it failed the more they fell about. When I went to the show John begged them all, 'Please, please, Sheila's out front. Don't make me laugh. Do absolutely nothing.' Their dutifully blank stares convulsed him and I watched a stageful of actors, all speechless with mirth, O'Toole openly doubled up and guffawing.

It's hard for people outside the business to understand this habit of corpsing, as it is called. It is a dreaded disease for actors. It can be triggered by something not particularly funny, and is I suspect a sort of hysteria that springs from the heightened state you have to be in to go on stage. It is usually not enjoyable and can dog you in a long run of a play so that you dread certain passages coming up, having completely forgotten what made you laugh in the first place. It's like laughing at funerals and giggles when the boss sacks you and your heart is breaking.

One day Jack Watling was ill, but agreed to perform. He was in the wings feeling sick and muttered to John, 'Oh Lord, I feel a bit funny.'

John hissed back, 'Well, for God's sake get on before it wears off.'

That entrance became another recurring giggle hurdle for them all.

Working with Peter was a delight and John wanted to repeat the experience. Richard Wilson, the director, and John invited Peter to play one of the two homosexual hairdressers in a play by Charles Dyer called *Staircase*. John's character suffered from alopecia. Peter's response was the following letter:

Dearest John,
The only reason that you can have for wanting us to act in Ding Dong Dyer's 'Staircase' is one of pure malice. We would never get through the first scene. You would be prinking about in a fucking turban and every time you get hysterics, which will be every other line, there is the stock room for you to prance in, while I am left clutching the curling irons, all alone on stage, where I will probably get Aids. Piss off. I love you. Kiss to Sheila and the kids. You can do the second act all by yourself. Piss off.
Peter

Most actors look for the sublime in a role. John looked for the common touch. I too noticed that at Stratford, put a crown on an actor's head and a sword in his hand and he swaggers around, justifying the most appalling behaviour. When I played Tamora, Queen of the Goths (Mrs Goth) in *Titus Andronicus*, who ends up eating her children in a pie – bodies in pies having become my speciality since *Sweeney Todd* – I had to fight hard to justify her behaviour to a cast full of avenging male actors, set upon being noble. Similarly, Paulina in *The Winter's Tale* was usually played as a strident nag and it took a lot of unacademic argument on my part to persuade them that she was right and that all the men in the play may be royal, but they were extremely silly and needed telling off. This sexist approach in all the plays began to be contested by the women. We formed support groups, including Harriet Walter and Juliet Stevenson, to give one another courage to stand up to the male hierarchy.

6 March

Started the day forcing myself to be positive. Long chat to Clare V.* helped. She is so wise. No sentiment, no bullshit but deep understanding. Felt a lot better, then suddenly out of the blue, totally doubled up with grief. Agonising pain in my chest and heart. OK. A heart attack? Good. Come on then. Let's be havin' you.

Trevor Nunn got his revenge for this female bonding by awarding me the artistic directorship of the small-scale tour. I was deeply honoured until I realised no one else in their right mind would take it on. My right mind had been perverted by my new obsession with Willy the Bard. I couldn't wait to take his glory to Scunthorpe Baths. There had only been one woman director at the RSC and that was ten years before. It was an uphill battle about which I have already written in another book, so suffice it to say that the whole brilliant company that I gathered round me for the adventure remember it with great affection. Dan Day-Lewis, who does not stick with things he does not like, was one of the most enthusiastic at building and dismantling our travelling auditorium, doing workshops and enchanting legions of Shakespeare converts in the backwaters of Britain.

During our travels in 1983 and 1984, we were well placed to see the state of the country under Thatcherism. It was riddled with discord. The industrial base was being dismantled and with it whole communities, whose cohesion was dependent on the local mine, factory or shipyard. Coal miners and teachers were striking. Everyone was fighting savagely. Phrases like 'the enemy within' and 'not one of us' were alienating whole sections of the community. Three million were unemployed, with all the

---

* Clare Venables. Actor, writer, inspirational teacher and opera and theatre director. One of the first women to run a theatre. Director of Lincoln Theatre Royal, Manchester Library and Forum, Theatre Royal, Stratford East, The Crucible, Sheffield. Principal of the Britt School. Director of Education, the Royal Shakespeare Company. Mentor to many of our leading directors including Stephen Pimlott, Michael Boyd and Stephen Daldry. Dearest of friends and solver of crosswords and people's problems. Died 17 October 2003, aged sixty. Why do the good die young?

implication of isolation and disaffection that that implies. Thatcher believed implacably that she was right. 'The lady's not for turning,' she said and, 'I am extremely patient as long as I get my own way in the end.' The bulk of the electorate loved her for it. Something was being done. She had courage too. When an IRA bomb nearly killed her at a hotel in Brighton she dusted herself down and carried on as if nothing had happened. She made the refusal of Oxford University to give her an honorary degree look petty.

7 March
John would have appreciated this letter:
'I met John on numerous occasions as indeed I met your good self when you came to the NCP to park your car (opposite his theatre). The thing that struck me most about him was his ability to treat me and other staff with a certain dignity that was certainly lacking in a lot of our customers. I found him to be a genuinely nice man who would pass the time of day with you. The huge star that he will always be, was just a normal decent human being. I returned and live in Ireland now so I very much doubt I will meet you again to tell you how very sorry I am for your loss in person, but I will say a prayer for you and light a candle for you in our local church. God bless you and give you the strength to carry you through.
Yours,
Mickey (with the patch)'

When we took the RSC tour to Belfast I was appalled by the wall. I hadn't imagined there actually was this hideous phys-ical barrier, covered in hateful graffiti, between the communi-ties, cutting streets in half and separating children from their friends. The slums and dereliction depressed me, but the ecstatic audiences were thrilling. I went round talking to people, trying to fathom this intransigence on both sides. Back in London an IRA bomb went off, killing horses and men in Hyde Park. Especially grievous to me, a bomb killed musicians and destroyed the bandstand in St James's Park which had given John and me such peaceful pleasure. During the tour, I managed to visit Greenham when 20,000 women embraced the base containing cruise missiles. The silence broken only by eerie keening flummoxed the soldiers on the other side of the wire. Peaceful protest felt very powerful. The healing power of Shakespeare in these troubled times was potent too. My company's performances of the *Dream* and *Romeo and Juliet* in sports halls and community centres were some of the most beautiful I have seen.

12 March
Found a tape made by John presumably from a broadcast, of the Elgar Quintet. It was in the key basket in London. It fell on the floor as I came back from Lucky. How the hell it got there I don't know. It was one of our absolute favourites. So guttingly lovely. I had to play it. The second movement seems to express profound sorrow. It transforms human despair into something beautiful and makes you realise you are bound to others by the experience. The whole world knows grief. I am not alone in this. It's part of life. Anyway, as John kept saying about his suffering: 'I have no choice.'

My passionate involvement in the RSC made me neglectful of my family. Ellie Jane had left home. She was pursuing her own RADA and acting career, as was Abigail, but ten-year-old Jo was dragged from pillar to post with me on the tour, as most of it fell during her school holidays. Some of the audiences had never seen a play, let alone Shakespeare, so it was vital to me that we should have no off nights. The company came to dread me accosting them after a performance, brandishing my pad with pages of notes. I couldn't leave them alone, which meant I did John. I popped back home occasionally but I was putting my job first and my marriage nowhere. John began to call me Muriel, his mistress, rather than his wife. Beneath the quips he was growing quite angry. We had a big party for one of Jo's birthdays. He had become curiously unhappy about having people in the house, especially those he didn't know. He and Dennis Waterman got very drunk in the basement and he started haranguing me every time I went down to get supplies. It was like an Ayckbourn farce. All gracious smiles for the guests upstairs, and spitting venom in the basement. We had always had rows but they were becoming more bitter though as yet the making up was still delightful.

While I was enjoying myself in Walsall John was mouldering in Margate. Peter O'Toole had been right to turn the play down. *Staircase*, with the author playing the other lead role with an unsure grip of his own words, was not a success. The only person who seemed to enjoy himself was the young ASM in his first job, Ross Kemp. He hero-worshipped John, watching in awe the way he worked. Ross enjoyed his nightly task of wetting John's coat with a watering can to make him look rain-soaked. They had time for a little chat as he sprinkled. He told John that he had been shocked to read that Marlon Brando had insulted his profession by saying that an actor was a person who's not listening if no one is talking about him.

'Pardon?' said John as he made his entrance.

John also taught Ross how to deal with aggressive fans, which would stand him in good stead in his own later tough guy roles in *EastEnders* and the like. He went to a café in Margate with John for tea. It was virtually empty, but one man came in demanding that they move as he had booked the table where they were sitting. John looked him in the eye and said overly politely, 'You want this table? OK, is it all right if we move over there? That OK with you? Are you sure now?'

As they moved, he winked sympathetically at the man's girl-friend. The couple spent their time at their chosen table having a hideous row. John could use his walking away from trouble to cause it and increasingly did so.

14 March
It seems every time I turn on the TV or read a paper there's a picture of John. I can't face it yet. The public reaction

*to his death would have astounded him and it disturbs me.
I have spent a long while in the public eye and I know
what is expected of me – at least by the media. After all I
have been a 'brave' widow before as well as a 'brave' cancer
'victim'. I know the ropes. Be an inspiration. Be brave.
Tragic Sheila. The letters are full of comforting ideas many
of which I appreciate but cannot aspire to. For me belief
in an afterlife seems simplistic and self-deluding although
I would be happy, God would I, to be proved wrong. I
feel insane. I walk around muttering – come back, please,
please come back. And I do expect him to walk in. How
can someone be there one moment and then completely
gone?*

John hated being away from home and he did a couple of
jobs where the locations upset him. *The Grass Is Singing*, set in
Africa, was filmed in sweltering heat in the Zambian bush. More
maddening than the mosquitoes was Karen Black, who played
opposite John and drove him insane with her Californian
gobbledygook. The three months away from home were hell,
although the film earned him a rave review from Margaret
Hinksman, respected film critic: 'A superb unstinting performance'. In 1985 he went to Belfast to play the devastated father
of a soldier killed by the IRA. Like me, he was poleaxed by
what he saw. *We'll Support You Ever More* was a superb television play by Douglas Livingstone. It was about an ordinary
man trying to understand the hatreds that had led to his son's
death, so in acting it, John had to do the same. It is one of his
best performances but the part affected him deeply. I could
understand why he was depressed when he came home. At other
times his depression seemed less explicable.

We had been married for over ten years. We had successful
careers and two lovely homes, but our frequent separations were
stunting the growth of our marriage. Problems got shelved rather
than discussed. There was still plenty of frantic sex but very
little tenderness. I was aware he was unhappy but hadn't got
time or patience to find out why. I knew we were working too

hard, but in our profession you have to take it when it's there because it often isn't. John in particular was wretched if he was unemployed and his drive to make sure it didn't happen was turning him into a workaholic. What I had not detected was that being away on location or alone at home was fuelling another more serious addiction.

After a run of serious roles, he was pleased to get a comedy role for a change, playing Reece Dinsdale's father in *Home to Roost* by that doyen of sitcom writers, Eric Chappell. It rehearsed in London but recorded up in Leeds. When he came home shattered each week I put it down to the stress of having to work in front of a studio audience, which he found difficult. When I played the part of his wife in one episode, I discovered that there was another reason. The night before the recording, we went out for a meal with everybody and, after we had eaten, I assumed we would go back for an early night before the heavy studio day. John did not come back to the hotel with me. This was extraordinary because he knew I was nervous and was usually over-protective of me. He reeled back in the small hours of the morning, blind drunk. The next day during the show, we barely spoke. I was shocked at his shaking hands and sweating brow. He got through the show and I'm sure nobody but I noticed the state he was in. All the time I was there jokes were flying around about his capacity for the booze, so I realised this was usual. I was appalled and showed it. They thought me a miserable killjoy. I comforted myself that when the series ended so would the problem. He had always been a drinker. I liked drinkers. My dad was one, so was Alec. It did not affect his work, and this was an aberration caused by him being at a loose end in Leeds. Of course it was.

15

It Takes Patience

IN 1985 TED CHILDS was Head of Drama at Central TV. His great gift was discovering and nurturing talent. A bright young academic called Kenny McBain was keen to break into TV adult drama, having worked on the progressive children's series *Grange Hill*. Ted told him to find a strong detective series set in the Central area. Kenny suggested the books by Colin Dexter, set in Oxford, which was about two feet inside the region boundary. The idea was opposed from all sides. When it was pitched to the big boys they were not at all keen. They thought Inspector Morse was a miserable old sod, and could not believe that a man who liked classical music and real ale and was a failure with women would appeal to the public. John Birt, then Director of Programmes at LWT, who had a say in all TV output and was later renowned for questionable decisions at the BBC, was vehemently against it. John too had his doubts about doing yet another policeman. Kenny, who had only seen him being crude and physical in *The Sweeney*, did not think he had the intellectual qualities necessary for the role. Ted fixed up a lunch between John and Kenny, they got on like a house on fire, and by the end of it, they had persuaded each other to go ahead. With John on board 'the Suits', as John called the bosses, reluctantly decided to give it a go.

Kenny recruited another academic, Anthony Minghella, to do the first TV adaptation and they were in business. Anthony insisted they needed two hours to unravel the complicated plots. This was unheard of in TV. Nobody believed the public could concentrate for so long in our sound-bite society, but they got their way. Again, one of John's programmes was breaking new ground. Ted, as usual, made sure the production values were first class. Top writers like Julian Mitchell, Stephen Churchett, Daniel Boyle and Charles Wood were recruited to adapt Colin's books. It was never difficult to get writers for John's shows because he was respectful of their work. Top directors too were delighted to be on board. Many people cut their teeth on *The Sweeney* and *Morse* and then went on to film success. One of these, Danny Boyle, came from theatre. John greeted him with, 'I hope we're not going to do any of those bloody trust exercises you do at the Royal Court. Or throw balls around.' They all enjoyed working with John and learned a lot from his expertise in front of the camera, acquired from years of experience.

Colin Dexter was quite happy when John suggested subtle changes in the character of Morse. John's Morse became less sleazy and more tentative in his attitude to women than the hero of the early novels. John respected Colin's academic background and encyclopaedic knowledge, which stood him in good stead when compiling or solving cryptic crosswords. Despite Colin's deteriorating hearing, they enjoyed having a laugh over a drink together, although Colin could become miffed when autograph hunters pushed him aside in their quest to get at John, particularly if they were pretty young ladies.

Kenny McBain's brilliant choice of team for the series was largely responsible for its immediate success. He had a great career ahead of him. During the fourth series he contracted a virulent strain of leukaemia and died when he was thirty-seven. John was devastated.

15 March
Jesus, I miss him. I miss the quest for the perfect cup of tea, watching EastEnders, *listening to* The Archers, *his*

conviction that the experts on the Antiques Road Show *deliberately value things low so that they can buy them cheap afterwards – 'Two thousand pounds my arse' – his blue, blue doting eyes, his silky white hair, his little stubby legs, his funny walk, his rage, his pride in me, him, him, him. His smell, the sound of his voice, his silent presence, just knowing he is there. But he never will be. 'Never, never, never never, never.'*

Kenny's place as producer was taken by David Lascelles. It was a difficult situation for David, but he knew they were all right when the first episode under his regime was aired and he read a critic in the *Observer* lauding an esoteric joke about Mozart on the same day as the *News of the World* pronounced John TV's Sexiest Cop. Although John's performance was totally unlike Jack Regan and in spite of the many other roles he had played since *The Sweeney* ended nine years before, the critic John Walsh wrote predictably:

Old *Sweeney* fans wouldn't have been alone in raising a mocking cheer at Thaw's new identity. It didn't or couldn't ring true. The combination of home brew and coloratura seemed forced. The Man with no Christian Name heroics only made you wonder if he was christened Cedric, and when Thaw let himself be bested by a wimpy student carrying a rugby boot, a million disbelieving hearts must have reassured themselves that had it been Jack, he would have well flattened him.

Despite Mr Walsh's misgivings, with Inspector Morse another TV icon was created. Towards the end of the series it was revealed that the initial E, which was all that Morse would disclose of his Christian name, was not for Ernie, as we had speculated, but Endeavour. Colin explained that Morse's parents were probably Quakers, amongst whom it would have been a usual name, as well as being what Captain Cook called his famous ship. For some people, his surname became Inspector Remorse, or Inspector Morose. Later on there was another version. When Clare Holman joined the cast, she was nervous of meeting John. She breezed into the make-up van and said, 'Hello, John, I'm Clare.' He replied curtly, 'Hello, Clare, I'm John,' after which there was silence. On the set she was confronted with a huge Range Rover to drive which, being small, she found daunting. She managed to get it on to its mark and got out, and nervously walked up to John. Looking at a piece of paper, her first line was, 'Excuse me, I wonder if you could help me, I'm looking for . . . Inspector . . . er . . . looks like . . . Mouse.' At the first rehearsal everyone laughed and laughed, including John, and from then on they were great mates, and he became Inspector Mouse.

The public felt that if they sat on Morse's shoulder he would solve the mystery for them, but at the same time they would never solve the enigma of his character. Morse was emotionally sensitive but tried not to reveal too much. Jenny Jules, an actress who worked with him later, describes a Morse scene: 'A woman had died and there was this scene at the end, just him for a whole minute, you can see him fighting his emotion, he's trying not to cry and he's just listening to Mozart and you just want to cuddle him. The fact that he found it hard to show emotion: to cry, to break down, I thought that was really beautiful.'

Actual tears were always John's last resort, in acting or in life, as the struggle to suppress them is more moving than paroxysms of grief. Instead, the audience cry for him.

16 March

Got through a whole day without sobbing. A couple sent me some Bach remedies – Star of Bethlehem and White Chestnut and Ignatius. Could they be helping? Mind you, I have a thudding dullness inside instead which is not enjoyable either.

John Madden admired the technique with which John handled all the information he had to impart in a way that sounded natural. He had a good ear for rhythm and would orchestrate any passage that could become dull in a way that kept it alive with changes of pace and pitch. Kevin Whately would find himself hanging on to John's coat tails if he felt a scene needed a kick up the arse.

As with Regan's relationship with Carter in *The Sweeney*, much of the richness of the characterisation of Morse came from his relationship with Kevin Whately as Lewis, his sidekick. John was never a man who had many close mates but with Kevin he was relaxed and trusting, as well as sharing a similar sense of humour; they became very fond of each other. On location they shared a Winnebago and at the end of a long day would chew the fat a bit, congratulating one another on 'getting away with it'. Over his vodka John would groan, 'That took years off me, that bloody scene.' Morse's exasperated cry of 'Lew-is' became much impersonated, but Morse had an awkward affection for him. In one episode Morse has been horrid to Lewis, then he confides he feels dreadful about someone's death. Lewis comes out with the cliché, 'Well, she's at peace now,' to which Morse snaps, 'The glass is always half full for you, isn't it?'

Lewis proudly quotes, 'Well, if you can meet with triumph and disaster / And treat those two imposters just the same . . .'

Morse: 'Kipling.'

Lewis: 'No, All England Tennis Association. It's above the door of the Centre Court.'

Morse: 'So it is.'

The way John delivered that line summed up their relationship with gentle humanity.

One of John's skills, invaluable in playing policemen, was that he was a good listener. Hard to do realistically, to *really* listen, not just act it. My friend Faith Brooks said: 'John listened. He listened when conversing. He listened when acting. He listened with intensity to music. It's good to talk, it's even better to listen.'

This made him easy to act with, and it was why everyone wanted to be in *Morse*, from Sir John Gielgud onward.

17 March
I just can't bear to sort his things. His trousers are still folded on the chair, his watch by the bed.

The beginning of the thirteen-year series was shot while John's life was in turmoil. It was obvious from the first showing that *Morse* would be a huge success. So why did he continue to be so wretched? He did not get demonstrably drunk as he had in Leeds, but his moods, which once he could be jollied out of, were now becoming more frequent and impenetrable. They seemed to descend on him for no reason. He came home from work and after his first drink was usually on a high, but after going upstairs for a shower he would become uncommunicative and dour, burying himself in his script to learn the next day's lines. Where he had been funnily cynical he became at times viciously cruel, not only to myself but to the girls, who came to resent and sometimes fear him. Never physically, but he could wound just as much with his tongue. It was incomprehensible. I tried desperately to fathom why he was like this. We would have anguished discussions, long into the night, which got nowhere. I instinctively felt it was something to do with his childhood giving him this growing hatred of women, and me in particular. I would say, 'I'm not going whatever you do or say to me, *I'm* not leaving.' There were times of blessed respite when he showered me with gifts and love. He became two different men – Jekyll and Hyde. If I tried to talk sensibly about it he claimed not to remember the things he had said. He sometimes denied them so vehemently that I began to question my own recollection and wonder if I was exaggerating. I felt completely disoriented; the rows often ended with me cravenly apologising. It was sick behaviour.

All this time I was trying to work at the National Theatre. Ian McKellen and Edward Petherbridge formed a talented company to work together for a year on several plays. I had one of the best parts of my life in Madame Ranevskaya in *The Cherry Orchard*. I was also the first woman to direct a show in the biggest auditorium, the Olivier. Insanely, I decided that at the end of Sheridan's *The Critic*, the whole set would fall down and catch fire around the actors. The scene is a patriotic pageant led by John Bull, with Britannia flying above on a cloud, and my idea was a metaphor for the British Empire collapsing

around our ears – it seemed apposite at a time when Thatcher
had declared that our absurd war in the Falklands, with 225
British and 652 Argentinians dead, had 'put the Great back in
Great Britain'. I very nearly killed Ian McKellen and several
other brilliant performers at the dress rehearsal of this spectacular scenic wonder created by Bill Dudley and engineer Peter
Kemp. But the worries at the theatre were nothing to what
awaited me at home.

I began to dread being there with John, subjected to his Back
Treatment. Sometimes his face contorted into a mask of pure
loathing towards me. Jo went to Bedales as a weekly boarder.
She hated leaving but she equally hated being at home, trying
to mediate between us. The months dragged on in utter misery
and chaos. We were on a rollercoaster. I could not believe that
all that we had built up together was falling apart.

It was almost a relief when I discovered the cause. Searching for something on top of the wardrobe in the spare room, I found a half-empty bottle of whisky. I was appalled as I unearthed more and more hidden bottles. I felt grubby spying on him like that but I knew enough about drink to know that if you were secretive about it, you were in trouble. I confronted John with my discovery. His shame was terrible. I phoned Anthony Hopkins, who made no secret of having had a drink problem himself. He was not surprised to hear from me, having heard on the grapevine that there might be a problem. He wisely told me there was nothing I could do to help John, that it was up to him. The best thing was to look after myself by going to Al Anon, a twelve-step organisation for people involved with anyone with a drinking problem. It was sound advice. At my first meeting I felt such relief when I heard the other people talking of their experiences. I recognised that John's behaviour was a symptom of what I came to think of as an illness, just as asthma is.

It also began to dawn on me that I was as unbalanced as him. All the men most dear to me were drinkers. It was not difficult, then, to conclude that something in my personality fitted in with that. I liked the drama, the volatility, the excitement of being with a man who was unpredictable. Maybe my wartime child-hood had affected me, but I thrived on danger. I was frightened of security. I feared knowing what would happen for the rest of my life. I felt comfortable with unease. Despite all the trappings of family and home, I was averse to settling down, and these mad men suited me. Not a recipe for maturity. Or contentment.

18 March
Some of the letters make me realise how lucky I am. Women left with fearful money problems who really have no social life except as a couple, who belong to a section of society that shun widows out of embarrassment or fear that they'll be next. People who have lost children – can't bear to even think of that. I can only read and reply to so many letters at a time. The weight of people's painful lives weighs heavily on me.

As a result of my help from Al Anon, John was tempted to attend an AA meeting. He came back very drunk indeed. It was not for him. Although there were many of his friends at the meeting who greeted him with warmth and support he felt the whole thing of exposing your weakness was wanky. Anyway he wasn't like them, was he? He wasn't an alcoholic.

I needed a break away from all this intensity so I was delighted when a project I initiated came about. I bought the rights for *Jumping the Queue* from Mary Wesley, and, with my mate Sally Head as producer, we all decamped to Devon to shoot it. It was Jo's holidays so she came too, and we were both relieved to be away from John. One of the chief joys of my profession is the comradeship. The work lays you bare emotionally and you become very close, then move on. Good old propinquity. I have always said I only joined the profession for the sex and the tea breaks. I often think the abuse poured on luvvies by the press is envy because, whatever they say about us, in the rehearsal room and on the set we are like a secret society whose members cling together, and nothing can touch us. Thus it was very healing for Jo and me to be in a lovely part of the country with a kindly cast and crew fussing over us. The other two girls were keeping an eye on John. One day Abigail phoned to say she had called round to find him desperately depressed, he was monosyllabic and sunken-eyed. She had taken him to the local pub in an attempt to cheer him up and he had vomited violently in public. She got Sally to come and help and she insisted on calling the doctor. He told John that his life would be threatened if he did not give up drinking.

20 March
Lovely letter from Sally:
I am so sorry, so sad about John's death. His fierce reserve never extended to his love for you, which he revealed almost every time he opened his mouth and from the moment he met you. I will always love John for giving me my beautiful daughter and for the friendship of you and Ellie Jane and Jo.

Very touched. A triumph for all of us that we achieved that, I think.

Maybe he would have heeded the warning and stopped drinking but I had to tell him news which pushed him further into the mire. While in Devon I was having a shower when I came across a small lump in my breast. I knew instantly, before the test proved it, that it was malignant. A few days before I had seen some stills of myself in a bathing costume and had been shocked by the sight of my backbone sticking out from my thin body. I was terrified when the doctor told me the verdict. I rushed home, expecting comfort from John, but my Bridge over Troubled Water collapsed at the news. Now I was going to leave him. Like the others. He couldn't stop me dying. So he turned his back. He walked away from trouble. He would not discuss it or see a doctor with me. I was just as likely to get run over by a bus. What was all the fuss about? Forget it. He hid in the spare room and barely spoke to me.

I knew he was in despair. I knew he was torn apart, but I needed support. I went for a week to the Bristol Cancer Centre with my eldest daughter. When I returned, the house felt dank with misery. It was October 1987 and terrible storms whipped across the country. I stood alone at my bedroom window and watched the branches bending and breaking and the Thames lashing. I really didn't care if I died. John was in another room, doing his best to kill himself with drink. By this time I was incapable of action. My daughter took control and found a little rented house for me to move into. John was indifferent, relieved in fact. Now he could drink in peace. I too enjoyed the respite of being on my own, with my children and my friends free to come and go.

The press got hold of the news. I told them a cock and bull story about needing space to come to terms with my illness; John said nothing. We were used to being secretive about John's drinking, so I accepted, without contradiction, that I should take the blame for having deserted this sweet man. One of the newspapers found out I had gone to Bristol and visited a healer at

St James's Church in Piccadilly. An article appeared asking how could I turn to silly New Age remedies and leave poor lovely John, when he yearned to look after me? A picture was published of him wearing a superimposed apron, maintaining he was henpecked and demeaned by my intransigence.

I had a lumpectomy followed by six weeks of radiotherapy. After the treatment and my visit to Bristol I began to feel better, but I could not get John out of my mind. Every now and then he would phone sounding wretched. Bristol had taught me to be aware of negative thoughts and language. When I thought about John, I was worried sick. Worried to death? Not a good idea. So when Derek Nimmo offered to take me off on one of his theatrical tours of the Middle East, it was an opportunity to put sea and deserts between us. Maybe then I could forget him.

21 March
A very odd thing. John had one of his DIY disasters with the light in the oven hood. He couldn't get it to work. He sweated and swore for a whole morning trying to fix it and then gave up. I came down this morning and it was on.

Derek's main motivation for setting up these tours was a passion for travelling and he was the best of companions on a trip. His relish for life made him the ideal person to be with. We hadn't decided on the show for the tour when I bumped into Kenneth Williams. We stood on an island beside Broadcasting House, with traffic hurtling past us on either side. He looked ashen and wretched, his mouth pursed in pain and his eyes flicking around abstractedly. He told me of worries about his health. The usual obsession about his bum'ole, I thought. There was no work; he only got offered crap. I suggested he get away from it all with Derek and me. We could do some of our revue stuff. Have a laugh. He snapped at me angrily, asking how I thought he could leave Louie, his mother. He had always loved his mother and she him. They were inseparable, but now he rambled obscenely about her incontinence and dependence on him. I knew he was in a bad way but so was I. I had had enough of unreasonable rage. I told him not to be cruel. He turned on his heel and sped off through the crowd, pinched face held high to avoid the stares. I shouted that I'd ring him. I didn't. Ten days later a newspaper placard told me: 'Kenneth Williams dead'.

The sun in the Gulf took the chill off my soul, as did the company. Derek led us off on strange and wonderful adventures. There was a world elsewhere. Every now and then my heart wrenched at the thought of John like a ghost alone in that huge, sad house in Chiswick. As Al Anon's twelve steps said, I was powerless, but I felt riven with guilt.

In Oman I went with a young teacher to visit a group of dwellings in the desert. We were invited into a mud hovel. The teacher sat with the man but I was ordered on to the other side of a sheet of sacking with his two women. We sat cross-legged on the sand floor. The women curiously stroked my hair and clothes and dabbed heady perfumed oil on my brow and wrists. They offered me strong sweet coffee, and dates covered with flies – they had nothing else. The place was bare apart from a blackened cooking pot. I had on my little finger one of the rings that had belonged to John's mother. It was gold with a tiny diamond. It was not very valuable but a fortune to these women. I put my finger to my mouth, signalling secrecy, took it off and gave it to them. I no longer wanted the ring of the woman whose cruelty had blighted John's life and, indirectly, mine. They glanced at the curtain and one of them slipped the ring down the front of her gown. I hoped it might buy them freedom, a future. Who knows, maybe the women now run a nice little business in Muscat.

24 March
A perfect day. We gathered at Lucky, all his close friends and family. Sally, housekeepers, gardeners, his driver, his stand-in, his dresser – his Scallywags, other close colleagues. A Quaker service – silence with people talking if they felt moved to do so. They had brought poems and

songs, Auntie Beattie a beautiful scrapbook that Uncle Charlie kept of John's life. I told them they could cry if they wanted and we all did. Everyone found it a comfort as his death had been a shock to them and they had had no chance to mourn. He would have been proud to hear how they admired his 'estate', which most had never visited. He had ordinary friends who loved him profoundly. I hope he knew. When the grandchildren joined us we scattered his ashes in the stream where the kingfisher swoops, by the bank with the primroses and our favourite cowslips. While the Elgar Quintet played in the background the girls recited:

Do not stand at my grave and weep
I am not there.
I do not sleep.
I am a thousand winds that blow
I am the diamond glints on snow
I am the sunlight on ripened grain
I am the gentle autumn rain
When you awaken in the morning hush
I am the swift uplifting rush
Of quiet birds in circled flight
I am the soft stars that shine at night
Do not stand at my grave and cry
I am not there; I did not die.

A bit death-is-nothing-at-allish but it fitted the occasion We unveiled the sculpture bench which says: 'The two John Thaws loved it here'. It was a loving occasion. Everyone said nice things. Nigel especially. 'I have such respect for you. I feel privileged to know you.' Pretty fabulous compliment to a mother-in-law, I thought. We did him proud. That's the personal goodbye. Now we must steel ourselves for the public one.

16

Fear and Despair

MY FLIGHT FROM MY problems had been marred by another frightening encounter with the medical profession. Derek Nimmo's touring production of *Bed Before Yesterday* played in Madrid before setting off for the Gulf. No sooner had we opened than I was rushed to hospital with agonising chest pains. I was diagnosed as having possible gallstones leading to pancreatitis, with further exploration needed on my return to England in the light of my cancer history. John's reaction was a letter implying that although we were separated he thought we would, as usual, soon patch up our differences – he had not grasped, or chose to ignore, the depth of the rift between us and the gravity of the possible spread of my cancer. His letter was full of loving intimacies, then, 'Not a day goes by, not an hour but I think of you; a look, a phrase, an incident, a touch, a kiss or even a map! I pray that we can overcome our/my problems in the not too distant future. Hope you are keeping the gallstones and the sheikhs at bay. But if you do meet a homeopathic sheikh, remember that this Mancunian git will always love you more.'

I probably would have been relieved and rushed back to fall into his arms again had I not had Joanna with me on the tour. Freed for a while from my obsession with John, I had time for my daughter. I saw her horror at my new illness and understood how terrified she had been by my cancer. I had made the classic mistake of thinking it better that she should not be told. At thirteen of course she knew something deeply troubling was happening, but had no one to talk to about it. It was another family secret to be kept. I saw how profoundly affected she was by our erratic behaviour. I could see that I had neglected her. It hardened my resolve. I returned to my little rented house and set about getting life in order independently of John.

I started with my health. I had the offending gall bladder removed and was scanned for and declared free of cancer metastasis. I wanted to keep it that way. I had pushed my body to excess and now it had given up on me; in quick succession, I had breast cancer, gallstones, shingles, and a dodgy cervical smear result. My approach was a mixture of orthodox and complementary medicine with a dash of any bit of superstitious hokum that came my way. On one occasion secondary cancer was suspected in my bones. I was given an injection of some sinister stuff to make my skeleton illuminate in an x-ray. I went to Regent's Park while it was taking effect. Wandering around anxiously, I saw a magpie. One magpie.

> One for sorrow, two for joy,
> Three for a letter, four for a boy.

In my manic state, I *had* to find another magpie to get me out of sorrow and into joy. My whole future health depended on it. I couldn't see a mate for Mr Magpie anywhere. Not surprising since my lone bad luck symbol was a singularly unprepossessing creature with one broken tail feather dragging on the ground. A very ill-looking omen. I reckoned that a park that housed a zoo must have at least two magpies. I was frantic. A woman asked me if I was all right and got the confusing reply that no, I was radioactive. I never found a second magpie and my bone scan was clear, so that put paid to that superstition. On the other hand I did salute the one I saw and recited, 'Hello, Mr Magpie, how are your children?' so that is probably what did the trick.

30 March
A dreadful day. I've no one to really talk to. Or not to talk to if we chose. We were utterly on the same wavelength. And I have that with no one else. I am drifting in a vacuum. Hot cross buns on my own. They nearly choked me. It would have been a 'highlight' to relish with him. I ache with misery – literally. I keep looking for him, calling his name. All our rituals have gone, I have nothing to anchor myself to. How the hell do I live without him? Queen Mother died today at 101. She managed. She obviously loved her husband but spent years in the public eye without him. Had a lovely letter from one of her ladies-in-waiting telling how when she asked the Queen Mother if the loss gets better she replied, 'It never gets better, but you get better at it.'

I believed anything. I went on a series of wild goose chases after perfect health. The nadir was reached in a Kensington mews house where a hefty gentleman hit me hard to remove the djinns that were polluting my body. Good complementary medicine did help me, but without the orthodox treatment as well I would have died. Just as after Alec's death I found myself involved with issues that related to dying and bereavement, I was now in danger of being regarded as a font of knowledge about cancer and particularly complementary medicine. People are so desperate for help and information that they will accredit someone in the public eye with far more expertise than they have. I tried to resist pushing myself as obsessively as in the past but I have never been able to resist a good campaign.

One of the most impressive campaigns of the eighties and nineties was that waged by the gay community for research into the illness that was killing so many of my friends. When Tony died the cause of his death had been mysterious, but when Aids was given an identity, we knew that several colleagues in *Annie* and, later, *Sweeney Todd* were afflicted. My profession lost many members to the scourge of the disease. Because at first it was thought to affect only gay men it was shamefully ignored until public pressure forced it to be taken seriously. The numerous young deaths taught us a lot about the process of dying. Lighthouse, a hospice for people with Aids, of which I was a patron, changed the process of death from a hole-in-the-corner affair to a fond farewell with rituals and leave-taking, that made it a good experience for the dying and the bereaved. In my childhood, death was at least marked, albeit rather glumly, with drawn curtains and black armbands. Nowadays the tendency is to pretend it isn't happening. With Aids, the gay community taught us to celebrate life as well as mourning death.

When the entertainment industry gets the bit between their teeth, they can be very efficient – Bob Geldof with Live Aid in 1985, and Kevin Cahill, Richard Curtis and Emma Freud with Comic Relief, started in 1988 and continued every year since. Both tackled injustice and deprivation, which are often the cause of war, more effectively than President Reagan. His diplomacy produced this statement: 'Five nations, Iran, Libya, North Korea, Cuba, Nicaragua are a confederation of terrorist states. The strongest collection of looney tunes and squalid criminals.' This from the country that produced the book *How to Win Friends and Influence People*. Reagan did, however, make his peace with the 'Evil Empire' now that a reforming president was in power in the shape of Gorbachev. In 1991 trouble broke out in Iraq during which many Iraqis and Kurds were killed. Bush Senior intervened in Saddam Hussein's invasion of Kuwait. In Operation Desert Storm, Baghdad was bombed.

Everyone rejoiced when the Berlin Wall came down in 1989. In the same year one of the most poignant images of people protest was the lone student standing in front of a line of grotesque tanks during a demonstration in Tiananmen Square. His brave defiance was followed by tragedy when the misnamed People's Liberation Army slaughtered and injured thousands of their fellow countrymen and women. There was much to protest against.

2 April
Lyn said, 'I have never known great passion or great grief because I wouldn't take the risk and I tell you that's no

*way to live.' Beautiful letter from a nun, of all people.
'There is a dark side to the golden coin of love; a paradox
of joy and sadness. You are bearing the sadness for him
now. He won't have to weep at your funeral, and feel bereft.'
Talking of his work she said, 'There was no side, no conceit
in his performance.' Absolutely true. Still the 'Death is
nothing at all's keep coming. Not true.*

I managed to fit in some theatre and TV engagements between
campaigning and my fasts and diets and fitness regimes. However
low he felt at my absence, John never let it affect his work. In
the midst of all the panic about my illness he did a stunning
performance in Arthur Miller's *All My Sons*, up in his home
town at the Manchester Exchange Theatre. At the final curtain
there was a long silence before the applause started. It is the
greatest compliment an audience can pay an actor: to be so
moved and involved that it is hard to come back into the real
world.

For eighteen months we lived apart, but were in agony about
it. We made some attempts to get back together but they failed.
On one bizarre occasion John phoned to say he was taking Jo
and me for a holiday in Ireland in a horse-drawn caravan. It is
a measure of my desperation that I could believe for a moment
that this could be anything but a disaster. The day before we
were due to leave, he phoned to tell us curtly that he had
cancelled and to forget the whole thing. Yet again Jo was hurt
and bewildered by broken promises. Ian McKellen came to the
rescue, whisking us off to a villa in France where he lit log fires,
cooked delicious meals and lovingly cosseted us both. We badly
needed it.

5 April
*We have all come to Barcelona. The trip the girls gave him
for his 60th birthday present. My dear friend Helen has
come in his place. She is wonderful and positive and loves
life. I need people like that. It's hard going for us all, but
two 'highlights': a couple of lads playing classical guitar*

outside a café and some old folk from Catalonia dancing some wonderful stately dances in front of the cathedral to the music of a small local band. Charming. There is nothing more lovely than seeing plain people transformed when they dance. It's like the old couples ballroom dancing at the Waldorf Hotel tea dances or the Tower Ballroom in Blackpool. Very moving. It's the same effect as fat people who are miraculously light on their feet. Roy Kinnear was like that. Funny little chap who became Fred Astaire when he danced.

Few people outside the family knew what was going on. On the set of *Morse* they were puzzled by John's moods. Sometimes he would emerge from his Winnebago and want to chat. At other times he made it obvious he wanted to be left alone. He was usually kind to small-part actors but once when one was pestering him for advice he snapped, 'Listen, sunshine, all you have to do is hit the Duke of York [chalk mark] and get the dickies [birds – words] right.'

He complained about directors 'shooting the arse off the scene' with shots that he knew would be edited out. 'I'm giving you a week's work for nothing.'

'Well, come on, shoot it before it shoots us,' would be his grumble at long delays, or, 'Now listen, I've got a nice house by the river, I'd like to see it before it gets dark.'

He could still laugh on occasion. Filming in Oxford, a sweating electrician with his belly hanging over his trousers heaved a lamp past an elegant woman who was watching. John was delighted to hear her say to her friend in a pained voice, 'Who would've thought such a wonderful programme could be made by such a bunch of thugs?' 'Morning, thuggies,' was John's daily greeting from that day forth.

John relished a repetitive gag. His 'Help me, help me' cries could be adapted to any situation. In the bedroom, 'Help me, help me, I'm trapped in this house with a sex maniac'; when learning lines, 'Help me, help me, my brain hurts'; in France, 'Au secours me, au secours me, I'm surrounded by foreigners.'

A loud, preferably indistinct 'Cut!' always demanded, 'Is he talking about me?' After his CBE in 1993, if he had difficulty with some lines, he would complain haughtily, 'I can't say this rubbish – I'm a Commander of the British Empire, I tell you.'

He had round him in all his shows a team of supporters with whom he felt safe and at home. More at home than in his home. They made no emotional demands on him and over the years they were his bulwark against interference. Micky his driver, Tony his dresser, Barry his stand-in and Pauline continuity, as well as regular make-up girls and a designer, Sue Yelland, nicknamed the Rottweiler. He called them his Scallywags and when away on location it was with them he would go out rather than actors or directors. They knew how to jolt him out of a mood, usually by having a funny conversation within earshot until he shouted, 'Fuck off, you're driving me mad. I'll swing for you lot.' He joined in one of their japes. Pauline's daughter Katie was having a smart twenty-first birthday party and Pauline told John she wished to leave the set in time to attend it. On wrap of filming for the day Pauline returned to the unit base to find the dining bus done up with balloons and streamers and the

Scallywags and John wearing paper hats and excitedly blowing squeakers ready to embark on a trip to join the celebration.

Despite being the fall guy or doll for many of his jokes, Pauline was devoted to John and he to her. On set she learned to prompt him with a gentle 'Did you mean to say that?' rather than 'You got that line wrong.' If he had no faith in the current director, after a scene he would look at Pauline for a nod of approval or a signal that 'No, you could do better.' He trusted all of them implicitly.

Beneath the surface jollity, the people closest to him suspected he was in a bad way. John Madden reckoned that John only felt safe when acting. He could control emotions when he acted them. Real ones were messy. Madden directed an episode of *Morse* set in Australia. John asked me to go with him but I refused while he was still drinking. I was frightened of being isolated with him away from home while his attitude towards me was so volatile. He was distraught at my refusal and his misery was converted into one of the most effective scenes ever shot in *Morse*. As John Madden, not aware of the personal relevance of the scene, described it in his obituary:

My most poignant memory of him is at the end of Julian Mitchell's episode, 'The Promised Land', which we spent four months shooting in New South Wales, when Morse travels to Australia in search of a supergrass. It all goes wrong and it is all Morse's fault. In the final scene he stands at the foot of the Sydney Opera House steps.

'What are you going to do?' he asks Lewis.

Lewis plans to meet his family. Morse wishes him well, looks after him as he goes and then turns to mount the endless steps, carrying in every agonised step the loneliness and pain of mankind. Is this an exaggeration? For me it was great acting. Every actor creates his part with the audience. John had built this character with all of us, we all knew him. We didn't want him to walk away.

7 April
Not besotted with Barcelona. Too noisy, too much traffic.
Hotel pretentious. But then I'm not in the right frame of
mind. Abs has summed it up in a poem, which I want her
to do at the memorial service if she can face it:

Last week we went to Barcelona.
A beautiful city; the kids had fun.
He really should have come too – I missed him.

Mum thought it would be a good thing too.
He had wanted to go for twenty years.
So last week we went to Barcelona.

So excited when he opened the card:
First class tickets and a suite at the Ritz.
He really should have come too – I missed him.

We held a simple funeral at home;
Sorted through his clothes and belongings
And last week we went to Barcelona.

When the cancer came back we'd changed the dates
Something to look forward to, the doctors had said.
He really should have come too – I missed him.

'He would have liked this' became our mantra.
Endless booze-soaked toasts, 'Happy birthday, Dad'.
Last week we went to Barcelona.
He should have come too – I missed him.

In 1990 both *Morse* and *Home to Roost* were in the Top 10
of the ratings. John was at the height of his popularity but off
screen he was fighting profound depression. During our eighteen-
month separation I wrote to him: 'I and the girls will do almost
anything to make you happy. You are deeply loved and we long
for you to discover how good life can be . . . it is terrible for

me and the girls to watch you being so, so sad. You feel lonely and persecuted but you only have to ring one of your daughters and they would be there. They daren't ring you, sadly.'

We were still living apart, incapable of communicating, when John chose his eight records to take on a desert island in *Desert Island Discs*. They were all a coded message to me. One Easter at the start of our marriage, we were going to go to Handel's *Messiah* at the Albert Hall. We couldn't get in, so we rushed over to the Festival Hall where they were performing the Bach *St Matthew Passion*. I was not a great Bach fan then, saying, in my supreme ignorance, that he did not write nice tunes. I was horrified when I discovered that the concert was five hours long with a supper break. It turned out to be an evening of revelation and pure ecstasy. We were higher than any drug could send us. Another of his choices was me singing 'Little Girls' from *Annie*. The Sibelius was the music we had listened to in his car when on tour with *So What About Love?* The Schubert was one he had gone to a lot of trouble choosing as incidental music for a production of mine. The Elgar Cello Concerto was a favourite of us both. One of Strauss's *Four Last Songs* was sung by Elizabeth Schwarzkopf, who, he quite truthfully told Sue Lawley, he often joked was the only woman he would leave me for. He was less truthful when, in parrying Sue's questions about his drinking, he said he had stopped and found it as easy as giving up sugar in his tea.

His denial of his problem should have sent out warning signals but the ploy was irresistible. All the reminders of why I loved him and the things we had in common touched me. He was filming an episode of *Morse* in Verona and I rushed out there to join him. Then he came to Los Angeles with me where I was filming *Three Men and a Little Lady*. We had a wonderful time, except on a visit to Disneyland, where it teemed with rain and Joanna persuaded us to wear absurd plastic hats.

21 April
A day from hell. The BAFTAs. Terrified getting ready. The indispensable Martyn propped up my face with make-up and gave me a pep talk. Jo, Ellie and I gripped hands and walked the red carpet.

Photographers and fans screamed, 'Sheila, Sheila, this way, this way.' Jo was terrified I had to collect an award for John. I was all right until they showed some clips of him. It was the first time I'd watched him. Thank God I had Dominique, the little girl from Buried Treasure *with me, so I had to pull myself together so as not to upset her. Made a speech I think. Can't remember what I said. Then had to wait to see if I had won Best Actress for* Russian Bride. *It was Julie Walters. Bit disappointed because I'll never have such a good part again, and everyone was very hopeful. But there you go. The little fat one with the white hair got his. At the do afterwards colleagues were lovely. I do love actors. They are thoroughly nice people. Such a small community really. I mean proper actors not celebrities. After all these years, between us John and I seem to know everyone. They all seemed genuinely sad at his death.*

Over the next five years John and I behaved like characters in a cartoon, ricocheting in and out of each other's arms. It became farcical. By the start of the nineties our two older girls had their own lives and loves; they were growing up, we were becoming infantile. In 1993 Joanna went off to Paris for a year. She could not keep up with our on-off relationship.

Every time we got back together again we would buy a new home or do something to an existing house or garden. It was as if we were trying to strengthen the marriage by improving the setting, instead of getting down to the root cause of our problems. In 1991 we found a tumbledown stone house in a *hameau* in the Luberon in France. It was surrounded by a cherry orchard, vineyards and lavender fields. There were no English people so we were blissfully anonymous. We sat in cafés and looked in shops instead of tearing around with our heads down to escape attention. John visibly relaxed and only occasionally let out a faint, 'Au secours moi, je want to reste ici.'

But we couldn't stay in France all the time. Back in England and back at *Morse*, it all fell apart again. The house by the river in Chiswick became associated with miserable silences and fierce rows. OK. Change it. How about a house in the country? In 1992 we acquired a Cotswold stone house by a stream with a field attached in Luckington, which became known, rather optimistically, as Lucky. That didn't work. So we bought a flat in Chiswick as well. We re-created two gardens, redid a kitchen and two bathrooms. Each piece of property development marked a rupture and supposed fresh start. It was absurd, and our girls got very angry with us. They could not understand or bear the pain we seemed to be inflicting on each other. They came home less and less, saying it was like having an invalid in the house to tiptoe around John's erratic moods and my distraught reaction to them.

Madness seemed to be in the air in the nineties, it wasn't just us. We were urged to be entrepreneurial, to look after ourselves and our families and not rely on the state, although curiously Thatcher herself was quoted as saying that for her home was somewhere to go to if you had nothing better to do. The increase of individual acts of violence was a distortion of the Me Society. One man took it upon himself to kill gays and people from ethnic minorities with homemade nail bombs. Thomas Hamilton shot dead sixteen children and a teacher in Dunblane in revenge for personal grievances. Another man did the same in the streets of peaceful Hungerford. Some youths killed a black lad, Stephen Lawrence, and a later report concluded that not only were they racist but the police showed institutional racism in the way they handled the case. In the US, a right-wing ex-soldier killed over a hundred people with a bomb in front of a federal building in Oklahoma. Two youths shot thirteen schoolfriends in Denver. A bomb exploded in one of the Twin Towers of the World Trade Center, though it was not given much coverage. There were constant IRA atrocities, most notoriously in Omagh where twenty-nine people died, and in Manchester in 1996, when the Exchange Theatre and a lot of the city centre were destroyed. A more positive event in the nineties was that thanks to Thatcher, John Major and later Blair and Clinton, and some Irish politicians, the greatly improved situation in Ireland meant that terrorist acts on the mainland became rare. Clinton also looked on as Arafat and Rabin shook hands over the Palestinian problem. In 1995 Rabin was killed at a peace rally and they were back to square one.

As the century drew to a close the atmosphere was tainted by disturbing murder cases. The squalor of the Wests' sordid lives led to savage butchery for which the suicide of Fred West and his brother seemed a fitting end. The whole nation was appalled that two ten-year-old boys could kill the two-year-old James Bulger. With the murder of Sarah Payne, paedophilia became the decade's evil of choice to get worked up about. We were forced to peer into lives that horrified us. Hidden lives.

25 April
Recording Bedtime *again. Everyone was wonderful but last time I did it John was alive. Dreaded going home to empty house. He would have welcomed me, 'How did it go, pet?', cooked a meal, fussed over me. But the house was empty, I had no food in and no one to dissect the day with. I actually would rather be dead than live like this. I can't do solitude.*

Keep thinking of what I was doing this time last year before this calamity. Today we were in France having a picnic up in the mountains of Silverque with Liz and David. We lay in the sun, ate, laughed and hadn't a care in the world.

In my childhood little was known about what went on behind the gates of Buckingham Palace. The Duke of Windsor's affair with Wallis Simpson was kept secret from the hoi polloi. Now the Queen's business was pried into by the scandal-obsessed press. She declared 1992 her *annus horribilis*. Windsor Castle had a major fire and all her sons and her daughter had relationship problems. Nothing more vividly illustrates the changes in society than the blank bewilderment on this good woman's face. Everything she had been taught to believe in was disintegrating. My world too seemed to be crumbling. In 1992 I did a TV series aptly named *Gone to Seed* in which I played opposite Peter Cook. I had known him during and just after his university days. He wrote much of the material of the revue that I did with Kenneth Williams. He was at that time a hilariously funny, extremely beautiful young man. Now he was a shambling, sweating wreck. Alcohol had destroyed him. He died three years later, aged fifty-seven.

It had begun to seep into our thick consciousness that our difficulties would never be sorted without confronting John's drinking and my attitude to it, which in his opinion was more of a problem. John made several attempts to stop but always fell off the wagon as he tried to pull off the impossible feat of doing it on his own. He filled his mind with work, which was not, as yet, affected by his drinking. But the situation was not helped by him doing two projects that were not a great success. *Stanley and the Women*, adapted from the book by Kingsley Amis, could not hide its misogynist theme. John's attempt to transform his appearance for the part, resulting in orange hair, did not improve it either.

In 1993 John seized the opportunity to live in his beloved French house while filming *A Year in Provence*, but I did not go with him. I had originally been asked to play his wife but a new director decided I was too old for the role. It is the rule on TV, if not in life, that even old men have pretty young wives. Peter Mayle has always been unpopular with fellow journalists, probably because he hit on an idea, which made him a fortune, that any one of them could have written if they had only thought of it. The series was a flop, though not as big as the one I was involved in – a misconceived, badly directed English version of *The Golden Girls* called *Brighton Belles*, which was dropped after a few episodes. That deserved to bomb but the vitriol heaped on *A Year in Provence* was out of all proportion to the gravity of a rather trite little comedy not quite pulling it off. The Americans loved it, but the British did not. John's confidence, still fragile despite his success in *Morse*, was shattered, plunging him further into depression. He decided to try the theatre.

3 May
One of the crew of Bedtime *said, 'Your tyres are worn out and dangerous, Sheila.' I didn't know what to do. John would have dealt with these things. But I got it sorted. I've bloody well got to learn to cope. Felt quite pleased with myself. Then had to do a shot looking in a mirror. Christ, I look old. Why does anyone employ such an ugly old hag?*

In 1993 an offer came from the National Theatre to play the lead in a new play by David Hare. *Absence of War* was the last of a trilogy about the state of the nation, covering the law, religion and, in John's play, politics. It was about a passionate Labour man confronting the adaptation needed to make his party electable to the masses. Although not meant to be Neil Kinnock, many of the characteristics of the role were his. It certainly was the dilemma that he faced with a party that seemed doomed to stay in opposition unless it changed its image. In 1992 John and I had watched the TV in horror as any possibility of election victory was destroyed by a ludicrous American-style jamboree rally in Sheffield. The worst moment was when

Kinnock, high on the orchestrated jubilation on his arrival, kept saying dementedly, 'A'right, a'right, we're a'right.' He resigned soon afterwards and the more sedate, highly respected John Smith became leader until he tragically died. Blair steamed in and on to victory, and brought about the changes Kinnock had attempted.

Hare's play was ambitious and large-scale. It was to be performed in the Olivier Theatre, which has a stage as big as a football pitch, with a 1,200-seater auditorium. It is a notoriously difficult space for actors to perform in. A new David Hare play is always an event, but this one even more so because it was known that he had been given access to the inner workings of the Party, and everyone was agog about what it would reveal. John could not have taken on a bigger theatrical challenge. It took real courage at a time when he was emotionally unstable.

He was also aware that many people would be curious to see if this telly actor would fall flat on his face. Richard Eyre, the director, got some sense of the effect of his fame when he walked down the Strand with John, and everyone, including the traffic, stopped to greet him. On another occasion, when they were doing the film version of the play, he asked John to walk amongst the crowd in a market in Stockport. He was mobbed of course, and filming couldn't continue. Richard was not used to this kind of recognition with theatre stars. People are more restrained with actors they watch from a distance on a stage than those who appear in their living rooms. John was real and moving in the play and had no trouble projecting his performance into the chasm of the Olivier Theatre, to the surprise of some of the stuffier critics. His fellow actors supported him wholeheartedly. One member of the cast, Clare Higgins, watched John closely. Oliver Ford-Davies and Saskia Wickham demonstrated their support with nightly cuddles when at one point in the play the three of them had to squeeze past one another behind the set. Cuddles were in short supply at home. Partly because I wasn't there, having fled to Leeds to play in the musical *Gypsy*.

6 May

In France. Must try and pull myself together. I am becoming alienated from the family. My misery is making me utterly self-centred. Little things get blown up out of all proportion. Went to Leclerc and they left me in the café while they shopped. I sat there with a group of French navvies who were constantly commenting obscenely about all the passing girls. I was invisible to them. An old crone in the corner. The girls were ages coming back and I snapped at them when they eventually arrived. It was downhill from then on. I do not have the safety valve of slagging them off to John so it all builds up inside. The focus of our family has gone. And though he didn't seem to be the strength of the unit, he was. Even when he was at his worst, that in itself was our focus. Trying to appease him, to avoid trouble. All our roles are changed. What am I now? Ellie Jane said, 'Our family is falling apart and you must be the matriarch.' I beg your pardon? How do I do that? And it doesn't seem a very good part to me. What's the costume? Buttoned boots and corsets?

Frantic to bury himself in work when *Absence of War* finished, although he was still doing episodes of *Morse*, John looked for even more TV. He needed the reassurance that at least his working life was a success. Ted Childs came up trumps again with a series about a barrister called Kavanagh: 'Why do they keep miscasting me as intellectuals?' Ted assigned Chris Kelly to produce. He was new to the job, having hitherto been widely known for a TV cookery programme. He started off by daringly sacking one of John's Scallywags who stepped out of line. Then he redeemed himself by asking Jack Gold to direct.

It was a new departure for Jack to do a TV series. Since they worked together on *The Bofors Gun* John had held him in high esteem. They met for lunch at the River Café. It was an awkward meeting. Both men were delighted to see each other again for the first time since their youth, but were too inarticulate to say more than 'Nice to have you on board.'

'Good to be on board.'

Jack could not find the words to tell John how much he admired him – that he considered he could express important moral values without sentiment. The others with a similar quality were, in his opinion, Henry Fonda and Spencer Tracy in film, and Ken Stott and Helen Mirren on TV.

During the filming of *Kavanagh QC* John was even less able to communicate than usual. He was often mute with misery. His colleague Oliver Ford-Davies received no welcome when he joined the series. John expressed his admiration obliquely one day when the set was a bit noisy and they had a difficult scene to play: 'Let's have a bit of hush here. Oliver has won an Olivier award and me a BAFTA, so you're gonna see some acting. Let's have a bit of respect.' In his touchy condition it could be that he felt under-appreciated as well as trying to help Oliver. He sometimes complained that people took him for granted and didn't credit how hard he worked. One day they asked him to learn a new long speech during the lunch hour. It was done at the end of the day and then everyone packed up and went home. He was distressed when he told me that no one had thought to say 'Well done' to him. When I worked with Bette Davis in the film *The Anniversary* she cowed us all with her Hollywood star behaviour. One day she did a very fine take and I ventured to say, 'Well done, Miss Davis.' She grabbed my hand and said, 'Oh thank you, honey. The nearest I ever get to a compliment is "OK, print it."'

It was becoming impossible for me to get through to John. The tempestuous love affair in which I had so revelled had turned rotten and become an ugly, chaotic battlefield. When our first grandson was born in 1995 we were in one of our periods apart and in danger of spoiling the event for everyone. I had to face the fact that we were destroying each other, so I suggested divorce. A bitter failure for both of us. As a last throw I told him that Maggie, my counsellor, knew someone she thought could help John. 'I bet he lives in Hampstead.' He did.

12 May

Camera crew at Lucky to film interviews for TV tribute. We had to do it but God it was hard. They had to keep stopping for us to pull ourselves together but we went on. We want an accurate portrait of the man. Jack Gold was very sensitive, especially with Jo. 'I've always had to be so careful what I say that I can't talk now.'

Got through that. Now for the memorial.

17

Change

JOHN WAS FULLY EXPECTING to pay only one visit to Hampstead to keep me happy, but Udi Eichler was a beguiling man. He had worked in television and was fascinated by John's complexity. Somehow he won him round and John began to enjoy their meetings. They had much in common: difficult childhoods, they even both had a crippled foot. Udi tried to make John value himself. He encouraged him to spend his hard-earned money on silly pleasures and to look for joy in his life. He analysed why John's repeated jokes were often to do with leaving. When I said I was going out, even just from the room, he would wail, 'Doon't gooo, doon't goo.' His reaction to bangs was always 'And stay out,' and his 'Help me, help me' jokes were potent as well. When he left a room he would often repeat the last words of Captain Oates: 'I am just going outside and may be some time.' Shades of his mother perhaps?

Udi made John write down his dreams. One reflects his heavy childhood responsibilities towards his brother: 'Kids on phone. Joanna and Sheila. Maybe Abigail. They're screaming and shouting "Raymond". "Oh great." I take it that it's Ellie's baby and say, "Is it the baby, what a good name for the baby," but they don't answer.'

Other dreams were grimmer. 'Came upstairs. Sheila came out

of study. Looks me up and down. I look down. See there is vomit over my jacket and trousers.'

13 May
Plucked up courage to sort out some of John's things. Piles of Stuff *magazine's 'Great Gear for Men' from when Udi urged him to buy some treats for himself. They look unopened. Discovered he'd got scores of suits I didn't know about. He has never even worn them. The times he said before going somewhere, 'I haven't got a dark suit' or 'I don't have anything to wear.' He had dozens of the bloody things. He must have bought them half-price from various TVs – he could never resist a bargain. Or was it because they were so beautiful – mostly Zegna or Armani – that he had to have them even if he never wore them? He is a little squirrel storing up things for a possible rainy day.*

John seemed to enjoy his trips to Hampstead. When I had a session with Udi I expressed my concern that he was not tackling the problem of his drinking, which I maintained was central. Udi wrote to me putting me in my place: 'The kind of work required to help John out of his life-long depressive misery is long and arduous. I have no illusions about the frustrations and anguish of living with such a person. Nevertheless, as his therapist, I must be his advocate, certainly in the one-to-one work.'

Not long after this, John returned from Hampstead and said he would never go again. I don't know what triggered his anger with Udi – probably something trivial. Or maybe Udi tried to enter the no go area of John's drinking. Udi got the Back Treatment. I knew how he felt when he wrote to John: 'I find it unimaginable that the relationship that we had can have evaporated into a meaningless nothing.'

Still John did not respond. Udi wrote again: 'So I live in hope that our paths will cross at some time in the future. Whilst I can imagine your stubbornness (actually a kind of wounded hibernation at your own expense) might well keep you at bay, I hope nevertheless that you might surprise us both and finally respond. Why do I keep on at you in this manner, beyond the call of professional duty? Because I have a personal affection for you which I have allowed to stray beyond the consulting room.'

John's efforts to drive people away did not daunt Udi. He continued to try to break John's behaviour pattern of leaving people before they left him as they surely would when they discovered how unworthy of their love he thought himself. I was in despair. So was John. I tried to stay with him and hold his hand but he was emotionally impossible to reach. Ted Childs noticed his behaviour was 'a bit iffy' and others noted he was often in tears. I tried to work. I didn't choose the ideal job. In 1995 the Almeida Theatre asked me to play in Strindberg's *Dance of Death* opposite John Neville. It is a cruel piece about the disintegration of a marriage. I was less able to use my present pain in my role than John. I could not cope with hatred at home and in my work so I did something I had never done before, I let them down by leaving in the first week of rehearsal, pleading illness. By this time all John cared about was his access to alcohol. His little black bag with the vodka bottles never left his side.

15 May

Still sorting John's things very slowly as I can't take too much at a time. Found a pile of letters from friends that I told him to answer personally. I doubt if he did. I hope they understand. But most poignantly I tackled his black bag, the dread black bag he took to work for his script, etc. In the drinking days it used to clink as he left. In it I found hundreds of fag ends. He must have been secretly smoking and hiding the evidence. There was no need to. I wouldn't have minded in the least, but I suppose it was part of the pleasure. To be naughty, to have a secret, to do his own thing and sod you. Once an addict, always an addict. I was glad. He remained his own man and did what he liked. He probably thought I would worry too. Whatever. I'm glad he did it. I drank in the smell of stale tobacco. And to think I used to hate it.

Clare Higgins was not surprised when I phoned her on the recommendation of a friend who had some experience of alcoholism. As well as being a fine actor, Clare is a counsellor particularly skilled in dealing with addiction. While working with John at the National she detected that he had a problem. She suggested a family meeting, without John, to discuss our best way to help him. She explained to us all how we were, to use the technical term, 'enabling' John in his habit by covering for him and tolerating unacceptable behaviour. In the vernacular, what we needed to exercise was tough love. When he asked for help himself, and only then, she gave us the name of someone for him to contact.

We were determined to try. Richard Eyre and his wife Sue Birtwhistle came round to Luckington for Christmas drinks. John tried to pour champagne but his hand was shaking so much it went all over the table. We all sat and watched, making no attempt to cover for him. After a dreadful Christmas the family and I left him on his own and went back to London. He made it clear he could not bear us around. Before I left, I told him if he wanted help I had something to suggest.

It was the worst few weeks of my life. I felt like a murderer. I loved him with all my heart but my behaviour seemed so unloving. Eventually he did phone. Jo and I drove down immediately. We were shocked by his appearance. He was a physical wreck. He had injured his arm in a fall, his face was swollen and he was in agony from gout. As advised, we just gave him the number and left him to take action. It had to be his initiative. No more hand-holding, no more cover-ups. Tough love. He had to want to help himself because he had hit rock bottom. Beauchamp Colcough was waiting for his call. A miracle was about to happen.

There is no nameplate on Beechy's door in Harley Street and the waiting room is like any other. He himself comes to take you into his room, a short Irish leprechaun with wild black hair. Although now dressed in trendy clothes, there is still an air about him that makes it possible to believe that he once slept in the gutter. He is not your usual doctor or psychiatrist. Nor is his room typical. He has comfy old armchairs, pictures and a table full of objects which his patients have left behind for luck. It is a cosy, womb-like room.

He knew that he had to get John's confidence in the first one and a half hours, so Beechy used every ounce of his skill and energy to grab John's attention. John was like him. He understood how he felt. He had been there himself. Similar backgrounds. Suffering from depression which, combined with alcohol, was like petrol on a fire. He was at dis-ease with himself. 'You're a miserable bugger but you're making yourself fifty times more miserable with drink. What's it like, fame?'

'A nightmare.'

'Doesn't the money help?'

'It buys me privacy, that's all.'

Beechy could see that John didn't believe any of the media hype about himself. He was too real for his own good. But wrong about himself. He didn't believe he was the real thing, he wanted to be someone else. Drink helped that.

'Can I drink a bit? Control it?'

'You're not here because you're good at it.'

Beechy hammered home his memory losses, his never feeling well, the family disintegration, the misery.

'I'm the last house in the block. Your last chance saloon. You're here because you're in the shit. It's killing you. Give me a week. By the end of the week you will have made a decision. If I haven't killed you with the coffee first.' Beechy made foul coffee.

As he left that first session John asked Beechy, 'Can I do this?'

''Course you can, John.'

'I'll give it my best shot.'

'You don't do that. That's not enough. You deliver – that's what you always do.'

Beechy says he spent an agonising night hoping with all his heart that John would return the next day. He did. After one week – just ten hours – Beechy had changed his life for ever. John never touched another drink. Beechy's method is unique to him. It is propelled by a profound hatred of the harm done by alcohol. Someone dies of alcohol-related disease every ten minutes. The waste of lives it causes fires him to inspire people to change. He only met John for one week but he cared passionately about him during that time as he does all his patients.

'I got lucky with John. We got lucky with each other. He touched me. A beautiful man. A gentle man. The devil was in him.'

He gave John a packet of the coffee which they had christened Thaw's Delight as a parting gift. As he left Beechy's room for the last time, John tripped over his feet. Beechy's parting words were, 'Watch your step.'

John described his sobriety as like a cloud lifting; it was for his family as well. Even when he was drinking heavily he managed to keep it secret from the world outside the home. Chris Kelly, his producer, had not known he had a problem until he stopped drinking and a different man emerged. 'Happier, calmer and more at peace with himself. More generous in terms of relationships.' As Beechy said, nobody had seen him really sober for years. John's relief at shedding his burden was profound. He turned his back on the booze completely. Everyone was amazed at his ability to refuse a drink, not even enjoying a good wine. He was unperturbed by people drinking around him. He had no desire to go back to where he had been, at rock bottom.

His mind clear, he now tried to put all the work he had done with Udi into practice. It was like learning to live all over again. He risked reaching out to people even though there was a chance of rejection. It was hard for him. He was tentative. The producer Thelma Holt had suffered a great sadness in her life, so everyone was surprised when she turned up to a RADA Council meeting. Fellow members greeted her with warmth and kisses. Not John, however. He did nothing. She was walking down the stairs after the meeting when she felt a hand fall on her shoulder. She looked up into a pair of blazing blue eyes and he just said, 'Watch yourself, girl,' and kissed her on the cheek. She felt she was drowning in affection.

18 May
Had a breakthrough today. Clare V. came to Lucky – and
I cooked a very good roast lunch on my own. And had a
lovely time with her. We talked and actually laughed. My
girlfriends are an immense solace. I have neglected friend-
ship in my life. John never felt the need for it at home. At
work, yes.

Two years into John's sobriety, in 1997, his father died after
struggling against lung cancer. If anything was going to drive
him back to the bottle this was it. When we arranged the funeral
service with no priest or religious context, just a family
expressing their love, I did not think John would want or be
able to participate. On the day, he stood up, the man who
loathed making speeches, and talked uninhibitedly about his
love for Jack, whom he touchingly called his 'brother, friend
and wisest of counsellors'. He told how, when he was awarded
his CBE, he phoned and said, 'D'you want to come to the Palace,
Dad?'
'Do what? What's on then?'
'What do you mean?'
'The Palace, you lummock! What's on in Manchester then?'
The most amazing breakthrough was that he was not afraid
to show his grief. He wept unashamedly in front of the congregation. Jack's friends from the pub in their best suits and flat caps
must have been a bit embarrassed, especially as I had given them
all posies of sweet peas to hold, which they did with good grace
to placate the weird southerners. I was relieved that John was not
turning his back on his loss. He was even moved by the public
demonstration of grief over the death of Princess Diana in the
same year. He did not, as one would expect, join the cynics who
found it absurd. He wept with me as we watched the crowd throw
flowers at her passing hearse. Suddenly the British turned conti-
nental and publicly howled with grief and rage at the death of
this damaged young woman. And their own private griefs perhaps.
It was odd behaviour and we were all surprised at ourselves. We
knew she was a mess, that is why we liked her. No one could

organise when and to whom we paid respect any more. Suddenly the people dictated when flags were lowered and how queens should behave. It was a strange little revolution.

John did not feel able to return to Udi. He could not remember the reason why he left so abruptly. There was so much in his life that he could not recall and some of it he preferred to leave unexplored. In 1997 he received a letter from Udi. 'The lengths I have to go to, to bring some kind of satisfactory – for me and for you – closure to our old but, for me, quite unfaded relationship. What do I mean? Thought you'd like to know and perhaps wish to respond to a shitty development in my life. A few weeks ago I had a relatively advanced stomach cancer diagnosed. Size of a huge brick, so my surgeon told me.'

They met and John continued to learn from this wise man, who set an example to everyone of how to die well, tidying loose ends and bidding farewell. At the memorial service John read the passage from Primo Levi that Udi had chosen for him:

To My Friends:

Dear friends, I say friends here
In the larger sense of the word:
Wife, sister, associates, relatives,
Schoolmates, men and women,
Persons seen only once
Or frequented all my life:
Provided that between us, for at least a moment,
Was drawn a segment, a well-defined chord.

I speak for you, companions on a journey
Dense, not devoid of effort,
And also for you who have lost
The soul, the spirit, the wish to live.

Or nobody or somebody, or perhaps only one, or you
Who are reading me: remember the prime
Before the wax hardened,

When each of us was like a seal.
Each of us housed the imprint
Of the friend we met along the way;
In each the trace of each.
For good or evil
In wisdom or in folly
Each stamped by each.

Now that time presses urgently,
And the tasks are finished, to all of you the modest wish
That the autumn may be long and mild.

The imprint of Udi and Beechy, friends met along the way, had indeed restored to John the soul, the spirit, the wish to live. Two near divorces, numerous separations, lots of houses, kitchens, gardens and bathrooms later, we were back together for good. It was like the first idyllic days. Of course there were still fights but they were the sort we enjoyed. No cruelty, no fear. We made a real effort to grow up.

25 May

Noticed it is a beautiful spring day. And I hate it because he can't see it. That's a waste. I have to learn to see the blossom. For myself, not just to tell John. A woman stopped me today and said, 'I've loved your work ever since Sweeney Todd,' *no mention of John. I was grateful. There is a danger of just being seen as his widow. I have always been in his shadow and never minded much when he was alive but now he's not here in person to cast the shadow and I need to get in the sun on my own.*

18

You Came Through

WITH THE FOG CLEARED, John used his new-found clarity to make amends and open up his life. In 1997 he wrote to me when I was on location for a film: 'I seem to have seen a lot of TV drama about alcoholics since I got back from Greece and it brought to mind the fact that I may not have said that I'm sorry for all the years of misery I gave you. I am *truly* sorry and thank God that you stayed with me. I love you and need you.'

He had no need to apologise. The delight in being together had only been deepened by the struggle to achieve it. As Udi had done, I tried to continue to make him value himself, so I was delighted when he faxed me on a trip to America:

My darling (Hi darlin')
I am proud of my family – I am proud of myself (pleased?) but most of all I am proud of YOU. You are the love of my life.
Missing you
Me.

4 June
To St Paul's for Jubilee service. Bit disappointing. I expected the music to be monumental but it was fairly conventional

stuff. Felicity Kendal had instructed me to wear a hat and
gloves – she knows about these things – so I rented a rather
splendid silver number from Hepsibah. My first public
appearance without John or the girls. Crowds held back
by barriers shouting greetings to me. Good luck darling.
One woman called me insistently so I went over thinking
she wanted an autograph but she took my hand solemnly
and said, 'You look beautiful, my dear.' People are so un-
believably kind. It was exactly what I needed to boost my
confidence.

On Christmas Eve 1998 we celebrated our Silver Wedding.
He bought me the Jaguar of my dreams and I commissioned
sculptors and artists to make various garden seats for Luckington. My card to him read:

Darling,
You will see my present at Lucky. It's something for us to
enjoy together. Because this is a celebration of being together.
I am so grateful to you. Not just for all you have given me,
love and beautiful homes (and my Jag!!) but what you have
permitted me to do. It is a great blessing in life to have
someone worth giving love to. Through all the dark times I
have always hung on to the absolute knowledge that it was
worth hanging on in there. And now after your courageous
battle, we are *so* lucky. It is a tough old world out there but
I always know I have you. Let us enjoy our next years
together. They can't be as long, but they can be ever richer.
Thank you my darling.

His to me read:

My darling,
You are a very special person – a one-off. You have brought
hope, encouragement and love into so many people's lives
(not least your family's). You have a great talent and a heart
as big as an oak. Whatever we have for twenty-five years of

marriage is mainly due to your giving, your loving and I thank my God for you. I love you with all my heart.
Your little husband.
P.S. you're also dead sexy!!
TWENTY-FIVE YEARS, KID?!

6 June
God this business. It's a joke. The humiliation never ends. It's endemic in the job. Just after being nominated for a BAFTA as Best Actress some young producer wanted me to go and audition for a telly part that was virtually one speech. I know the author and the director so surely they could assess my ability to act or even look at a tape of my work if they needed to? Well, at least you can never get above yourself. Normally I would've slunk along and done what they asked but, prompted by my agent, I actually told them to stuff their part up their arse. Taking Holly Bach remedy for anger and bloodymindedness. Think I need it!

A few years after he had told John to watch his step, Beechy was alarmed when the doorman of his rooms phoned to say he had arrived without an appointment. Beechy was with a desperate patient so he could not see him for over an hour. He expected the worst when at last he went down to the waiting room. He feared that John would have gone or be in trouble. He was still there, looking fit and happy.

'I just came to say thank you. That was all.' A hug and he left.

Of all our daughters our youngest, Joanna, had probably suffered most from our antics over the years. She had been on the receiving end of rejection by her father followed by over-compensating effusive love, which she learned to mistrust. One day they were sitting together and he said very quietly, 'I love you, kid.'

'Me too, Dad.'

And the past was forgotten.

Our first grandchild, Jack, whose birth John had been too ill to enjoy, presented him with another challenge. In 1999, when he was four years old, he was suddenly diagnosed with a brain tumour and had to have a massive operation at Great Ormond Street Hospital. Simultaneously I was rushed into hospital for an emergency appendectomy. John was left holding the fort. I was beside myself with anxiety. John comforted and supported us all, darting between hospitals, places he had hitherto avoided like the plague. Confined to my hospital bed, all I could do was write Jack a letter:

Jack,
When I grew old enough to know better I had an irresistible desire to go on a seesaw. I sometimes wanted to play hopscotch too. Or pull faces at strangers. But I was sixty years old. My hair was going grey and I was respectable. So I had to behave, but I was very very depressed. You see, I didn't *feel* old but people, even your mummy, told me to 'act your age', which meant taking things slowly, being serious and driving a Saab and feeling very very bored.

Then a wonderful thing happened. You arrived. Your daddy was holding you wrapped in a blue blanket and I knew then that I loved you not that much (I am doing the arms thing), not that much – but that much (very wide arms). We celebrated with a bottle of champagne and lots of laughter and that's how it's been ever since. Because I've got you with me I can go on seesaws, go down slides, dance in the streets, go on funfairs, watch *Babe* over and over, have pillow fights and bite people's bums. I got a sports Jaguar telling people that I thought my grandson would like it. That was a fib. I like it. I like everything I do with you. Being in the garden in the rain, throwing things in streams, feeding ducks, flying kites, sailing boats, giggling till it hurts, even reading Snow White and the Seven bloody Dwarfs! With you I don't have to be an old lady. I'm very lucky, mind you, that you have turned out to be such a very nice grandson. In fact, come to think of it, I'm the luckiest Nana in the world.

Having coped with many crises in my life, I was useless when confronted with the anguish of my daughter and the suffering of Jack. I could think of no words of comfort for Ellie Jane or Jack's father, Matt, because I was too distraught and terrified myself. Anyway, I was holed up in another hospital. So John took control. My daughter Ellie Jane's letter, written when Jack had left hospital and was on the road to recovery, says it all: 'Dad was a very good, calming and strong presence to have in the hospital and a very good messenger one to the other.'

Calm and strong were not qualities she had been used to from her father. He was proud of that letter.

22 June
Lola's dancing school concert. She was brilliant. Four years old and this little wild child was suddenly concentrated, centred and poised. She did everything double-time but obviously felt the whole thing needed a bit of pace. She was right. When the audience applauded she looked at them in astonishment and then glowed with pleasure. Oh, I know that feeling.

I loved being a grandparent. John had to work harder at it. He could certainly act it. He was warm and loving with the little girl in *Buried Treasure* and one of his best performances is of an old man befriending a young evacuee in *Good Night Mister Tom*, adapted for television from the book by Michelle Magorian in 1998. The part demanded many skills – carpentry, playing an organ, roofing and a difficult East Anglian accent – all of which John mastered. The role was so different from Morse that he needed to transform himself. While we were in France he didn't bother to shave and I suggested he keep the beard.

I filled him in with my memories of the Blitz and being an evacuee. With Jack Gold's usual sensitive direction, *Mister Tom* has become a classic TV film. John brought all his understanding of loneliness and loss to his growing affection towards the young boy. He could say with passion lines like: 'The need for love is a priority for a child above all else.'

The purity of his feelings, devoid of sentimentality, when he comforts William about the death of a friend is profoundly moving. He stands by the grave of his own wife and child and says firmly: 'Except I didn't lose them, you see, not really, because they're still here, inside here [tapping his head] and always will be . . . in every little thing you'll ever remember about him. And that is something that nobody can ever take away from you – nobody – ever.'

When his second grandchild, Molly Mae, was born to Abigail and her partner Nigel in 1997 he went to greet the baby. The next day Abigail received this letter:

> I wanted to tell you how proud I am of you and my grand-daughter. What a great shame that Grandma Mollie and Grandad Thaw and of course Grandpa Bill are not around to feel as I do. I am certain they are watching from somewhere though. Mollie is a beautiful little girl and I was very touched by the sight of you and Nigel being with her – if you know what I mean. It was pure LOVE! You see, I can see it and *know* it, when I see it, but sadly for me I find it hard to create

ble to laugh again. On set with a supporting player in *Morse*. The beer was a prop.

John enjoying himself with his creative team, Ted Childs, Jack Gold and Chris Burt.

Richard Briers relishing playing an evil character with dyed hair in *Morse*.

RADA friends reunited in *Kavanagh*, Tom Courtenay and John.

John's friendship with Kevin Whately was one of the pleasures of *Morse*.

Discussing a *Kavanagh* script with Chris Kelly.

ohn sending up his stand-in, one of his
Scallywags', Barry Summerford.

Pauline, another Scallywag, keeping an
eye on a tense scene in *Monsieur Renard*,
whilst the crew wait for the sun to shine.

izing up a shot behind the camera in
Goodnight Mister Tom.

Me playing Dora Blossom in
The Russian Bride, who
reminded John of his mother.

Clare Venables, my inspiration and comforter.

Beauchamp Colcough, miracle worker.

Clare Higgins, friend and rescuer.

Udi Eichler, wise counsellor.

Back to Manchester to receive an honorary doctorate at the university, with (*back row from left*) Ellie Jane, Abigail and Joanna and his proud dad and stepmother beside him.

This photo was all John's mother Dolly had to remember her son by. It was found in her bag when she died.

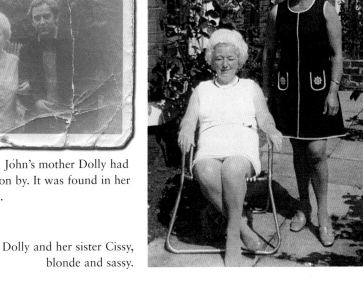

Dolly and her sister Cissy, blonde and sassy.

'Au secours me': John in France fathoming out yet another state-of-the-art radio.

A couple of old farts: still picnicking, this time in a field looking down on Blackgang Chine, my birthplace.

In a secret backwater of Venice reading to John from the *Links'* guide.

John learning to be a good grandad with Molly Mae.

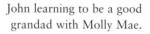

Matthew Harvey

All four grandchildren Lola, Molly Mae, Talia and Jack (playing table tennis in the corner).

On my own by the stream in Lucky after John's death. The bench is inscribed 'The two John Thaws loved it here.'

Molly Mae's impression of she and Lola in their velvet dresses at Grandad's memorial.

Wilts and Gloucestershire Standard

After planting a tree in a children's home for the John Thaw Foundation.

With Cherie Blair after the service for John at St-Martin-in-the-Fields, waiting to release sixty balloons in Trafalgar Square with labels saying 'Today we remembered John with love.'

Town and Country Photography

I was auctioning a holiday for two in the Bahamas for a cancer charity of which I was president. A mystery bidder kept pushing up the price. When I asked the winner to come and claim his very expensive prize, John stepped forward. We never took the holiday.

it myself. But I promise I will really try to be a proper Grandad to Molly Mae as your Grandad was to you!

24 June
The sons-in-law round to supper to choose a suit each of John's. Ermenegildo Zegna are going to alter them to their various sizes, as a gift. Nigel amazed me by suddenly breaking down and saying, 'I can't do this.' Tough, together Nigel. I have decided to give the rest of John's clothes to the Actors' Benevolent Society. I like the idea of some old actor laddie wearing John's Armani and Italian handmade shoes. Some needy out-of-work actor going to an audition in John's overcoat.

When Ellie Jane had her second child, Lola, in 1998, she was a challenge to John. He christened her, as his father had Jo, 'the little bugger'. He found her quite scary. When she wouldn't eat her carrots he said: 'Right, leave her to me. Come on, eat up.'
'No.'
'Now come on, Lola, do as I say. Eat up.'
Slightly louder: 'No.'
'Lola, do you hear me? . . .'
Bellowing: 'NO.'
Feebly: 'Oh, all right then.'

For the grandchildren's sake John overcame his phobia of being in public. We took them to see *The Secret Garden* in the West End, featuring my mate Dilys. He cuddled Lola on his lap as she slept through the whole event, only waking to join enthusiastically in any applause. He did not mind at all when strangers laughed and spoke to him as he carried her out of the theatre still sleeping soundly.

I risked working with him again in *Kavanagh*, after our disastrous experiences with *The Two of Us* and *Home to Roost*. The Scallywags were relieved he was so much happier, although they had not realised until he stopped drinking that that had been the problem. The man who looked after his Winnebago proudly showed me how the fridge was now stocked with orange juice and water. Not that I spent much time in his grand domain. Like all the other supporting players, I was allocated a minuscule caravan. When John asked me to join him for lunch, in front of the unit, I told him not to be cheeky. I make it a rule not to get off with the star. This time we had no rows. Chris Kelly said, 'He dropped his guard when they were together. They were just like two teenagers really. Obviously in love and obviously very happy to be working together. It was delightful.' A bit different from Leeds.

When depression consumed him, John was in danger of losing his sense of humour. Now he enjoyed a joke again. Just like my father had been when relating jokes – he was incoherent with laughter as he told me about Spike Milligan on a doorstep, with a stocking over his face, saying to the person opening the door: 'I'm a Jehovah's burglar.' An actor came to rehearsal with a rather poncey crocodile bag and John went into a brilliant riff about man-eating briefcases. He literally fell out of his chair when told that the very ladylike Virginia McKenna was in the wings with Frances Barber when Brian Blessed stomped off the stage muttering. Frances asked Virginia what he was saying and in her upper-class, cut-glass voice she replied, 'I think it was something about cunt.'

As his drinking had become worse John, and therefore I, had become reclusive. He did not like people coming to the house and was not interested in friendships. Now, when Tom

Courtenay agreed to take part in *Kavanagh,* it was a joy for them both. Tom wrote: 'Just to say how much I enjoyed being reunited with you. Your warmth, sweetness, humour and talent gave me the greatest pleasure.'

28 June
Busy, busy preparing memorial, fighting Carlton to get the
long version of the tribute programme shown rather than
a cut version. Every now and then I literally double up
with grief. He is still so – not real, sadly – but potent.
Lovely poem by Raymond Carver from Rufus Norris,
young director at Royal Court:

And did you get what
you wanted from this life, even so?
I did
And what did you want?
To call myself beloved, to feel myself
beloved on the earth.

John's workaholism was the next ogre he tried to fight. In 1999 he did a television film called *Waiting Time,* a lot of it shot in bleak East Berlin, where he had a sequence reminiscent of the *Sweeney* days, giving chase over rooftops. It nearly killed him. The redoubtable Pauline had loyally chosen to be with John even though she had been offered a job on the Delia Smith cookery show. They were filming in a stinking herring boat in a freezing cold gale, tossed around in the Baltic Sea. John noticed Pauline had tears running down her cheeks. He put his arm round her and she wailed over the wind and lashing rain, 'I took the wrong job. I could be in Delia's warm kitchen now.' John said, 'Never again, kid. We're getting too old for all this.'

Wanting to lessen his workload, he agreed with Colin Dexter that they should finish their thirteen-year run with *Morse.* Colin would not entertain the idea of any other actor ever playing Morse; everyone was shocked when it was decided to kill the character off. Even the camera was unhappy. When they were shooting Morse's fatal heart attack in a college quadrangle the camera broke down five times. That had never happened before. John found the final episode upsetting. Before each shot he had to remind himself he was a sick man and he began to feel really off colour. It was nevertheless a consummate piece of acting from both him and Kevin. When Lewis kissed the dead Morse on the forehead and said, 'Goodbye, sir' there were many wet eyes amongst the three quarters of a billion people that watched worldwide. When we went shopping the day after the episode went out, people were stopping him, genuinely distressed. It was the Princess Diana syndrome.

The talent to act is difficult to explain or pin down. However much technique you acquire, a performance can work magically in front of one audience and inexplicably fail to click the following night. Because of this dependence on chance, actors are a superstitious bunch, forever warding off demons that will come between us and our ability to meld the words, our minds, our emotions, our bodies into expressing ephemeral events. Some people believe it is absolutely necessary to feel nervous before a first night and get nervous if they don't. I have always found my fear of critics and audience destructive, so I use regular hypnotherapy to help me overcome it. As you stand in the wings waiting to go on, there is nothing but you. No computer, no tool, no machine, just you, facing an empty space with a head full of words. It can be scary and performers often lose their nerve and need help. A pill, a drink or a shrink. Kenneth Williams knew that his personality was not altogether normal, but rejected any suggestion of psychiatric help lest it should take away his talent. Yet John did some of his best work after treatment. In the final *Morse*, there is a long shot when the camera tracks into Morse's face as he sits alone in his flat. He is confronted with retirement and loneliness. John does nothing. No movement of the eyes or puff of a cigarette. He just is. It is as powerful a piece of work as he ever did in his career. An example of screen acting at its finest. Something he had striven for since those trips to the Burnage Odeon.

With John now on a relatively even keel, I set about looking at my own state of mind. The vicissitudes of my life since my cancer and my glimpse of death had made me question my atheism. I would never believe in a biblical God, but I felt the lack of a spiritual dimension in my life. I embarked on a quest, similar to my childhood religious adventures with my father. The Anglican Church was a non-starter, with its absurd reluctance to accept women priests. We had a splendid woman in Betty Boothroyd as Speaker of the House of Commons, easily controlling all the little boys, but the hierarchy of the Church of England was much too scared of women to let them do more than arrange the flowers and make the tea. All those men in frocks, refusing to let women give communion and threatening that the upstart hussies would divide the Church, made it impossible for me to contemplate even entering one of their buildings.

I tested many weird and wonderful approaches to the religious life. The all-time low was reached in an expensively vulgar house in High Wycombe, where a roomful of coiffed and manicured ladies crouched humming in front of a television. After a lot of 'ohm'ing an attractive female guru in a fetching red kaftan was beamed to us from New York and we were asked to approach and lay a rose in front of the telly. 'Oh noo, not for me,' as Jack would have said.

Although admiring of the various Eastern religions I explored, I always felt a bit silly participating. I am British or, as I like to think, European, and my inclination is towards something based on Christianity and my conditioning. I eventually found a home in the Society of Friends.

The Quakers are an odd lot. There is no one in charge, everyone believes something different, but the silent meetings are potent and you can continue to question faith but with others equally curious. The Society of Friends is, like Al Anon, dependent on the wisdom of ordinary folk. The homeless always welcome the Quaker sandwiches and soup the most because we don't judge or preach. My interest in prison reform is also something Quakers support and, of course, pacifism. Quakers are to be found negotiating secretly on most war fronts. Theirs is an active pacifism. They too like a good demo. They have a proud history of reform in all spheres of life and are not sexist or homophobic.

30 June

Went to Brighton to spend the day with Neil and James. How I value my gay friends. They have always brought style and affection to my life. Their lovely homes, their taste, their cosseting, their humour. All through my life I have been supported by gay men – and women. Now more than ever. We went to a very odd secluded beach where naked, rather unattractive guys were eyeing the trade. The sadder side of their lifestyle. On the other hand, on other beaches heterosexuals are doing exactly the same thing. But I was sure some of these were bank clerks living with their mothers, and that only on this beach could they furtively be themselves. Probably not true. I'm stuck in my memories of gay friends in the fifties, terrified of being found out. Dear Jack who committed suicide. An immaculate charming man who was forced by society to be ashamed of loving – or I suppose lusting. Nothing wrong with a bit of lusting, in my opinion.

I am not a good Quaker. I hypocritically hide my Jaguar round the corner when I go to meetings, as it hardly conforms to their ideas of simplicity or, in its petrol consumption, their regard for the environment. Sadly, because Quakers don't put themselves about, most people still confuse them with folk in white collars and pointy hats, but they are in fact the most unpuritanical people you could wish to meet. I am lucky to have found them.

Religions based on a book make me nervous, whether it's the Koran, the Torah or the Bible. Extremists can use them to justify anything. The Quakers' only book of importance is called, endearingly, *Advices and Queries* – no laws or creeds for them. One 'advice' is 'Speak truth to power'; right from the start Quakers have stood outside and questioned authority. Suits me. I like a bit of anarchy. In the nineties I had a sneaking admiration for

Nick Leeson who stood the Stock Exchange on its head and nearly ruined Baring's Bank. I also enjoyed the discovery of a very old lady in Bexleyheath of all places who had been a spy. It was claimed she gave atomic information to the Russians on principle, to keep the balance of power. It obviously wasn't for money or surely she would not have chosen to live out her life in a bungalow in Bexleyheath.

By the nineties my campaigning zeal was beginning to wane. I did not join the anti-poll-tax riots under Thatcher or the demos against pit closures under Major. When I worked with Harold Pinter in a revue at the Lyric Hammersmith in 1997 we agreed we were probably even angrier than when we were young, but unlike Harold I had that disease of old age – resignation. When I got to sixty, things began to repeat themselves and I questioned the effort I had wasted in attempts to change the world. I was, however, delighted when, at last, Labour was returned to power in 1997. My favourite moment, as it was for many, was the defeat of Michael Portillo by a rather startled gay man. Portillo has now become a softie, but I could not forget a truly shocking speech he made at the Tory Conference in 1993 when he lambasted Europe and came on strong about law and order and the proud SAS, which would not have been out of place at a Nuremberg rally. The blue-rinse brigade lapped it up. Now they were choking on this landslide defeat.

My happiness on the home front was reflected at work where I did some good and interesting stuff. In the theatre I landed two great roles, in David Eldridge's *Under the Blue Sky* at the Royal Court and then in *In Extremis* by Neil Bartlett at the National. In *The Russian Bride* on television I received a BAFTA nomination for playing a blousy, tarty woman who destroys her son's life, who John said reminded him of his mother.

John was less lucky. *The Glass* was not a great success but he enjoyed working with Sarah Lancashire. He loved it when Sarah was terribly nervous about kissing him passionately as he was 'a national treasure and shouldn't be rummaged about with'. He had high hopes of another of Ted's ideas. Monsieur Renard was a priest in wartime France. Chris Kelly was again producing and all the Scallywags decamped with him to France. John brought his usual self-discipline to the role. He learned to do a High Mass in Latin from a priest at my old school, St Ethelreda's in Ely Place. He was word and gesture perfect.

1 July
Chris Kelly tells me he had a Mass said for John at St Ethelreda's. I wonder if some little girl was sitting in the church holding her nose as the incense went by.

To lose weight for the part he did not eat at all at night. In the land of good food and fine wine he could enjoy neither. Everyone was thrilled with the first series. It was a perfect part for John and the series was impressive in its historical accuracy. Nick Elliot, the head of the network centre, who chooses what we see on ITV, wanted more. Two money men who have since left Carlton, Lord Waheed Ali and Michael Foster, dithered for some time and then decided to ditch the series as they deemed it too expensive. Caught in political infighting, the series was abandoned. Everyone was dumbfounded by the decision and John was bitterly disappointed, as well as being disillusioned by the new criteria for commissioning shows, so different from his early career, when good quality was paramount rather than immediate financial returns. As with any of John's shows, the programme would have ultimately repaid them handsomely in overseas sales. He consoled himself by thinking it would have been gruelling work for the next four years of the proposed schedule and he could have a few holidays instead, as Udi had recommended.

5 July
At last an antidote to 'Death is nothing at all'. It's by Edna St Vincent Millay and was sent by another stranger:

> *Time does not bring relief; you all have lied*
> *Who told me time would ease me of my pain!*
> *I miss him in the weeping of the rain;*
> *I want him at the shrinking of the tide;*

The old snows melt from every mountainside,
And last year's leaves are smoke in every lane;
But last year's bitter loving must remain
Heaped on my heart, and my old thoughts abide.
There are a hundred places where I fear
To go, – so with his memory they brim!
And entering with relief some quiet place
Where never fell his foot or shone his face
I say, 'There is no memory of him here!'
And so stand stricken, so remembering him.

That's more like it. As we Quakers say, that 'speaks to my condition'. Good old Edna. She knew a thing or two about loss. I can barely lift my eyes and look around me without some memory jumping up and biting my brain. As I drive around London – this café, that doctor's surgery, that stage door, everything I lay eyes on makes me 'stand stricken' – not wise when you are driving a Jaguar XKR and I can't even look at that without remembering his joy when he gave it to me and saying it was for putting up with him for twenty-five years. I am a human-shaped container filled to eye level with water, which spills over, cascading down my face, whatever I look at. A startling apparition to draw alongside at the traffic lights.

John was not good at holidays. In the past, a trip to Lake Garda had nearly ended in disaster. To avoid the British tourists, we took to hiring a pedalo and, singing 'I'm a pedalo and I don't care', we'd pedal as far away from the beach as possible. One day a gale blew up and it took us an hour and very achy legs to get to shore.

My obsession with guidebooks and determination to see everything in them ruined a visit to Rome. When I was not dragging John around museums and ruins, we were sitting on the lavatory, with our feet soaking in the bidet, to ease what John christened our Marble Foot Rot. In 1998 we had a better experience with a guidebook. The *Links' Guide to Venice* took us to glorious hidden corners and selected some special treasures from that cornucopia of a place. John never complained as he limped round Mr Links's suggested walks. Being carnival time, masked figures floated past and musicians serenaded us in hidden squares that the *Guide* led us to. It was a magic holiday. The relish of this most beautiful of cities is increased selfishly for me by thinking that one day it might be completely submerged under the sea so we are transiently privileged to experience it. We also took a wonderful holiday in Oman where John ventured with me into the desert, but he had to wait outside the winding alleys of old Muscat where only women visitors were allowed. I searched for two special women but never found them. Nor did I tell John about the ring I had given away. Discussion of his mother was still out of bounds.

But the place he loved best was France. He relished good wines and I worried that he would miss them when we drove down to the Luberon with Jo and her partner Matt (Ellie Jane's partner being Matt Byam Shaw and Jo's Matt Harvey, I collect son-in-laws called Matt), stopping off in the wine and champagne areas. John enjoyed our descriptions of the wines we tasted but was not tempted to join in. We cooked together from our battered Elizabeth David book, which we had bought it from her shop in Pimlico when we were first married. She taught the English, ourselves included, to appreciate good food. We ate in cheap cafés and posh gourmet places. John would choose our wines with care. We enjoyed watching him enjoying us enjoying them.

His first five years of sobriety, apart from the usual marital spats, were a time of great joy for us. We almost grew up. Ours was not a conventional love affair, but whose is? It was not textbook. We made up our rules as we went along. And then ignored them. It consumed us for twenty-eight years. It was not mature until the very end.

The millennium celebrations nearly scuppered us again. John hated Christmas. It had always been his worst time. He had obviously had some sad Christmases as a child, but so, I would point out, did I. So did many people. His sock at the end of the bed with just an apple, an orange and one toy was not unusual. I did not even have that when I was evacuated. The build-up to the millennium celebrations made John grumpy. The vacuous Dome and the Wobbly Bridge and the badly organised fireworks display over the Thames were depressing. After Christmas the family went back to London to celebrate with their mates, and we were left alone in Luckington. I felt suddenly left out and old. John was angry that I couldn't be happy with him alone. We watched the proceedings on television and ended up having a row. It seemed a good time to look through my old diaries and I was appalled by what a miserable cow I had been. I tried to end the twentieth century by burning the most dreary ones in a bonfire in the field, but it was raining and my melodramatic gesture fizzled out. We greeted the new millennium in sulky silence. The girls made a decision for us. Next Christmas we must go away on our own. Forget the family and enjoy each other.

Our week in Paris over Christmas 2000 was the best of times. We had a suite at the Crillon Hotel and relished it guiltily like the urchins we still felt we were. It was a long way from Stowell Street and the King's Cross Road. We celebrated our twenty-seventh wedding anniversary in one of the best restaurants in the world, Les Ambassadeurs. We marvelled at the complicated ballet performed by the waiters as they carried out their impeccable service. We were fascinated by the *sommelier*, tasting a sip of each bottle before it was served, savouring it in his mouth and then elegantly spitting it into a silver spittoon. John was panicked into buying a very expensive one, lest the Mighty One sneered as he spat ours. The food was the best we had ever tasted, the coffee better than at the Grégoire, our yardstick brew from Apt, and the other diners oozed French chic. As we raised our glasses to each other, mine with fine wine and John's with water, his toast was: 'Nous avons cracked it, kid.'

We attended a sung Midnight Mass at the Madeleine and squeezed hands and pressed elbows at the sublime choir. We held hands in front of some exquisite late flower paintings by Manet and I made John laugh by weeping at their beauty – 'Diddle-oh.' We went to a concert of Gregorian chant, given by the St Petersburg choir in a beautiful church on the Ile St Louis.

Afterwards we ate in one of those tiny French bistros where everybody joins in the conversation until the small hours of the morning. We lingered over coffee in the Place des Vosges. We wandered the streets, arms round each other, in the winter sunshine. Years before, I had lost my wedding ring. It is probably at some costumier's in the pocket of a dress I wore for a show. John bought me a new one in Paris. It was gold with a little sapphire set in it. Later, at Luckington, I was groping in the earth for potatoes, and I lost the stone. It left a gaping hole. I have not replaced it.

In April 2001 John played Captain Hook at the Festival Hall.

In May 2001 his dear friend Tom Courtenay presented him with the highest accolade you can receive in television – a Fellowship of the British Academy of Film and Television.

In June 2001 he was diagnosed with cancer.

For the next eight months the fearful man became brave beyond belief. The boy who was not taught to love became the most loving of men.

On Valentine's Day 2002 I gave him this card:

Darling husband,
I hope you know how much I love and cherish you. I am so grateful for my love for you. It is the very centre of my life and has been since I first set eyes on you. You are my husband, my lover and my friend.
Guess who?

He gave me two teddy bears to add to the collection he had given me over the years. His card said:

I love you more than I can say. You have given me more than any one man deserves and I know I'll never be able to repay you. BUT I'LL TRY.
You are the love of my life.
Me!

Seven days later he was dead.

7 July
Found in the bedside table drawer the notebook I gave
John to write his dark thoughts in. It had only one entry,
written when we were in France:

It's so beautiful here and peaceful and I think healing.
For the last two days I have had long moments of feeling
normal (i.e. forgetting that I have the cancers). If only my
bloody voice was stronger because it's that that reminds
me I am not myself. Poor Sheila has to listen very hard
when I speak as she is having a problem with one ear so
we're a right pair!

We went to Saignon for morning coffee and it was lovely
up there. Sitting there with Sheila outside the church was
very, very healing I know. I am full of love for my
wonderful, wonderful wife. What would I do without her?
Don't ask! I'm a very, very lucky man.

19

A Single Woman

IT IS INEVITABLE WHEN someone is an addict or suffers from depression that you seek for reasons. Some schools of thought maintain that it is genetic and I am inclined to agree but I was tormented with guilt that John's problem's were somehow my fault. Certainly my ignorance of the condition for a long while contributed to its progress.

8 July
Keep wondering if my ordinariness kept John back, stopped him from reaching his full potential. Or was it a welcome sanctuary? There is no doubt he could have achieved more, Hollywood, more stage work. Would some other woman have pushed him harder? But he used to say, 'I'd rather be a big fish in a small pool.' Can't really imagine him coping with the rat race in LA but then he coped with worse. Did I stunt his growth because I was as fearful as him? Perhaps he needed someone bold and brave.

It is a good ploy to blame everything on our mothers until we too become mothers and find ourselves behaving just like them. John would seldom talk about his. When asked he usually replied, 'I have no mother' in a way that brooked no further discussion. What little he told me made me angry. I felt contempt for a woman who could just walk away from two little boys; it was not a feeling I enjoyed. It was a weeping sore that continued to fester because it was covered up. I wanted to expose it to the light and see if it would heal. There is no doubt that her inexplicable desertion deeply affected John and, indirectly, myself and his daughters. I felt I had the right, when he was no longer here to be hurt by my curiosity, to find out more about her. It was not easy. She had been erased from his life.

I start with Beattie. The blood of Mary Veronica Mullen (John's grandmother) flows through the veins of his Auntie Beat. A lifetime joyfully dedicated to the service of others is an old-fashioned concept but with her it continues now she is over eighty, an apple-faced, smiling woman. It is impossible to get her to say a bad word about anyone, so she is reluctant to criticise Dorothy, despite her disbelief that anyone could desert their children. Similarly Mildred, Jack's second wife, still glamorous at eighty with black hair and beautiful skin. When the boys had left home she married Jack who, together with Dorothy, had worked in her fish and chip shop. Dorothy was 'a good worker', 'very clean', 'well turned out'. Apart from the Ablott nose, a bit too large for the rest of her face, she was 'very attractive'. Because they felt protective of Jack and his boys, she and her then husband severed all connection with the Ablotts when Dorothy had gone. Nor did she ever discuss Dorothy with Jack when they were married as 'it was in the past tense'.

I discover from John's old schoolfriend Harvey Bryant that John had visited his mother when she worked at the Shakespeare Pub in Manchester and he was at Ducie Tech. On the several occasions Harvey went with him, they seemed relaxed together in a way that signified it was a fairly regular occurrence. Keeping these visits secret from his father and brother must have been torture, but then he was used to keeping secrets for his mum. Then there was the visit in 1960 with Barry J. Gordon and again in 1969 at my insistence. I am fairly sure he never saw his mother again after his marriage to me. Which is significant.

In December 2002, as I approach the first anniversary of

John's death, I decide to visit Manchester to try to get some sense of the woman. I do not have much to go on. A Christmas card from a Mr and Mrs Calland, purporting to be an aunt and uncle, and a copy of the decree absolute of Jack and Dorothy's divorce from the Family Records Office that gives me nothing except the date and place of their marriage and that the Respondent had 'deserted the Petitioner without cause'. No records of the custody proceedings exist. After John died I found a bill for the administration of her estate in his drawer. It mentions paying some debts, correspondence with a Mr B. H. Welsh, and personal effects to be collected from Llandudno by a Mrs C. Simpson. None of it means anything to me.

10 July
Friends Helen and Hattie to stay in France. They love it. It is a beautiful place. Why can't I enjoy it for myself? First it was for John and the family, now it is in danger of being for my friends or the kids. Must I always live my life through others? Hattie and Helen have learned to live well on their own. So must I.

I find Mr and Mrs Calland in a pleasant sheltered housing estate on the edge of the Peak District. Terrie Calland had been a singer with Bonelli's Band for fifteen years at Belle Vue. Dolly's brother Alan, 'a lovable rogue', had wooed her away from her first husband and eventually married and then divorced her. Those people who knew Dorothy best called her Dolly, and that is how I now begin to think of her. It seems to suit her better.

The Catholic Terrie obviously found Dolly a bit much. No surprise there then. She was 'flighty', had 'a bit of a mouth on her' and 'used language'. Terrie is still a twinkly woman born, unbelievably, in 1917, whose memory is beginning to fail, but she prefers to forget her brief marriage to Alan anyway. She does remember Jack as a lovely man and thinks Dolly was a fool to leave him. Did Jack really tell Terrie that he wished he'd met her sooner? Was he a bit of a romancer? Or is it wishful thinking on her part?

I move into central Manchester and stay there, as I have many times on tour with shows. Despite the rain, Manchester has always appealed to me. It was built by ordinary men with vision. There is no aristocracy or ruling family, just bluff *nouveaux riches* making money by the sweat of their brows and, of course, other people's. It was the Dissenter Churches, mainly the Unitarians and the Quakers, that pushed forward social reforms, and the city was accepting of anyone from anywhere who had something to offer, accounting for the diverse mixture of Germans, Jews, Armenians, Turks, Austrians, Portuguese. Since the rebuilding after the massive IRA bomb in 1996 and the holding of the Commonwealth Games it has cleaned itself up and is very perky. Those early intellectuals would be thrilled at the refurbished art gallery, the imaginative use of the Royal Exchange to house one of our leading theatre companies, and the new, perfect concert hall, the Bridgewater Hall. The city feels alive and kicking, as it must have done to John as a boy, even though it was coated with grime then and usually seen through a thick smog. The trams are back. How John would have loved that. Now they are sleek, purring beasts, so he might have missed the rattling and shaking of those childhood journeys.

20 July

Really laughed with Hattie and Helen today. We got lost somewhere near Bonnieux looking for the Gare Café. Also trying to buy a screw to mend the chair. Saw a group of hefty half-naked workmen doing the road. Hattie, demure in cotton sunhat, wound down the window and in rather posh franglais asked the way. One spoke a little English so she followed up with 'Do you think we'll get a long screw in Bonnieux?' The double meaning was possibly lost on them, but our raucous laughter was not. They obviously thought, 'These old English biddies are game.' Lots of nudging and leering ensued. We set off on our quest – a long screw being a very inviting prospect – but kept getting lost and passing them again. God knows what they thought.

I set about getting someone to drive me around and I land on my feet. Shaun is short, pink-faced and shy. He has never met a 'superstar'. I quickly disabuse him of that idea and it isn't long before he comments – with some disappointment – how 'ordinary' I am. When I invite him into the Malmaison Hotel to have a coffee while we map out our journey, he says he can't, look at him. Oh Lord, do people still feel they have no right to enter the portals of the posh? If unworthiness is bred in you, how do you convince yourself you are as good as the next person? I assure Shaun that I think his bright anorak and jeans are great and, of course, the trendies and businessmen having their breakfast meetings don't turn a hair. It's all in the minds of the cowed. Shaun and I get on like a house on fire. I say I want him to park in various areas and I will go for a walk, knock on a few doors and come back to the car. He will not hear of leaving me alone. Although he only comes up to my shoulder I assess he will be a more ferocious bodyguard than any real superstar's big bruisers.

Our first stop is the rough triangle that encompassed Stowell Street, now a desolate wasteland. A few prefabricated car auction

places and tin huts stand where once was that teeming working-class area, full of suffering and love. The old living conditions were shameful, but to destroy the community and replace it with nothing seems mindless. Similarly, where the beautiful Belle Vue gave gaiety to these hard-working folk, there are a few rather nasty housing estates and yet more undeveloped sites. The multi-plex cinema provides some non-participatory entertainment, and a huge hypermarket caters for our modern recreation of shop-ping. There is still a greyhound track and a snooker hall, but gone are the elegant walks and meeting places that brought the people together and the enterprises that provided much-needed employment for the locals. Only the old remember the place now.

On to Daneholme Road, and this is depressing. What must have been a showplace of an estate is now neglected and bleak. I ring the bell of No. 2 and the flat above, but there is no move-ment apart from the rubbish blowing around in the garden. The other doors I knock on are opened with much clanking of chains and bolts. One front-door window is boarded from a recent break-in. This old man comes to the door looking neglected and grubby and is obviously too frightened to undo the chain. Peeping through the small gap, he tells me that he and his wife knew Jack but now he lives alone. He would not have been so isolated in the days when the neighbourhood rallied round to watch over John and Ray.

Another two houses I visit welcome me warmly with mugs of tea. I have the usual battle recording my chats over the back-ground of continuous daytime TV. These homes of the old resi-dents are immaculate little havens in this wilderness. Full of knick-knacks and crocheted cushions and homemade rag rugs, they are, I imagine, unchanged since the fifties. The TV makeovers have not influenced them. They tell tales of the decline of their district. How it is the dumping ground for those needing a short-term stay, who naturally take no pride in their tempo-rary homes. Some are refugees and it is easy to understand how incipient racist attitudes have arisen.

22 July
Hattie and Helen have left. Alone in the French house for the first time. I felt him around me – a benign presence.

It felt comfortable. Went to a recital of the Goldberg Variations on a clavichord in the church at Saignon. Chatted to a few people. The concert started with shafts of sun lighting the church and ended with candles flickering. It was quite lovely. But still I am thinking I wish he was here to be thrilled with me.

Shaun is getting worried about his car. He reminds me that the Gallagher brothers lived in Burnage and I think that colours his judgement somewhat. All I sense is a numbing apathy. We pass the Burnage cinema, scene of John's former glories, which has been a supermarket at some time but is now boarded up and falling into ruin.

The old Victorian building of Green End Junior School is intact, but surrounded by forbidding high wire fences and padlocked gates. Inside it is brightly painted and warm and cheerful. One little boy has been reported for 'using language'. Does he have a mum like Dolly, I wonder. I am told that broken families are now the rule rather than the exception. All the notices are in four languages, demonstrating the extra skills needed by teachers in a school like this. The Deputy Head produces an ancient form photo, and at the end of the back row, a bit on his own, is a sad, fat little boy – recognisably John.

As we leave, Shaun bristles at the sight of a large group of youths in a huddle, lighting a suspicious-looking cigarette. One looks over and begins approaching menacingly. Then he leaps about shouting, 'It's Steve's mum.' They know every nuance of *EastEnders*. Shaun is thrilled as I sign autographs for the growing crowd. He later describes his trips with me as the 'highlight of his life'. He deserves more.

I have one more call to make. I do not hold out great hopes for it, but it turns out to be pure gold. The will solicitors can only give me one document – the grant of probate for Dorothy's will, dated 14 June 1974. It says that she had died intestate as a 'single woman'. The resonance of that phrase strikes me as so lonely. There is an address for Dorothy at the time of her death on 2 February 1974 in Longsight. It is a forlorn hope that anyone will remember her in 2002, but on Shaun's insistence – he is now totally involved in the quest – we go to Leedale Road. I knock on the door with little expectation. A gaunt man of about fifty opens it: 'Hello Sheila. Come in.'

24 July
Am in Belfast having agreed to do a radio play with an all-Irish cast in a Tipperary accent. Am I mad? But with their help I got there. And over the many drinks after the recording, they christened me Sheila O'Hancock. I do love Irish actors. I've enjoyed it. Feel guilty saying that. But it has been good to be Sheila, who is quite a good actress, rather than the grieving widow of a famous man.

It is not the usual 'I've seen you on the telly' recognition. This is the son of Dolly's favourite sister, Cissie, short for Cecilia, same name as my only aunt. This house is where Dolly had been living when she died in St Anne's Hospice. Stuart Simpson (the name on the bill being Mrs C. Simpson) has personal memories, some from conversations with his mum who died recently, that fill in numerous gaps in my knowledge of John's mother. He also has some photographs that tell me more than anything.

Up until now I have only seen one photo of John's mother.

In it she looked oldish, plump, with stiff-lacquered hair – a fairly ordinary woman. Now here are two of the young Dolly. A slim figure striding along the wall of the vinegar factory, critically eyeing the chubby queen of the Whit-walk. In front her two

boys wearing their best grey flannel suits. She is wearing an elegant, long-jacketed suit, teetering heels and maybe a velvet bow on the back of her long blonde hair and gloves. She looks a knock-out compared with the rest of the women. Poignantly, judging by the ages of the boys, it was taken just before she left. In another family wedding photo she has on the same suit, but this time with sexy ankle-straps, a witty bow-tie and a cheeky hat. It is not her wedding but she has taken centrestage. She is the star and the bride is nowhere. John is in the corner being held affectionately by one of the men. What a wrench it must have been to lose touch with this huge family of Ablotts. Significantly, John Senior is in neither picture; nor is Ray, but he was probably playing foot-ball which would take precedence over a soppy wedding.

There are later photos of the older Dolly that I have seen before, but this time I notice she always has her shoes off. All that standing behind bars in unsuitable shoes? Or a gesture of abandon? The most poignant photograph is one found in her handbag after her death. It is a faded, crumpled Polaroid of herself and John on the

visit I persuaded him to make. She is wearing a jaunty aquamarine blouse with ruffled neckline and bare, aging arms. Her still-blonde hair is stiff from the hairdresser's. Her hand is loosely linked in John's arm for the photo. His hand holds a cigarette and does not touch her. His handsome face is unsmiling and haunted and she looks tentative. They do not look like a mother and son, although their features show that they are. It was taken in the garden of the house I am now in.

There is also a photo of John as a toddler in Stowell Street perched on the handlebars of a tricycle, playing on the cobbles with four other more typical ragamuffins.

John looks like the child of an aristocrat. An immaculate smock suit such as you buy in Belgravia, clean white socks and a shining, well-cut head of hair. She really turned him out well. So why on earth did she desert them all?

3 August

Braved the Proms. Took poor Jo. It was Rachmaninoff's Third Piano Concerto. We sat there sobbing. Out loud. Will I not be able to go to concerts any more? It was such a shared thing. Elbows pressing against each other at the best bits, orgasmic experiences, dissecting the perf afterwards, trying to understand New Music, 'Oh noo not for me.' Obviously Jo and I are useless together. Embarrassing to behold.

An actor has to fill in the details of a role that the script does not give. We piece together, or invent, our character's back story before the play begins, to deepen the interpretation of the particular moment in their life that we are showing. However unpleasant that character may seem to the audience, the actor has to empathise, if not sympathise. I will attempt to get inside Dolly's skin as if I were going to play her and try to understand what John never could or would.

The births of the ten Ablotts were spread over twenty years. The eldest had to help look after the youngest. Sometimes supper was a bag of chips between them, or anything they could scrounge. Dolly, being a lively kid, was especially good at this. There was no question of further education. Dolly had to leave school at fourteen, although she was as bright as a button. She would give some of her wages to her mum and any of her brothers or sisters who needed it. They pooled their resources. First up was best dressed. A girl's best chance of betterment was to hook a good bloke. She had to look smart.

When things became scarce during the war Dolly painted her legs with gravy browning and drew a pencil line up the back for seams. She used beetroot juice on her lips and soot round her eyes, and kept her hair in metal Dinkie curlers, concealed under a turban, except when she went out on the town. Once a week she touched up her roots with peroxide and styled her hair after the stars she saw at the local cinema – Betty Grable and Rita Hayworth were her favourites. She and her sisters cut a dash when they hit Belle Vue. Wherever Dolly went she attracted attention. Her clothes were daring and stood out in the crowd. She once wangled some precious nylons out of a GI stationed in the park and flaunted her lovely legs. There was something about her. She wanted to have fun, but often she had to look after the baby. Why the hell did her mum keep having kids?

One day a tall, good-looking youth asked her to dance. They revolved around the wooden floor under the stars with the lake illuminated beside it. Like James Stewart off the films, he was gentle and shy so she made all the going. He didn't say much, but when he did he made her laugh. No one could have been less like her father. They agreed to meet again. After a few dates he introduced her to his family. They were warm and fun to be with. His mother cooked a wonderful meal and they all had a sing-song round the piano. Jack was besotted with her. She had never been so loved. She felt like a film star – the centre of his world. Her bloody father messed up the engagement party, but once she was married she would move in near the Thaws and be shot of him and having to look after everyone.

Her little house in Stowell Street was her pride and joy. She scrubbed her front stoop, as she saw the other Thaws do, and cooked imaginatively with the meagre rations. For the first few months she acted the perfect housewife and, whenever Jack was free, they went out to town or Belle Vue. She understood when Jack got moody about the horrors he was facing on the bomb sites, but she could easily cheer him up. She was nineteen and sexy and, despite the war, full of hope.

4 August
I like the vicar from St Martin-in-the-Fields, Nick Holtam. Getting the religious content right is tricky. John used to have what he called 'my God' but never went to church. I told him I didn't want stuff about meeting in another

*place and he emailed me this lovely piece not to be used
in the service but just for me, which was used at the funeral
of the theologian John Taylor. It was apparently a prayer
from somebody just before the outbreak of the First World
War.*

*'To have given me self-consciousness for an hour in a
world so breathless for beauty would have been enough.
But Thou has preserved it within me for twenty years and
more, and has crowned it with the joy of this summer of
summers. And so, come what may, whether life or death,
and, if death, whether bliss unimaginable or nothingness,
I thank Thee and bless Thy name.'*

When, after only three months of marriage, Dolly fell pregnant it terrified her. She dreaded the drudgery of her mother's
life. She went to her mother's house to have the baby and it
was a difficult and painful birth. She had to give up work and
Jack started doing even more night shifts to make up the gap
in their keep. She had never slept in a bed on her own in crowded
Norman Grove, so she would take little John into bed with her
for company. She enjoyed dressing him up and parading him in
front of the neighbours. By the time he was toddling and more
independent she began to love her sweet-natured babe. She got
her figure back and managed to work a morning shift in the
pub at the Longsight Gate of Belle Vue, where they let her bring
him with her. She was a good barmaid and she enjoyed it. Life
wasn't so bad.

Then, at twenty-one, she fell pregnant again. Clumsy birth
control was useless for someone as passionate and impetuous
as she. Was her life going to be endless children and housework?
Jack was now sent away to work in the mines and she was all
on her own with a new baby and a toddler, tied to the house.
The Thaws were supportive but they would never understand
this burning desire to improve herself. She knew she was known
as a two-bit millionaire and was thought to dress too tartily for
a young mother. She knew she wasn't cut out for looking after
kids, she found it boring and exhausting, but she was good at

every job she did and full of ideas. People always commented on her ability. She never had a problem getting work.

One of her bosses asked her to go away with him. He said he loved her and he had a bob or two. He promised her a future with him where she could provide for her boys and have more freedom. Always impulsive, she went. Only to discover that what he wanted was a dirty weekend. She had to return and face the street again. Jack was a kind man and, in spite of everything, adored her. He took her back and they decided she would be happier if they lived with her family. There was always someone to keep an eye on the kids there so Dolly could go out a bit more and take on longer hours at the pub. So off they went to make a fresh start. Dolly brushed up well, despite her two kids. The spirit of the war led to flirtations with one or two men. What the hell; we might all be dead tomorrow. Jack was always so tired and grumpy. There were endless rows between him and her father, which ended with the bastard putting her few sticks of furniture out in the front and telling them to bugger off. They traipsed off to Wythenshawe, a dirty flat in a slum area.

About this time a salesman called Alan West came into the pub. He was selling sticky tape and his patter was so good he off-loaded a caseload during the lunch hour. He had red-blond hair, a snappy suit and a car. Dolly had only ever been in a van before, so he took her for a ride. He confided his plans for his future. He was going to make a lot of money, get a bigger car and buy a house at Alderney Edge. He was going to make it somehow. He looked like Van Johnson and acted like Mickey Rooney. She believed every word he said.

Jack thought their dream had come true when he landed a flat on the new estate in Burnage. A nice area for the kids to grow up in, a bit of garden even; everyone wanted to live in the model Kingsway Estate. But not Dolly. She couldn't help it. She wanted more. It was the suburbs. She hated the bloody garden and lace curtains and the endless tram rides to town. It was miles from Belle Vue and dead as a door nail. Alan understood. He could see she was a good businesswoman and a bobby-dazzler. She was wasted. Why not come with him and they would set up in business together? They would make a great team. But what about Jack and the kids?

She really tried to make a go of being a wife and mother. She arranged a tea party for Ray's fifth birthday. She made cakes and jellies and both families came round. The tea-cups clinked. 'This is very nice.' 'Well, you couldn't want better than this.' 'When are you going to have another littl'un?' Was this it for the rest of her life? She had to get away or she would die. Jack would get used to it, he was very easy-going. She vaguely thought she could get the kids later, but Alan wasn't having that – they would get in the way of his big plans – and neither was Jack.

Suddenly the worm turned. Jack swore he would never see her again. She didn't believe him; he had always given in before and she knew he still loved her. Then he went to court and she was banned for ever from seeing her kids. She hadn't a chance: she had deserted her children and her husband. A lot of husbands, returning as strangers from the war, were leaving their wives, but the other way round was unheard of. Her own mother was bitterly ashamed of her and all her brothers and sisters told her what a fool she was. Alan West was a spiv. He was a 'I love me, who do you love?' kind of bloke. Couldn't she see that?

No, she couldn't. He was her key to a great future. For a while they lived in her sister's front room. Then they got tenancy of various pubs and were successful landlords. The pubs got bigger and she did catering – an innovation in those days. Dolly became quite well known. Especially when *Coronation Street* started and she had a pub near Granada Studios. She managed to push thoughts of Jack out of her mind, but she worried about the children. One day she was distraught and Alan offered to drive her to Burnage to try to catch a glimpse of them. They saw her and didn't seem much interested. John showed up with a friend one day when she was at the Shakespeare Pub in Central Manchester. Was he just trying to show his pal he really had a mother or did he love her in spite of what she had done? He often turned up after that. She gave him sandwiches, but he was an odd lad – quiet one minute, then showing off and putting on voices the next. She would be in trouble if Jack found out, but she knew her son would keep it secret. He was good at secrets.

10 August
I have really lived this grief. I have been totally centred on my pain. That's some sort of achievement. Most of my life has been postponing feeling or thinking what comes next. But grief like this can't be avoided. It's utterly real and has to be experienced there and then. I am doing what I have always striven to do – live the moment. I am here now. Shame I had to learn through pain rather than pleasure.

She did not tell John or anyone that the man on whom she had pinned her hopes and for whom she had given up every-thing was a phoney and a drunk. That it was she who worked her arse off running the business while he drank the profits. She kept going as long as she could, performing the happy barmaid, while behind the scenes she dealt with a cruel drunk. Her son's visits petered out but he began appearing on her TV screen.

He visited her once with a friend when he was working in a theatre in Liverpool, but didn't stay long. Now, even though she knew he was working in Manchester, she only read about it. He never mentioned her in the papers; or, if he did, it was to say he didn't know her. She never told anyone in the pub she was his mother and, although friends told her she could make a fortune talking to the papers, she would not stoop to that. When she managed to get away from Alan she gave up running pubs and went to live with her sister Cissie while she sorted herself out. She was at a low ebb. She had put on weight and at the age of forty-nine it wasn't easy to find work or attract men. Cissie heard that John was working in Manchester with that Sheila Hancock and took the risk of phoning and asking if he would visit his mum. When he agreed, Dolly was in a right flap, trying out various outfits, spending hours in the hair-dresser's, manicuring her nails.

He arrived in a snorting blue MG with the roof down. He looked every inch the star. When Dolly linked her arm in his for a photo he felt a bit stiff, but his jacket was soft and expensive and his green silk shirt had obviously cost a bob or two. He told her his shoes were handmade in Italy. She had always turned him out nice, so perhaps something had stuck. She couldn't think of much to say to him – his was a different world, the world she had dreamed of. She was so pleased for him – not proud, she had no right to be proud.

30 August
Have been searching for John's old Gucci jacket that we bought in Rome on idyllic hols. Went for a manicure at the Nail Place and found it on the clothes peg. It must have been there for months. No one had taken it or thrown it out – it was patiently waiting to be found.

She got a job near her sister's house and again made herself indispensable to her boss (possibly Mr Welsh, the other name on the bill). So much so that when he was too ill to continue running the pub he sold up and took Dolly to Llandudno to run a boarding house in partnership with him. It was a lovely little business. Her mother and her sister came on a visit and were very impressed. Things were looking good again. Six months after everything was up and running she began to have back pain. Then she started to haemorrhage down below. Her sister took her back to Leedale Road. She had cancer of the cervix, womb and spine. Her family cared for her. She endured chemotherapy and radiotherapy and acute pain, always convinced she would get better. She spoke often of her sons. Her family tried to contact John. Ray had moved to somewhere in Australia. John was either unable or unwilling to see her. Reduced to skin and bone, just before she died, she sat bolt upright and said, 'Right, pay t'bill and let's be off.' At fifty-two she had paid all right, but would go no further. They had a whip-round and sold her radiogram to pay for the funeral. Cissie insisted that her rings be given to young John for that was what Dolly had wanted.

As I am leaving, Stuart indicates not one but two fifties-style cocktail cabinets – all gilt and mirrors, faux walnut and sliding glass doors. They were Dolly's. Of course they were. And the Bell's whisky bottle converted into a lamp with the gold satin shade. Surely John would have enjoyed that. 'Yeah, go for it, girl.'

I find her grave. Her mother outlived her by two years and tended it every week until her death but it is neglected now. She ended up at fifty-two a single woman, in a cemetery in West Gorton, buried in the same hole as her mother and father because it was cheaper. She didn't get away, but her sons did. As I look at the shabby tombstone on this freezing cold grey day, I find myself crying. My new friend Shaun touches my arm, puzzled, but I suppose I am weeping for all the people who have mucked up their lives, thinking the grass is greener on the other side, only to find it's a desert. For my mother's generation and their mothers before them, who have been given no encouragement. And because the Ivys and Dollys never wept for themselves.

5 September
We did it. Sick to death of 'in celebration'. 'Memorial' was too grandiose so settled for Remembering John. After all the preparation it worked a treat yesterday. I actually think John would have enjoyed it. The balance of laughter and tears was just right and Jack, Lola and Molly Mae running in at the end lifted all our hearts. Trafalgar Square came to a standstill for the balloons. Letter from Dr Piggott, our doctor for many years, summed it all up.

Dear Sheila,
We felt very proud to have been able to share with you, the family, your friends and your colleagues at that wonderful outpouring of love and caring. It was simply an amazing occasion. I could not help but wonder how John's father would have thought and felt had he known that his precious son had had a service remembering him and devoted to his honour in St Martin's, that the Prince of Wales and the wife of the Prime Minister of the day were

there, that some of the most notable of his and your professional colleagues were there, that numberless members of the public, his fans, were there, that the bells rang out for him over Trafalgar Square and the police were needed to control the public and the traffic: surely he would have burst with pride, surely you and your daughters must have too. Was ever a man more deeply honoured, was ever there more beautiful music on such an occasion, was ever there more beautiful moving verse written and spoken so perfectly by Abigail, were ever so many emotionally in tatters at such an occasion? And did he not greatly deserve it?

20

I Thought One Was Enough,
It's Not True

6 September
TV tribute went out. Jack Gold did a great job. God how
he was loved. I wish I had told him more how wonderful
he was – but then he wasn't always. We are all in rags
now but we did him proud. Wish he could be here to see
it all. Ray was very brave and has become a star after his
contribution to the tribute which he did superbly. Tom
made me laugh at the memorial. Said how he and John
knew this very camp musician who used to speak in a
strange and affected way. One of the things he used to say
was, 'Let's commit telephonage.' That was the last thing
John said to Tom, 'I tell you what, Tommy, let's commit
telephonage.' They never did again, but it was a sweet note
to go out on.

11 September
Dull dead feeling now all the tension of our public perform-
ance for John is over. Life goes on – and on and on. I don't
think it should. The world should stop as mine has. I'm
sure the relatives of those that died in the US last year feel
the same. Rumblings of pre-emptive strikes on Iraq. The
big boys want to show their powerful toys off and frighten

the little ones. Never mind that bloody phrase 'weapons of mass destruction'. The carnage of 9/11 was caused with the help of a few penknives and fanatical hatred. War is not a sensible option. It creates more terrorists, especially if they lose. We have backed some appalling people like the Majahadein including Osama Bin Laden in Afghanistan and then are surprised when they turn on us, using the weapons we sold them to kill us.

12 September
To Oxford to open a scanner at the Radcliffe Hospital. Nice dinner in University College with medical types. Forced myself to be entertaining and acted enjoying myself and eventually I did. Nice people.

13 September
Took Jack and Lola to Somerset House. They loved running into the fountains. Ended up sopping wet. Shrieking with laughter. They are upset by John's death but can still experience pure joy. Albert Camus: 'In the midst of winter I finally learned that there was in me an invincible summer.' There certainly is in kids. My summer is a bit more vincible at present.

16 September
I feel I have reached a fork in the road. One route leads to recovery, the other to life-long martyrdom. There are no oughts or shoulds but I could choose the positive route. I almost feel I'm in danger of clinging on to my grief for fear of losing him if I let it go. A poem someone sent me sums it up:

You can shed tears that he is gone
Or you can smile because he has lived.
You can close your eyes and pray that he'll come back
Or you can open your eyes and see all that he's left.
Your heart can be empty because you can't see him

Or you can be full of the love you shared.
You can turn your back on tomorrow and live for yesterday
Or you can be happy for tomorrow because of yesterday.
You can remember him and only that he's gone
Or you can cherish his memory and let it live on.
You can cry and close your mind, be empty and turn your
*   back*
Or you can do what he'd want.
Smile, open your eyes, love and go on.

20 September
Felt happy today. The family gathered at Lucky. The chil-
dren rolled on the grass. The sun was soft and warm. The
garden full of autumn flowers. It was a different kind of joy.
Without the edge, without the excitement but a loving day.

22 September
I don't believe John would have 'wanted you to be happy'.
He would have been pretty miffed if I wasn't gutted in fact.
But I do believe it is a negation of our life together to be
unhappy for the rest of mine. I can't help it now, for a
while. But he relied on me to get things done. And I must
get this grief done. Eventually. The difference with my
ability to cope is now I don't have him as a sounding board.
To bore, to make light with, to unpick problems with, to
vent my spleen on. So? I do it alone. Or with my lovely
family. Or with my friends. – Or somehow. I have to learn
to be alone. You can do it, kid.

27 September
Went to see hypnotherapist. Lots of talk about starting a
new life, closing the last chapter. Came out feeling very
positive. Passed the Wallace Collection in Manchester
Square and thought: 'Well I don't have to hurry home,
there's no one waiting, I'll pop in.' I've often heard how
good the restaurant is so went into the courtyard and, sure
enough, it was beautiful. Sat in the sun feeling very proud

*of myself when a young woman came up and snapped,
'Have you booked? No? Then I'm afraid you must leave.'
Slunk out thinking she wouldn't have been so rude if I'd
had John with me, or any man come to that. It's true that
women on their own are not treated well, even by other
women. Sat in my car and had a sandwich, thoroughly
depressed. I have started on Ativan to help me sleep. Those
small hours in the morning are intolerable.*

29 September
*Lot of stuff about Edwina Currie's affair with John Major.
Little rat says, 'It is the one event of my life of which I am
most ashamed.' He let himself stay ashamed for quite a
while, as it lasted from 1984 to 1988. She's getting all the
flak of course. One article said adultery was necessary to
keep a marriage alive but you must keep quiet about it. I
swear I have never for one moment needed to commit
adultery. John was all I ever wanted. And I'm sure it was
true for him too. Maybe we were freaks of nature.*

30 September
*Horrendous accountants' meeting. Don't understand a
word they say. I don't know my ISA from my elbow.*

1 October
*Felt really wretched today but found a quote from Flaubert
that cheered me up: 'To be stupid, selfish and have good
health are the three requirements of happiness but if stupidity
is lacking all is lost.' Another nice one of his: 'The mass of
men lead lives of quiet desperation.' And they're all trudging
down Hammersmith Broadway by the look of it.*

3 October
*Talking to people about John. Interesting how different
people saw him. I suppose we are all like that, not just
actors. We try to be what people want us to be. Or not.
Either way we are sort of acting a role. Especially women.*

I've been Mummy, wife, lover, public person, charity worker, leader, learner, bossy or dependent and a million other things according to the company I am in. My big problem now is what am I to be on my own? I don't have to be anything for anyone and I am lost. No one's telling me they need me so I feel redundant. No one's saying I'm beautiful so I am ugly. Above all, no one finds me sexy so I am becoming what I actually am – old and past it.

4 October
Decided to let the family go to Luckington on their own. I stayed in London and saw friends. I think I have to create my personal life as a firm base before I can contribute strongly to the family, otherwise I depend on them too much. Expect too much. Want them to dote on me like John did. And why should they? They have their own lives and families. We are extremely close but it is a family relationship. They want me to be strong – their mother – not some feeble old fart constantly demanding attention.

5 October
A breakthrough. Clare V. to stay. Can't believe she's dying. She's so full of life. Watched Robin Williams on the Parkinson Show *and this bereaved woman and one with terminal cancer literally fell on the floor laughing. Even though the laughing hurt Clare's ribs. What a tonic laughter is. Mind you, the champagne helped. She had been given a bottle of amazing Dom Perignon champagne. We made our gravy with it as well. Delia hasn't thought of that.*

6 October
Email from Clare. She is so gutsy.

Darling person WHAT a lovely weekend. I go into the week with renewed energy and fits of giggles. I had a fab relaxing and enlivening time. You are such a dear. I know John is sitting on his cloud beaming with pride – I know because

I asked his pyjams – for which great thanks. Let me know how you are at regular intervals whether gloomy or not. You are doing brilliantly.

How can she be so concerned for me when she is ill and facing death? She is a miracle person.

10 October
Curious day. Found myself by mistake at corporate lunch for donors to the National Theatre. Everyone talked about how they would have liked to meet John. I actually rasped bitterly to the umpteenth, 'Well you'll have to make do with me.' Showed Ellie Jane a tiny picture of Alec in his flying kit and she burst into tears. She has been so stoic up to now. She's had so much sadness in her life, losing two fathers and the worry over Jack.

11 October
Followed Helen's advice and cooked myself a proper meal instead of a ready-cook or sandwich. Laid the table and ate it with a glass of wine. It felt good.

12 October
Took Jack and Lola to cinema in Kensington then over to Holland Park and the Commonwealth Institute. Looked up at Troy Court. Who would have thought when I looked out of those windows, drowsy with love, that I would one day be out here – an old woman playing with her grandchildren? But we had fun. Pretending to hide from the police when they came round to lock up the park. They both had those divine giggles where you can't breathe. So did I.

13 October
Appalling bomb in Bali. A small one first to get people in the street, then a huge one that killed at least 184 and injured 300-odd. Wicked, wicked. Those lovely, gentle, beautiful people. But it turns out it was a club where

Indonesians were not allowed. And I remember the stories of brutality when we were there. Perhaps it wasn't as idyllic as we tourists think.

14 October
The world is such a mess. I feel old and miserable. Do the two things go together? You end up singing the blues. At the end of Twelfth Night, *when everyone's happy, Will has the clown sing a song that keeps repeating, 'The rain it raineth every day'. I seem to remember the song also has the word 'tosspot' in it. One of John's favourite terms of abuse. The world is full of tosspots. The turmoil they cause is palpable. But the rain doesn't rain every day. Not in Provence anyway.*

15 October
Went to see Clare Higgins in Vincent in Brixton. *She was wonderful. Jo and I went backstage to thank her for her help with John. Said how hellish it would have been if he had died during the drinking days. I would have been so full of regret. We may even have died hating each other. Of course we never did really but it would be too late to make amends.*

16 October
Broke the curse of the Wallace Collection. Had a lovely lunch with wise James Roose-Evans and no one told me to leave. Later went to a concert at Wigmore Hall and enjoyed that too. I'm groping my way out of the dark. I accept every invitation I get and force myself out and about. Come on, girl, get your act together. This is it. Make the most of it before you too lose it.
  Life, I mean.

25 October
Enjoying France with Clare V. Lotta laughs. She has the ability that John had to disregard her illness completely but

she, unlike *him, is calmly preparing for death. Telling her friends she loves them and allowing them to tell her, as Udi did. Sorting John's clothes in France. Two things I cannot part with. His dogs. A hideous pair of shorts he brought back from Canada with Scottie dogs around the legs which he wore with socks and sandals. A ludicrous sight, far removed from Ernie Morse. And his mincing boots. A strange pair of hand-stitched ankle boots that some extra conned him into buying. They made him walk even more oddly.*

26 October
Offered some of John's clothes to David. He was very moved. He didn't see John that often, only when we came to France, but said he felt he was a sort of father figure. Just by being there John appears to have been so many things to so many people. John was fond of David but never put himself out much for him yet David felt his strength and he made him into what he needed. Just like the public have.

28 October
Dreamt John and I were making love. Woke with my body aching for him. It is chilling to think I will almost certainly never have a lover again.

6 November
Since John died I find myself looking back all the time – something I have seldom done. I feel a bit wobbly about it – the way time and life passes so quickly. I still get a shock when I see myself in a shop window reflection and I am old. But face it, when I was young I would have been thinking how awful I looked so it's no worse now really.

12 November
To Cosby Hall in Cheyne Walk. Ancient palace being restored by a man called Christopher Moran. He is wonder-

fully vulgar about his wealth, like Carlton's Michael Greene – oh I do like that – as John would say, if you've got it, flaunt it.

17 November
Papers full of vilification of Myra Hindley who has died. I've never been able to read the details of the case, it so horrified me at the time. But why are we reluctant to think people can repent? Why do we need hate figures? On TV now we have wretched people in so-called reality shows, who have done no harm, that the press and the public relish hating. To read some of this stuff about them you would think they had murdered someone. It does us no credit, this organised hatred. It is either that or blind worship of celebrity. All very odd.

20 November
To St James's Palace to a reception given by Prince Charles for the Actors' Benevolent Society. I think he really feels at home with actors. I suppose his whole life is a performance. He made a funny speech. If he wasn't lumbered with being the heir to the throne people would think him a nice man. Two old guys came up to me and whispered that they were wearing something of John's. They looked very smart.

27 November
Lovely concert with Richard Digby-Day. Mahler's Sixth Symphony. Never liked Mahler before, all a bit too Death in Venice *for me, but this blew my mind. Helped by Richard's advice before it started about what to look out for. Thoroughly enjoy concerts with my new friend. It's a different experience than with John. In a way more grown-up as he is so informative, although still an enthusiast. A very pleasing step forward. Two girls just started at RADA came up to us in the foyer, asking for an autograph. All wide-eyed and bushy-tailed. Lovely, lucky girls, just starting.*

28 November

John will be forgotten. There will be occasional reruns of his programmes, but they will start to look dated. There's a wonderful website dedicated to him*. Someone has worked really hard to get it together. The message board is becoming less busy already. If he had done films they would last longer. Does it matter? Isn't that the virtue of TV, that it is of its time? Then it moves on. Like life. When Margaret Fox, one of the founders of Quakerism, died she wanted no marked grave. She is buried somewhere in a field in the Lake District. That field encircled by a stone wall vibrates with energy but there is nothing there. When we redid the garden in Chiswick for my fiftieth birthday, we had a mosaic fountain put in with the inscription, 'The best in this kind are but shadows'. Maybe someone will deduce a couple of actors lived there once. Then again, maybe it's already been bulldozed, like my dad's garden.

29 November

Saw Ken Parry at the rather staid University Women's Club. We had a riotous lunch. He wore black slacks and T-shirt with gold necklace and bracelet and jaunty black leather Beatle cap. The retired lady professors and writers were enthralled. Particularly when he announced that John thought that he was the only man who could make the word 'cunt' sound funny. 'Cunty wunty,' he trilled for me over the hors d'œuvre. The song from Bitter Sweet *that John liked went down well too. He knows everyone in the profession. When he attended John's memorial, 'which we could have done without, dear', Barry, who was sitting next to him, observed he was doing the same thing in St Martin-in-the-Fields as he used to in the Seven Stars, waving at all the pros. He had tears in his eyes when he said, 'Yes, he was having a bloody good laugh at us, up there, couple of old poofs together.' This lovely man does not seem to be*

---

* johnthaw.topcities.com/johnthaw

*hurt that John and a lot of his other 'Alices' have lost touch
with him. 'I'm lucky – I'm still here, pussy.' And he still has
John's ironing board and an A to Z that has written inside:*
    This book belongs to Tom Courtenay.
    This book belongs to Vic Symonds.
    No it doesn't it belongs to Kenny.
    No it doesn't it belongs to John Thaw.
*As he left, he asked, 'Do you think I was important to
them? Very? Oh, I'm glad to hear that. It's the end of a
puzzle.'*

30 November
*Saw Barry J. Gordon in his sheltered housing in Ealing. A
dapper, smiley man, he has transformed a rather dreary
building into a haven of good taste. Actors are divine. You
could be in a flat in Eaton Square surrounded by the beautiful pictures, ornaments and antique furniture collected
throughout his life. There is Earl Grey tea in bone china
cups with homemade cakes. Yet the tales of his childhood
make John's seem like an episode of* The Darling Buds of
May.

1 December
*Thank God for the press. I never thought I'd say that, but
without them this whole Iraq business would go unchal-
lenged. All the opposition to Blair's mad rush to war has
come from his own party or the press. The Tories have just
rolled over lest they should be thought unpatriotic.*

6 December
*Women in Film luncheon. Great day. Everyone lets their
hair down, knowing that it's not exposed on TV. Germaine
Greer got huge reception. Jenny Eclair said, 'We owe it all
to you' and the room rose to its feet. Germaine was obviously moved. One actress said to me, 'I hate bloody men.
You're different. Yours was a real partnership.' A real partnership. Yes, that's it.*

10 December
Took Lola and Jack to Santa's World in Wembley. Got stuck in hideous traffic jam so Lola had to wet her knickers. We took them off and she greeted Santa with a bare bum. I was worried about her sitting on some out-of-work actor's knee, knickerless, but beneath the beard Father Christmas was a girl anyway.

18 December
Jo phoned to ask if she could come round. I thought it was going to be bad news but it was – a tiny black very scared kitten. 'He's no substitute for Dad, but he might help a bit.' He spent the day cowering under the sofa with me lying on the floor trying to coax him out.

19 December
Getting to know Benjamin. He is very sweet if a bit wild – so he should fit in then. Had some friends round. Spent the evening talking about illness and dying. We used to talk about sex and life. Ah me.

21 December
Felt very low shopping surrounded by couples preparing for Christmas together. Newspapers full of those awful end of year lists. John in Dead National Treasure List. 'Not a very good actor, but probably the most popular.' Stupid bastard. He was a superb actor. His range enormous and his subtlety and utter truthfulness beyond compare. (This guy thought Stratford Johns was better. Perlease.) The thing was you couldn't see the wheels turning so they couldn't tell how skilled he was. Some of them. Did this schmuck think that all the people that made him 'probably the most popular' for four decades were complete idiots?

24 December
Our wedding anniversary. Jo and I went to a St Martin-in-the-Fields service and then supper at the Savoy. It was

very ordinary, full of lost foreigners and I suspect, part-time waiters, but it was different. Took our minds off what we would have been doing with him.

25 December
Ellie Jane laid on a lovely Christmas Day but it was total agony. I felt detached and dead and guilty that I couldn't be more gracious. It's the going home on my own with no one to talk to about the day's events.

31 December
In Lucky. Family gone back to London. Felt wretched and sorry for myself while the rest of the country celebrated. I've been invited to a lovely party by Amanda Redman, but chose to be miserable with my sister. Am I finding comfort in my grief? This feeling that wells from the pit of my stomach, tightens the back of my throat and contorts my face into a parody of a Greek tragic mask. Is the pain beginning to be a substitute for you? I think of you – you're not there, but the pain is. So something is. Better than nothing. It is proof of your non-existence. If that goes what is left of you?

3 January 2003
John's birthday.
Dear God, how these anniversaries come round. I'm not usually one for birthdays – I've been known to forget my own children's and I never know how old anyone is, but suddenly since John's death I've started marking events. This time last year, etc., etc. It's pointless and negative and I'm going to stop it. The two biggies are looming: his death and my 70th. Not looking forward to either. Jo and Matt came round and did some DIY for me and Ellie Jane came with the kids. New life, new focus.

8 January
Lola's first day at proper school. She looked like Little

Orphan Annie standing on the doorstep in the snow in her uniform, which Ellie Jane has bought to last – till she's sixteen, by the look of it. We are on the brink of a war with Iraq. Poison gas found in Wood Green. These bastard politicians had better watch their step and not ruin the world for the Lolas, Molly Maes and Jacks. Or I'll . . . I'll what? God knows. On top of that I discovered that our little local Hammersmith Post Office has been held up by armed robbers for the umpteenth time. What a world. No wonder Auntie Ruby said before she died that she would be happy to go, she didn't belong any more. I used to want to take on everyone. Wave banners, write letters, make speeches, but like my parents I see the patterns repeating over and over and I have lost heart.

14 January
Party for the tenth year of Breakfast with Frost. *Hell of an achievement. He has had every top person on his show. A lot of them were there looking rather grey and small. Why are most 'great' people a disappointment? I went into my usual mode of being rude and discourteous. What is it with me that I have to insult important people? Is it an engrained inferiority complex, an I'll-show-you mentality? Or years, generations, of ordinary people being shat on by the likes of them, that I want to get even for? Whatever it is, it's singularly unattractive. Went for supper with Esther Rantzen.*

15 January
Extraordinary coincidence. I described the restaurant I went to last night to Billie and she told me that during the war she had come back from a tour with a friend and went down this self-same passageway, to find the pub that this girl's parents owned had been destroyed by a bomb. They went on a frantic search, finding her parents alive, but her brother dead in a temporary morgue. Billie must have been about sixteen or seventeen. The actual fact of war is so

awful. This generation, including Blair, has not experienced it first hand or they would move heaven and earth to avoid it, instead of being drawn to it as they seem to be.

18 January
A lovely day (never thought I'd say that again). Wrote in the morning then went to see Mnemonic at Riverside Studios. An extraordinary, beautiful show. Then on to a new – to me – restaurant, the Patio in Shepherd's Bush with Geraldine McEwan and Alan Rickman and their friends. All new to me, but we stayed until 1.30 a.m. I really laughed.

22 January
The German Ambassador says that Germany will not fight Iraq, as they have started two world wars and will not be involved in another. Amazing. People are really standing up and being counted on this issue. I'm terrified for us all. I do not see how this war against terrorism can possibly be won.

23 January
Went to lunch with Chris Kelly and Ted Childs in the place in Charlotte Street where they used to go with John. It was curious. I had a lovely time with them, but I'm sure they were aching for John instead.

24 January
'Bleeooming great war clouds are leeooming' as Kenny Williams would say. Signed a letter to be published trying to stop the war. Fat chance. Benjamin is a darling and keeps me occupied. He is someone to care for – I need that. No, Sheila, some thing, he is not a person. Oh dear, I must not become a silly old woman doting on her pet.

25 January
Heard Condoleeza Rice talking about the US mission to save the world. She is intelligent and put her case persuasively.

But the impression was of a group of messianic people in Washington bent on a mission that they believe with all their hearts is right. I worry that their obsession with Iraq is making them take their eye off the ball in the search for terrorists. Quaker Advices and Queries, 'Consider it possible you might be mistaken.'

30 January
Dreamt John and I were separated and I thought – as I used to – oh, it's OK, I'll go back to him later, then remembered he was gone for ever. Woke up gasping and shaky. I keep thinking I'm getting better and wallop it's back again. I miss him, I miss him. I know now I have to allow myself to have shitty days. Just give in to it, but stop inflicting it on others. Hide away and scream and shout and it will pass.

1 February
You see? Today I felt OK. A good night's sleep is always a help. In the early days I couldn't sleep and that made me exhausted and that made me wretched – it's a vicious circle. My doctor has set a personal trainer on me, John. He puts me through my paces with various implements including ferocious weights. I need to get physically fit in order to be mentally better, I know that. I have been neglecting myself. Ellie Jane arrived at 8.30. He opened the door and she was confronted with me in tights lying over a large rubber ball with this rather dishy young man looking on. I hope she believed my explanation.

2 February
Memorial concert for Joan Littlewood at Stratford East. There we were, old codgers remembering the days when we were full of passion. Joan would have pulled her woolly hat over her eyes in disgust at such sentiment. Sitting on that stage I remembered the terrified girl in the wings. Oh Joan of blessed memory, an idealist, and God they are rare.

She remained true to her beliefs right to the end. I shall miss her postcards and phone calls.

4 February
Heard radio programme about bereavement. 'Everyone avoids me.' 'People should be taught about bereavement at school.' Oh, get a grip! It's part of life for God's sake. Surely we don't have to have classes in grieving now. Sheila, beware self-pity, it's so unattractive.

8 February
It's his bass notes I miss. Without John my life is thin and reedy, insubstantial, without depth. I glide over the surface of events. I don't discuss them after to analyse and put in perspective. When something happened in the past I couldn't wait to tell John and we'd talk and laugh about it, now it just evaporates or, worse, just whirls around in my mind, unresolved. I'm not grounded any more. How do I get round this one?

12 February
Coming up to the anniversary of his death. A year? Unbelievable. He is still so – not near – but potent to me.

14 February
Extraordinary Valentine's Day. The children round with cards and presents (they were pretty startled by John, the personal trainer, the handsome hunk). Then to a Story Competition do for the Great Ormond Street Hospital at Waterstone's. Felt pretty grumpy on arrival, then posed for photos next to a youth in a chair. Twisted body, can't walk or talk. He has a gadget to tap out words and I put in 'hello' and got talking to him, rubbishing the photographers who were taking ages. I was thinking, 'This could have been Jack – he had a similar tumour.' Later, his parents called me over and said he wanted to give me something. It was a single red rose. I told him I was dreading Valentine's Day, but he had made it lovely.

15 February

Biggest demo ever in London against the war. If there is one good thing to come out of this madness it is that the public has found a voice and a passion. Youngsters are revolting in the best sense of the word instead of the worst. People are actually concerned about the so-called enemy. In the old days if we were told someone was an enemy, we'd have believed them and started hating to order. Now people worry about the women and children, and separate out the leaders and the led. I only hope the people we are bombing know how we feel.

18 February

Tom Courtenay's first night in show about Philip Larkin, produced by my son-not-in-law, Matt. It is curious that poetry has always flummoxed me before but this year has been a revelation. John and I used to switch off poetry programmes. 'Wanky.' 'Oh noo, not for me.' But it was often the sanctimonious style of delivery, or worse, the mock-ordinary flatness of the Liverpool poets. Whatever – it irritated. And now the poems that people have sent me have helped enormously. There were several in Tom's show and the phrase 'What will survive of us is love' spoke to my condition totally.

21 February

A year since my best beloved died. Strange. I have been dreading this day and it was lovely. The three girls and I went to the church near Manchester Square where I had lit a candle for Jack when he was ill and we lit one for John and sat quietly for a while. I love London churches. The city sounds in the distance and the calm inside. Then to lunch at the Wallace Collection and a look at the pictures. I had my babes to stay the night and went to the cinema with them and Matt and Jo and tea after. Lots of laughter at bath and story time. This – they – are the future. That can't be bad. Larkin on the death of a hedgehog:

Next morning I got up and it did not
The first day after death, a new absence
Is always the same; we should be careful

Of each other, we should be kind
While there is still time.

22 February

Seventy. Seventy? No, not seventy? Yes. Bloody seventy!
My babes greeted me with lovely presents. We had fun with
me acting a very old lady. We went to the Wallace Collection
again. An eighteenth-century day – when I was born, prac-
tically. Lola, Abs and Molly Mae danced a minuet. Lola
got in a strop because she couldn't make a fan and Molly
Mae could. That evening I went, supposedly for a quiet
dinner, to Ellie Jane's and was amazed to find the place full
of my friends, from the past and new ones that I have made
this year. I'm so blessed. I felt full of love for them all.
Another lovely poem through the post. It was sent to me
by Lynda Tavakali, whom I have corresponded with for
years, since her friend died of breast cancer. It was in
Nicholas Evans' book, The Smoke Jumper. *A riposte to*
Edna. The fact that it works for me now shows that I have
moved on since Edna's despair consumed me.

If I be the first of us to die,
Let grief not blacken long your sky.
Be bold yet modest in your grieving.
There is change but not a leaving.
For just as death is part of life,
The dead live on forever in the living.
For all the gathered riches of our journey,
The moments shared, the mysteries explored,
The steady layer of intimacy stored,
The things that made us laugh or weep or sing,
The joy of sunlit snow or first unfurling of the spring,
The wordless language of look and touch,

The knowing,
Each giving and each taking,
These are not flowers that fade,
Nor trees that fall and crumble,
Nor are they stone
For even stone cannot the wind and rain withstand
And mighty mountain peaks in time reduce to sand.
What we were, we are.
What we had, we have.
A conjoined past imperishably present.
So when you walk the woods where once we walked
    together
And scan in vain the dappled bank beside you for my
    shadow,
Or pause where we always did upon the hill to gaze across
    the land,
And spotting something, reach by habit for my hand,
And finding none, feel sorrow start to steal upon you,
Be still.
Close your eyes.
Breathe.
Listen for my footfall in your heart.
I am not gone but merely walk within you.

8 March

I am really not at all keen on this old age thing. I am on the receiving end of respect and I hate it. The PA even calls me 'my love' – 'Let me help you, my love' – as if I were a helpless geriatric. But worse – they ask for my advice as if I were a fount of wisdom, which I'm not. About their love lives and such, whereas I fancy the focus-puller who I suddenly realise is twenty-six and I am seventy. I have to watch all the usual flirtations instead of having one. I am the cause of no gossip at all. I suppose I never was but I could have been and now I can't. It's a bugger. After the broadcast everyone was going for a drink and the director said, 'I don't suppose you'll want to come.' Why bloody not? I'm too old to get across the road? Too grand? In the old days I would have wanted to rush home to John who didn't find me old at all. He found me rude and feisty and sexy and as young as when we met. But now I just went home and watched the telly on my own – with a bloody great drink.

18 March
It is countdown to war and already 'the boys' are excited. Detailed descriptions of all the various toys including cluster bombs. You can feel the playground atmosphere. The antis are expected to come to heel now. 'Our boys' or 'our lads' are out there. I always get worried when men call one another lads and boys – like football hooligans. I don't support the lads. I weep for them and rage that they might die or be traumatised in such a misconceived venture.

20 March
Trinity College as guest for the Domus dinner. Standing in for John. Lovely evening but felt a bit ratty when I arrived. Greeted by some academic who kept saying 'No trouble at all.' I hate that phrase. Everyone says it all the time. What does it mean for God's sake? He's educated, he should use language accurately. I should bloody well think it's no trouble to hand me a paper, or press the lift button on number 3. And while I'm at it, how disgusting is the phrase 'shock and awe' to describe an operation to kill people? Awe is caused by looking at the Grinling Gibbons carvings at the chapel here at Trinity. Awe is the thought of all the scholarship these walls have witnessed since the sixteenth century. Not frightening badly-defended Arabs to death by an obscene show of might. But yes, I'm shocked all right.

Epilogue

2 April

France. Bought a new washing machine made by Laden. Not Osama Bin, I hope. The bombs, the wounded children, the woman caught on a bridge between firing men seem far away here. My sorrow has broadened, it is no longer just for me and mine. As you get older you cannot help but be melancholy. The turmoil of the world is palpable. But there are still rapturous moments. I went down to the stream through the cherry orchard. I came to a glade where the sun was beaming in rays through a roof of blossom. Beneath was a carpet of wild narcissi, the perfume took my breath away. I could hear the stream rippling. I was panting and trembling, it was so beautiful. Oh I wish – No, stop. Then I tried:

Be still.
Close your eyes.
Breathe.
Listen for my footfall in your heart.
I'm not gone but merely walk in you.

And it sort of worked. Cracked it, kid?

Gallagher. Reproduced by permission of The Random House Group Ltd, UK and ICM Talent, Inc., USA.

Nicholas Evans, 'Walk Within You' from *The Smoke Jumper* by Nicholas Evans, published by Bantam Press. Reprinted by permission of The Random House Group Ltd, UK and A. P. Watt Inc., USA.

Philip Larkin, 'The Mower' from *Collected Poems* by Philip Larkin. Reproduced by permission of Faber and Faber Ltd, UK, and Farrar Straus & Giroux Inc., USA.

Primo Levi, 'To My Friends' from *Collected Poems* by Primo Levi. Reproduced by permission of Faber and Faber Ltd, UK, and Farrar Straus & Giroux Inc., USA.

Edna St Vincent Millay, 'Sonnet 2: Time Does Not Bring Relief' from *The Collected Poems of Edna St Vincent Millay*. Reproduced by permission of Random House USA, Inc.

Other

John Madden, John Thaw Obituary ('His shyness was the source of his genius'), *Observer*, 24 February 2002, reproduced here by kind permission of John Madden.

The author and publishers gratefully acknowledge permission to quote from the private letters of Sally Alexander, Alma Cullen, Udi Eichler, Peter O'Toole, Dr Brian Piggot and Peter Thompson.

Photographs

All photographs, unless otherwise stated, are from the author's private collection and are used with permission.

For the photographs on the following pages the publishers would like to credit: John Alexander Studio, p. 187; First Leisure Corporation plc, p. 29; FremantleMedia, p. 52; Matthew Harvey, p. 57; John Haynes, p. 201; ITV/Carlton Television, p. 243; Manchester Picture Library, pp. 25, 50; Beattie Meyrick, p. 268; Murray and Carstair, Torquay, pp. 85, 91; Press Association, p. 97; Royal Court Theatre, p. 130; Stuart Simpson, pp. 267, 268; Abigail Thaw, pp. 117, 119; Nigel Whitney, p. 245; *Woman's Realm*, p. 149.

A NOTE ON THE TYPE

The text of this book is set in Linotype Sabon, named after the type founder, Jacques Sabon. It was designed by Jan Tschichold and jointly developed by Linotype, Monotype, and Stempel, in response to a need for a typeface to be available in identical form for mechanical hot metal composition and hand composition using foundry type. Tschichold based his design for Sabon roman on a font engraved by Garamond, and Sabon italic on a font by Granjon. It was first used in 1966 and has proved an enduring modern classic.